"Maybe It Should Have Been a Three-Iron"

"Maybe It Should Have Been a Three-Iron"

My Year as a Caddy for the World's
438TH Best Golfer

LAWRENCE DONEGAN

St. Martin's Press ❧ New York

ISBN 0-312-18584-7

First published in Great Britain by Viking, a division of Penguin Books, under the title *Four-Iron in the Soul*

First U.S. Edition: June 1998

10 9 8 7 6 5 4 3 2 1

For Roscoe, a sporting hero

Dost thou not hear their horses neigh, their trumpets sound, and their drums beat? Not I, quoth Sancho, I prick up my ears like a sow in the beans and yet I can hear nothing but the bleating of sheep.

MIGUEL DE CERVANTES
Don Quixote

If I needed advice from my caddy, he'd be hitting the shots and I'd be carrying the bag.

BOBBY JONES, 1930

Contents

Acknowledgements   xi
European PGA Tour Schedule   xiii
1. Turnberry   1
2. Rowley – My Teacher   10
3. Sun City   16
4. Buck's Fizz and Death Threats   33
5. A Momentous Day!   45
6. Walkman   52
7. King Hassan and I   72
8. 'Belgrano'   84
9. Early Exits   98
10. The Ballmark Kid, Elvis and Frank Sinatra   111
11. The Giant is Awake   125
12. Now's the Day, Now's the Hour   139
13. Mr Magic   146
14. The Sweat-box   158
15. Wobbly   169
16. The Van   183
17. Roasting   195
18. John Daly's $100,000   202
19. The Death of Don Quixote   211
20. Home   224
21. Together again   236

Acknowledgements

I would like to express my thanks to all those who helped me write this book, especially the members of the European Tour Caddies' Association. In particular, I would like to give special thanks to Andy Prodger, Martin Rowley, Julian Phillips, Gary Currie, Ritchie Blair, Pat McSweeney, Barry Courts, Kevin Woodward, Neil Wallace, Colin Byrne, John McLaren, Paul Aparechos, Pete Coleman, Myles Byrne, George Mosheshi, Andy Sutton, Philip Morbey, Jimmy Hillhouse, Brian McFeat, Joey Jones, Stuart Dryden and Lorne Duncan – all were generous beyond what I had any right to expect.

I am also grateful to the many professional golfers who took time off from the serious business of making cuts to speak to me, in particular Stephen McAllister, Gary Orr, Adam Hunter, Dean Robertson, DJ Russell, Paul Lawrie, Chris Hall, Jason Widener, Stephen Field and Thomas Gögele. Thanks also to Brian Gunson of Turnberry Golf Club and Jos Vanstiphout – golf guru supreme!

Alan Rusbridger, the editor of the *Guardian*, was kind enough to give me time off work, while my colleagues David Davies, Gordon Simpson, John Huggan, Andy Farrell and Norman Dabell always answered my stupid questions with unfailing patience.

Thanks also to Jonny Geller, Tony Lacey, Clare Alexander,

John Colquhoun, Hazel Orme, Claire Drummond and Ed Pilkington.

Finally, thanks to Maggie. You were great.

European PGA Tour Schedule

8–11 February	Dimension Data Pro-Am	Sun City
15–18 February	South African PGA	Johannesburg
22–25 February	FNB Players' Championship	Cape Town
29 Feb.–3 Mar.	Open Catalonia	Tarragona
1–7 March	Moroccan Open	Rabat
14–17 March	Dubai Desert Classic	Dubai
21–24 March	Portuguese Open	Aroeira
28–31 March	Madeira Open	Madeira
8–21 April	Cannes Open	Cannes
25–28 April	Turespaña Masters	Valencia
2–5 May	Italian Open	Bergamo
9–12 May	Peugeot Open de España	Madrid
6–19 May	B&H International Open	Oxfordshire
24–27 May	Volvo PGA Championship	Wentworth
30 May–2 June	Deutsche Bank Open	Hamburg
6–9 June	English Open	Coventry
13–16 June	Northumberland Challenge	Northumberland
20–23 June	BMW International Open	Munich
27–30 June	Peugeot Open de France	Versailles

4–7 July	Irish Open	Bray
10–13 July	Scottish Open	Carnoustie
14–15 July	Open Championship (Qual.)	Southport
18–21 July	Open Championship	Lytham St Annes
25–28 July	Sun Dutch Open	Hilversum
1–4 August	Scandinavian Masters	Gothenburg
8–11 August	Austrian Open	Waldviertel
15–18 August	Chemapol Czech Open	Mariánské Lázne
22–25 August	Volvo German Masters	Stuttgart
29 Aug.–1 Sept.	British Masters	Collingtree
5–8 September	Lancôme Trophy	Paris
19–22 September	World Invitational	Loch Lomond
26–29 September	Smurfit European Masters	Dublin
3–6 October	German Masters	Berlin
10–13 October	Oki Pro-Am	Madrid
24–27 October	Volvo Masters	Valderrama

1. Turnberry

The first thing to understand about caddying is that it's not brain surgery. It is more complicated than that.

Being neither rich nor a professional golfer, I had only ever hired a 'caddy' once in my life. I had a grudge match against a golf cheat of my acquaintance and thought I needed all the help I could get. William was a university student who worked his summers carrying golf bags on one of Scotland's more famous links. He spent the entire round detailing his narcotic and sexual adventures in the Union bar, except, that is, when he wasn't sniggering at my attempts to play golf. This disheartening habit of William's reached its nadir as I went to play my second shot at the last hole – a 175-yard three-iron to a green the size of a fireside rug – and his eyes grew as big as saucers.

'Jesus Christ,' he giggled. 'You'll never make it over the water.'

A proper caddy would never have said such a thing to his player. He would have adopted the manner of a family doctor and said, 'A solid swing here – like the one you made on the second hole – and you've won.' With any luck these soothing words would have set in motion an emotional chain reaction . . .

. . . he's not laughing at me, perhaps I'm not such a bad person after all . . . He hasn't mentioned water either, so I don't have to worry about that . . . The second hole? God. I'd forgotten that shot it was so long ago. He's right, that was a good shot

. . . and now that you come to mention it, William, I do want to win . . .

. . . which might have resulted in me at least connecting with the ball. As things turned out, I missed it completely.

I know now that William was a *bag carrier* and not a caddy. I also know now that they are not the same thing. Both carry golfers' bags, but only in the way that both the Beatles and the Bay City Rollers made pop records.

The difference is that a bag carrier requires little skill beyond that of being able to walk with a golf bag on his shoulder. But to be a caddy, especially a tour caddy, requires special talents: the golfing brain of Jack Nicklaus, a thick skin, the psychological sophistication of a £500-an-hour shrink, low cunning, the motivational powers of a five-star general, a robust constitution, strong legs, the organizational skills of a Psion 3a, loyalty, guile . . . The list is endless. Just ask a tour caddy.

I was a bag carrier once, though now I like to think of myself as having made the first faltering steps towards becoming a caddy. I think I'm a quarter of the way there, though some who have seen me at work on the golf course think it may be less. It has been a difficult journey and at times I didn't think I'd even get this far. Another fifteen years and I might actually make it all the way. If I do, I will be able to look back fondly to the wintry afternoon Ross Drummond and I stood on the ninth tee at Turnberry golf course and say that's where it all began.

Bruce's Castle is the most recognizable hole in all of golf. It graces the cover of every golf book ever published. Actually it doesn't really, it just seems that way. Let's say it graces the cover of half of the golf books ever published. The classic picture was taken in summer and shows a rich green fairway bathed in sunshine. The shadows are long and a thin red mist appears to be rising from the sea. There is a lighthouse in the top left-hand corner, like a huge white exclamation mark. In the background

Ailsa Craig, an uninhabited lump of granite two miles off the coast, watches over the scene like a benign godfather. Standing on that same spot in mid-January, it seemed that I was in a different place altogether. The lighthouse was in the same place, and so was Ailsa Craig, but winter had washed the colour from the landscape. An inhospitable wind hit me straight in the face like a slap. The fairway was two hundred yards away, directly into the wind. To reach it from the championship tee required either a career shot across a frothing inlet on the Firth of Clyde or, my preferred option, a stroll along the coastal path to the ladies' tee and a careful dink forward with a driver.

I watched my playing partner tee up his ball. He shook the tension from his neck and shoulders and shaped up to take on this awesome challenge. I could contain myself no longer.

'Jesus Christ, Ross,' I said. 'You'll never make it over the water.'

Typical. I look back on my sporting life and realize now that I always lacked confidence. That, and ability. Both were to prove fatal to my ambitions of becoming a professional sportsman.

Two sports dominated my early years: football and golf. I was once something of a schoolboy prodigy at both. Aged six, I could keep a football up for at least fifty kicks and hit my sawn-off seven-iron the length of the five-a-side pitch outside our block of flats. The downward spiral started, aged ten, when I became interested in girls, specifically Yvonne Richardson of class 6B. She tempted me from football training and for what? A clench-lipped kiss and unfulfilled promises of exciting times ahead.

Then I lost my seven-iron, the only golf club I had.

I barely made the football team at secondary school and, without a golf club, the blissful Saturday afternoons spent carving up the five-a-side pitch faded into distant memory.

My football career revived briefly in my late teens. I played in goal once, just once, for Central Region schools. (It was in December, at the height of a flu epidemic. The first-choice goalkeeper was sick. As were choices two to seven.) Thereafter, I lived my dreams vicariously. Two of my best friends at school became professional footballers, John Colquhoun and Robert Dawson. John was capped for Scotland and was even briefly on first-name terms with Kenny Dalglish. And I went to the same university at roughly the same time as Brian McClair, who dropped out after a year to play for Celtic, then Manchester United. We have never met but I've never forgiven McClair for stealing my destiny.

My twenties came and went. I had a sneaking suspicion that my dreams of becoming a professional footballer would for ever remain unfulfilled. Confirmation came when John and Robert began to be described in match reports as 'veterans' and the captain of the Tap and Spile pub team took me aside, thanked me for my services, but said there was no longer a spot for me between the sticks. For one sickening, careless moment I thought I might cry.

My golf career has been less auspicious.

I got a new set of clubs for my twelfth birthday but by then the moment had passed. Central Region schools didn't have a golf team. Even if it did it would have taken a nuclear holocaust in the neighbouring towns and villages before the selectors reached my name. It took ten years for me to break ninety for the first time. And another five before I did it again. But like all amateur golfers, I knew the perfect round was only another day or another expensive piece of equipment away. I guess it finally dawned on me that I wouldn't make it as a golfer either when Tiger Woods turned pro and signed a $40 million sponsorship deal. He was thirteen years younger than me.

I didn't even have the consolation of knowing anyone who was remotely good at golf until Ross Drummond floated into my life, or rather, I floated into his.

Ross was everything I had ever wanted to be: a professional sportsman.

I first met him when I was researching a newspaper article on journeyman pro golfers – a description that might have been invented for him. I don't mean that derisively. On the contrary, I had always seen something heroic in journeyman pros. It seemed so much more noble to try and fail than to win all the time. Or, at least, it did to me; perhaps I would have felt differently after trying and failing to win for nineteen years.

That's how long Ross had been playing the European Tour without ever graduating from the chorus. He was one of those players who filled in the landscape against which golf's superstars performed their heroic deeds. Norman, Faldo, Ballesteros, Price, Torrance, Woosnam, Montgomerie – he had competed against them all over the years. He was on first-name terms with some of them.

Ross had come close to winning a tournament only twice: the 1986 Scottish Open, when he came fourth, and the 1990 Atlantic Open, where he was joint leader until he bogied the second last hole. He spoke fondly of both tournaments, like a melancholy old soldier recalling lost comrades. He was the 438th best player in the world as we stood on the ninth tee at Turnberry. I checked that morning – one place above Mike Tschetter.

'Mike who?' I asked the man who ran the Sony World Rankings.

'Tschetter. You must have heard of him, his sister plays tennis.'

I caddied for Ross at one tournament as part of my research for my article. Or, rather, I carried his bag. To my uncontainable excitement we played the last round with the seventh best golfer in the world, José Maria Olazábal. It was a blisteringly hot July afternoon in Versailles and our pairing – okay, Olazábal – attracted a vast crowd, all pushing and shoving for the best view around the greens, releasing huge throaty roars for great shots and aaaahing disconsolately for missed putts.

I swear I caught one man, around fifty with thick greying hair and a beautiful, trim wife, staring enviously at my caddy's bib. I could tell he was deeply impressed at the easy familiarity I seemed to have with the world's seventh best golfer. I know this because I recognized his expression. I had been there so many times myself – standing beyond the boundary ropes of professional sport peering at those taking part in the spectacle I had paid to watch, wondering what it must be like to feel what they were feeling at that instant, trying to understand how they had made it to where they were and I was, well, a mere spectator. Now I was the object of someone else's curiosity. The thought sent a tingle down my spine.

And the excitement didn't end there. Olazábal shook my hand on the last green and said, 'Thank you for the round, Lawrence.'

That made up my mind. I wanted to become a full-time caddy. How else could I be on first-name terms with a sporting superstar or become a figure of envy for a handsome, wealthy Frenchman whose wife looked like Catherine Deneuve?

But it wasn't just that. I wanted to fulfil my childhood dreams of taking part in professional sport, to travel the world. I wanted to experience the feeling of winning a golf tournament, of walking on to the last green at the Open Championship one shot ahead of Faldo, shouting, 'Quiet, please!' at the gallery at Augusta. I wanted to play in the Ryder Cup, to see the fear on Fred Couples's face as he stood on the first tee for our singles match, then dance a victory jig across the fairway with Seve Ballesteros and lift Ian Woosnam off his feet in a victory hug and spray champagne on the crowd. I wanted John and Robert and Brian McClair to be sitting at home watching it all on television, saying, 'I wish that was me.'

So what if I didn't have the talent to do any of that? That was the beauty of being a caddy – you didn't need talent. Well, not the physical, hand-to-eye co-ordination talent that only a few are blessed with.

I clapped the world's seventh best golfer on the back. 'Yeh, you too, José Maria. Good round.' A world-class sportsman without skill. That was me. Caddying was my destiny.

Ross Drummond wasn't my first choice, Nick Faldo was. I know for a fact that I wasn't Nick's first choice. I was sure too that I wasn't at the top of Ross's list either. A week with a writer on his bag was an amusing diversion, a whole season might be career-threatening. He was understandably reluctant. That's why I dragged him along to Turnberry for a getting-to-know-your-possible-future-caddy game of golf.

Ross started his life as a golf pro at the famous old Scottish course back in 1977, the year Tom Watson and Jack Nicklaus contested the greatest finish to a major championship in the history of the game. He spent that magical day in the tented village selling emblemed balls to Japanese tourists. If he had had any doubts before, he knew then that he wanted to become a touring professional. I thought a return to Turnberry would make him nostalgic for freshness and excitement and the dreams he'd had in those days. I hoped he would see something of his young self in me and give in.

We finished eighteen holes. I played brilliantly and Ross had a terrible day. He only beat me by twenty-seven shots.

Standing on the last green I told him I had a picture in my head of the two of us traipsing across Europe together, like Don Quixote and Sancho Panza. So what if he hadn't won a European Tour event in nineteen years? I was Quixote – I had dreams and visions enough for both of us. He could be Sancho, the practical realist, the corrective lens through which I could experience what it was really like to compete in world-class golf, against Faldo and Ballesteros and Norman. I promised him the governorship of an island if he would take me on. And still he was reluctant.

What persuaded him in the end? Something daft – a conversation about the pop-psychology book I'd seen on the desk at his house called *Awaken the Giant Within* by Anthony Robbins.

It was open at chapter four, 'Belief Systems', which started with a homily about an alcoholic drug addict who was serving life for murdering a liquor-store assistant. His brother was a regional manager for a major national retail company. The point of the story, and this was where I got lost, was that 'It's not the events of our lives which shape us, but our beliefs as to what those events mean.' From there it was only a short hop to world domination, as far as I could make out.

'You're reading this?' I sniggered.

Ross nodded.

'Why?'

What alcoholic drug addicts and bank managers and belief systems had to do with getting a small white ball round a golf course in less than seventy-two shots was a mystery to me.

He became animated, not angry but steely, determined. 'I've been treading water for too long. I need to try something different, I've got to push it to another level. I need self-belief,' he said.

I liked the sound of this.

He said, 'I want to win a European Tour event before I finish my career. It's why I play golf.'

'And that's where Anthony comes in – he can help?' I interrupted.

'Yes.'

'And what about me, your new caddy?'

The firmness drained out of his voice like water down a plug hole. 'Well, yes. I suppose so.'

I wanted to sit him on my shoulders and run into the street in celebration. 'Brilliant! We'll be great together.'

He had probably heard this a million times before but was

polite enough to smile and nod. 'Let's just play it by ear,' he said.

Too late, too late. I wanted to read to him from *Don Quixote* . . . *look yonder, friend Sancho, there are thirty outrageous giants, whom I intend to encounter and, having deprived them of life, enrich ourselves with their spoils* . . .

He looked uneasy.

. . . *pray look better, sir, those things yonder are not giants but wind-mills, the arms you fancy are their sails* . . .

'I've never really had much faith in caddies, they always let you down. It's almost as if they want to let you down on purpose, make you sack them so they can go and work for a more successful player.'

Not me, Ross, no way.

. . . *I tell thee they are giants: and therefore, if thou art afraid go aside and say thy prayers* . . .

'I've got reservations, mind,' he said.

. . . *For I am resolved to engage in a dreadful, unequal combat against them all* . . .

'Well, forget them,' I said. 'You and me, we'll be like Don Quixote and Sancho Panza. We'll make a great team – and I promise not to die at the end.'

He shifted uncomfortably in his seat and reached for the beer bottle on the table in front of him. He didn't say a word. I don't think he'd read the book.

2. Rowley – My Teacher

Martin Rowley made a noisy entrance to the reception area of the Star Hotel, bumping through the double front door like a suitcase falling downstairs. The assistant manageress stared at him disapprovingly as he shambled from one end of the room to the other and back. The Star was one of Worcester's haughtier establishments and sweating, though not banned, was evidently frowned upon.

I didn't pay him too much attention, I thought he was much too smartly dressed to be the man I was waiting for, but ten minutes after my arranged meeting time had passed it dawned on me that he and I were the only people on the customer side of the reception area. I walked over to his table.

'Martin?'

He looked up and greeted me in a perfect English accent, clear as a Radio Four announcer but gruffer than the Queen. 'Lawrence. How are you doing, old boy?'

I liked him straight away. 'Martin,' I smiled. 'God, you look smart for an off-duty golf caddy.'

He was dressed in a three-button grey pin-stripe suit, blue cotton shirt and a firmly knotted tie. His thinning blond hair covered the tips of his ears and was teased into a wispy quiff. His shoes were highly polished. He looked smart enough to be mistaken for a county solicitor and mischievous enough to be mistaken for a county solicitor's client. It was easy to imagine him trudging along to the magistrates' court one day to defend himself on some piffling misdemeanour.

He chided me. 'Chairman of the European Tour Caddies' Association, if you don't mind.'

I was certain that willpower and fate would carry me, and Ross, to glory but there was no point in ignoring the technicalities of caddying involved in the journey upon which we were about to embark. After all, even Don Quixote had a prosaic *alter ego*, Alonso Quixano.

My meeting with Rowley was stage two of my master plan. I'd found myself a golfer; now I had travelled to Worcester seeking the Caddies' Association's official blessing. I thought Rowley could guide me through the rules of the tour and give me some advice on becoming a professional caddy.

I sat down. 'What do you want to ask me, then?' he said, pulling hard on his Silk Cut.

I explained that I was going to work for Ross Drummond – 'I caddied for him once, a few years ago. Good player,' he said. 'Just couldn't put it all together. Don't know what the problem is' – and that I wanted to know what it took to become a good tour caddy.

He stubbed out his cigarette and laughed. 'Let's go for a pint, old boy, and I'll tell you all about it.'

Rowley was a good talker, better than any county solicitor I'd ever heard in a magistrates' court. He had picked up the art in a previous life as the youngest Conservative councillor in the Midlands when Margaret Thatcher was at her peak. He said, 'I thought Maggie was great,' and I just looked at the carpet.

'How long have you been on tour?' I asked.

'Nine years,' he said. 'I went to Spain to watch a golf tournament and ended up caddying for a mate of mine who was taking part. After a couple of days I thought to myself, God, this is better than working fourteen hours a day, seven days a week.'

The Caddies' Association was full of people who'd made the same discovery as Rowley: Cambridge graduates, toilet cleaners, college drop-outs, plumbers, hippies, ex-punks, mobile-phone salesmen, professional golfers who hadn't quite made it swinging clubs and decided they would be better off carrying them. It sounded more like a synopsis of the *Yellow Pages* than a professional association.

I asked him what attracted such a disparate set to caddying.

'I'm going to Kuala Lumpur for the Malaysian Open on Monday,' he said, waving his hand towards the mid-afternoon crowd gathered at the bar. 'How many in here can say that? How many of them would tell you they can't wait to get into the office on Monday morning?'

Rowley went off to make a phone call, something about a slide show about caddying he was presenting that night. I looked round the room. The bar was uncomfortable, packed and smoky. Voices were raised, but not roaring-drunk loud. He was right: no one in there looked to be the kind who was desperately keen to get back into the office on a Monday morning.

Rowley walked back into the bar wearing an undertaker's frown. I noticed he had a perfectly shaped pot belly, which wobbled when he walked, like a bowling ball made of jelly. He sat down beside me. 'You want to learn about caddying?' he said.

I detected a slyness in the question but ignored it. 'Yes, that's why I came to see you.'

At last, I thought, I was getting somewhere. In between guzzling beer, Rowley said I didn't need his or anyone else's blessing, just show up in the car park on practice day, call myself a caddy and if a player was daft or desperate enough to employ me then I was a caddy. Not a real caddy, of course, he said, more of a bag carrier. Real caddies had experience and guile and the courage to make decisions when the player was under pressure. Bag carriers had strong legs and knew when to keep their mouths shut.

Becoming a tour caddy seemed all too easy. There were few rules: no shorts, no jeans. And it was best not to be late: players tended to dislike carrying their own golf bag up the first hole.

He asked me again. 'You really want to learn about caddying?' 'That's right.'

'Well, you can operate the slide projector at my talk tonight. My mate can't do it – he's got to play in a skittles match.' He smiled triumphantly. 'You have got a car, old boy, haven't you?'

The journey from Worcester took forty-five minutes. Rowley grew quieter as we got closer to our destination, a golf club on the outskirts of Solihull. He was nervous. He had only recently started giving his talks – 'Martin Rowley on life on the golf tour' – in an effort to top up his earnings during the winter. This was his fourth. Ever.

It was pitch dark when we arrived. We were early but the car park was already three-quarters full. Rowley got his projector from the boot of the car while I wrestled the screen from the back seat. A red Ford Escort pulled up at the front door of the clubhouse. I could hear the sound of muffled laughter as the car drew away again. Female laughter.

'Fuck,' Rowley said. 'I was hoping it was going to be a stag night. I'm not as good if there's women there. I can't let rip.' His accent had shaded to an earthier Midlands drawl.

'Don't worry, Martin, they'll love you,' I said. It was a wet Friday night in Solihull and I suspected expectations were never going to be high, even with tickets priced at eight pounds (including buffet supper). I was right. Even his obscure joke about Nick Faldo, which ended with a punch line about Britain's greatest ever golfer now having to look after three fannies, drew giggles from the table where the ladies' committee was seated.

Rowley was delighted, more so when the social secretary

came over and squeezed a tight ball of used notes into his palm. He put his lager on the bar and stuffed the cash into his pocket.

'Thanks for helping,' he said airily, in my direction.

'Don't mention it,' I said, making a mental note never to take up a position as a caddy's caddy. It had been a long night and although the trip hadn't been a complete waste of time – I had learned how to operate a slide projector, after all – I felt under-appreciated and under-informed. Perhaps I had expected too much from Rowley.

During his speech, he explained that a caddy must know the rules of golf, that he had to combine the golfing awareness of Jack Nicklaus with the psychological skills of Anthony Clare. He must keep the clubs clean and remember to keep his player's balls warm. He dropped a few names, Seve, Ollie, Ernie, Greg, and there was other stuff about the length of television cable needed to broadcast the Open Championship. This wasn't the knowledge I had been seeking. I was looking for something definitive, if not the Ten Commandments of Caddying then at least a rudimentary philosophy. The best Rowley could come up with during the course of the day was, 'Always remember the player pays the wages.' It was hardly enough to get me through what promised to be a long season.

Ross had been vague about his schedule. He intended playing in Morocco, Spain and Dubai. After that, he wasn't sure, probably France and Italy, then into Britain for a few tournaments up to the Open. The tour then swung into Holland, north to Sweden, then Germany, Austria, the Czech Republic. He might play them all, then again he might not. The one certainty was that I would soon be leaving for South Africa for our first tournament together.

Rowley was in a deep discussion about possible future engagements when I went over to say goodbye. He broke off negotiations with the social secretary for a minute.

'When are you out on tour?' he asked.

'South Africa,' I said. 'God, I'm so excited I could wet myself. If only I knew how to caddy.'

'I'll see you then. And don't worry.' He put his hand on my shoulder and promised me I'd pick things up as I went along.

3. Sun City

The Dimension Data Pro-Am was my first tournament as a caddy. I considered it the greatest single sporting event of the decade, though apathy was rife among the other caddies and players. Most of them thought it was nothing more than a warm-up before the tour headed back to Europe. The only other pocket of enthusiasm was occupied by the directors of Dimension Data, who had the privilege of stumping up £400,000 in prize money.

This was a lot of money but the company could afford it. Dimension Data, according to its press officer, was the second biggest IT systems supplier in South Africa, with a strong software division and an eye on joint ventures in the American market. Its directors sounded like a thrusting bunch of people, young and dynamic. I was glad I didn't meet them – they would only have sold me a computer I didn't want – but I was kind of sorry I never had the chance to say thanks to them in person; thanks for the tournament at which I began my career as a caddy and thanks for taking me to Sun City . . .

Sun City, South Africa. In my adolescent mind the place had been hell on earth, a gaudy gambling den where fat Afrikaners went to flaunt their sweaty pink bodies and bulging wallets in the face of the black majority. Remember the single by Little Stevie, 'I Don't Want To Play Sun City'? It was terrible but I still bought five copies. That's how much I despised Sun City back in the old days.

The resort had been the idea of Sol 'Baby' Kerzner, a reclusive Russian businessman whom his friends described as a good-looking garden gnome. As far as I was concerned, his creation had about the same amount of class and sophistication. It wasn't just the politics, there were the offences committed in the name of 'entertainment'. Sun City hosted the Miss World contest. Rod Stewart and Queen played there at the height of apartheid. Jean Michel Jarre was paid $2 million to stage a concert and laser show on the opening night of Lost City, a 'rediscovered' tribal city which had been converted into a marble-floored hotel. But the world had changed. Nelson Mandela celebrated the sixth year of his release from Robben Island the day I left home. It felt strange to be boarding the flight in London, knowing that soon I would be able to say that I, too, had played Sun City. If I could find a place to stay, that is.

One of the unwritten rules by which tour caddies live is that to pre-book accommodation is (a) to be a complete and utter sissy and (b) to be ripped off. Being new to the game I wasn't aware of this and called one of the travel agents who service the European tour in advance. He offered me flights and a room at the Sun City Casino Hotel with *en suite* bathroom, colour television, free bowling alley, water sports and twenty-four-hour room service for £2,000 (Club Class supplement, £1,000).

I turned him down – £2,000 was almost two months' wages – and called the Sun City tourist board to ask if there was somewhere I could pitch a tent.

There was a pause while my question registered. Eventually a male voice said 'I am sorry, sir. Have you got the correct number? This is Sun City.'

I felt him put his hand over the mouthpiece. After much

muffled sniggering, he came back on the line and explained that Sun City did not have camping facilities. Nor, unlike London, sir, did it have people sleeping in doorways. It did, however, have 2,338 hotel rooms and he asked if I would like to reserve one. Prices started at $169 a night. Or perhaps I preferred the King's Suite at the Lost City, a once-in-a-lifetime treat at the bargain price of $1,500? 'Would sir like time to think it over?' he asked.

I hung up.

Thunder clouds rolled over the Pilansburg mountains as our 'luxury' airport transfer, a battered white minibus with wire mesh over its windows, pulled up at the gates of Sun City. Immigration at Johannesburg airport had taken two hours and, once through Customs, the scramble to secure one of the eight available seats on the minibus was about as dignified and orderly as a school dinner queue. With Ross's help I secured a place, a minor triumph I regretted as soon I was introduced to our driver, a Londoner called Gary with a homicidal glint in his eye. He drove fast. Very fast.

The prospect of dying cheaply in the back of a converted prison van left me breathless and sweating for most of the first two hours of the drive through the Transvaal countryside. The final hour of the journey was ruined too, when Ross mentioned that he, like Rod and Freddie Mercury, had played Sun City during the apartheid years.

'It's a good golf course,' he said calmly, as a look of horror swept across my little liberal face like a forest fire.

'You didn't, did you?' I pleaded.

'I even think I made the cut,' he said.

The drive from the entrance to the hub of the Sun City complex was short and steep, along a silky stretch of dual carriageway. We disembarked at the steps of the Sun City Casino Hotel. I left Gary to retrieve my suitcase from the boot of a battered Volvo that had followed us from Johannesburg airport and wandered into the hotel foyer. It smelt of stale beer and cigarette smoke. The artificial lighting was feeble after the strong sunlight and gave the place the feel of a high-street amusement arcade. I counted three grey-skinned souls amid the rows of one-armed bandits.

I walked back towards the daylight. Ross was coming the other way, wearing the soporific look of a man who knew he was about to fall backwards on to a queen-size bed, order room service and curl up under a chintz duvet for the rest of the day. I felt as if I'd turned up for the first day of term at the wrong school. I still didn't have a place to stay.

'Don't worry, something will turn up,' he said dreamily. 'I'll catch you later.'

I went outside to get my case. Another caddy had arrived with the news that rooms were available at the Cabanas, a dormitory complex three hundred yards back down the hill.

This was the cheapest place in Sun City and justifiably so. The palm trees and constant clicking of exotic insects couldn't disguise the fact that it had been lifted wholesale from the blueprint for an inner London town hall, but with more sullen and unhelpful staff who appeared to be competing with each other to extract the greatest revenge from white guests for decades of racist injustice. Every bedroom had its own cast-iron valuables safe bolted to the floor, and the restaurant, the *à la carte* Morula restaurant, was not a restaurant but a building site.

A twin room cost fifty pounds a night, the most expensive accommodation of the entire season, but desperation was beginning to set in. A dozen caddies and players were mingling around the reception desk, each more unwashed and more exhausted than the others.

'It's a bit dear,' someone said. 'Shall we try and find out if there's a camp site?'

This was the signal for everyone who'd ever had dealings

with the Sun City tourist board to check in. We then paired off, a hurtful ritual conducted in every hotel foyer in which tour caddies gather. There was only one rule as far as I could make out: avoid sharing with the new boy at all costs, he's an idiot and an amateur.

For a moment it looked like I might be rooming with a thin, pale-skinned English caddy who had been reading *Time* magazine on the journey from the airport. He quickly found another room-mate and I was passed to a horrified French pro who spoke perfect English, as in 'I'm not sharing with the new boy, he's an idiot and an amateur.'

In the end I paired up with Paul Aparechos, a Spanish caddy. We were the only two left standing when the ritual ended, thrown together by the mutual contempt of our peers, but it didn't seem to matter. I was pleased to get a bed and he seemed ecstatic to have a chance to practise his English.

As I unpacked he told me his life story. He had been born in Zaragoza, where he had once been a physical education teacher. He was twenty-six. He hosted a golf show on a radio station and wrote a newspaper column about bullfighting for a local paper. He caddied for Miguel Angel Martin, a Spanish professional who had had a good year in 1992 but had since lost his form and had only just kept his card for the new season. Paul dreamed of caddying for Seve. He loved Seve and he loved golf.

'Tony,' he said conspiratorially – (he hadn't been able quite to get his ears round my Scottish accent and misheard my name). 'Tony, do you know that I was almost married once but six days before, whooooosh, I'm off. I thought – what do you say? – no contest, it is golf for me, please.'

I felt sorry for the girl but not for long. I had made my first friend on tour.

Now that I was privy to intimate details about Paul's life I felt I should let him in on my secret. I explained that this was my first time. I was an idiot and an amateur and that, as far as the other caddies were concerned, he was banished to social Siberia as a punishment for sharing with a new boy.

He took the bad news well. 'Never mind,' he said. 'I'll show you how to be a caddy. But first, let's go for to look at the golf course.'

I was in bed by now, exhausted, and suggested we go for to look at the golf course on the morrow but he wouldn't be deflected. Wearily, I put my clothes back on and followed him into the dregs of the daylight.

Ross had been right. The Gary Player Golf and Country Club was a great golf course, though virtually impossible for anyone who didn't play the game for a living. It threaded its way through Sun City's artificial rain forest for over seven thousand yards. The ninth and eighteenth greens were guarded by lakes. The fairways were tight, just twenty yards wide in some places, and the rough was about as friendly as a pit bull. Beyond it there was snake-infested forest. 'The toughest course on the sub-continent' was the boast in the clubhouse brochure and hundreds of tourists queued up daily to take their punishment.

The pros played there twice a year. The first was during the Sun City Million-Dollar Golf Challenge, a 72-hole event to which twelve of the world's top players were invited to compete for a first prize of $1 million. The player who comes last in the Challenge still 'wins' $50,000.

The Dimension Data championship was a far less prestigious event. Three rounds were to be played over the Gary Player course and another at the Lost City course, a newer, less demanding lay-out near the summit of the Sun City complex. The tournament was a pro-am, in which the professionals played with an amateur golfer in every round.

Normally pro-ams are staged the day before the main tournament, as a sop to the sponsors. They are meaningless events, the prize money is lousy and the standard of golf played by amateurs generally worse. If you ever overhear a tour golfer saying he loves the pro-am, it gives him the chance to meet interesting people, assume he is lying. They hate them.

To have an entire European tour event run as a pro-am was highly unusual and the prospect of taking part in one made me nervous. I had visions of Ross being paired with a white supremacist who was pissed off that he'd been paired with a Scottish golfer whom he'd never heard of and his pinko caddie. This wasn't an idle fantasy. Golf is not a black man's sport in South Africa and the white liberals were too busy fighting decades of institutional racism to be bothered about lowering their handicap.

Ross was more sanguine. He'd had every conceivable kind of pro-am partner over the years. Some were great, like James Garner, the star of the *Rockford Files*, with whom he'd once spent a very pleasant day on a golf course in Buckinghamshire. Others were awful, like Foster Brooks, now dead, an American comedian whose speciality had been playing a drunk pilot. 'He did this stunt on the seventeenth hole which involved knocking his ball back down the fairway with his putter.' It was just before midnight in the casino bar and Ross was reminiscing. 'Anyway. He thought this putter thing was a great laugh. To me he was just being a tosser.'

'He sounds great,' I said. Ross looked at me as though I'd just produced a cockroach from under my tongue. We agreed to disagree and arranged to meet the following morning for our first practice round on the Lost City course.

Paul was sleeping when I got back to the room. Silently, I laid out my outfit for the first day. I had chosen it weeks before: a clean, pressed polo shirt (red, no golf logo), trousers (chinos, Levi), one new pair of flat-soled trainers (Nike, white – I discussed this with Ross and we agreed that white was the classic colour for a caddy), socks (anything but red – colour co-ordinated socks and shirt would have been too sad). I had a plan of the course, a pencil, some sun-block and a pair of sunglasses like Sterling Morrison used to wear in the Velvet Underground. I thought I was ready for everything, and I was – everything except the ordeal of putting Ross's blue and white leather bag on my back and walking six miles across what purported to be a golf course.

Did I say golf course?

Viewed from the restful cool of the clubhouse, the Lost City course was undeniably spectacular, like a cross between Kew Gardens and the set for a Sergio Leone movie. Lush green strips of grass fought for space with vast waste bunkers and dense forest. Euphorbias and giant cacti were dotted everywhere.

The clubhouse itself had the appearance of a kiddies' sand-castle which had been stood on by a clumsy dad. It was an interesting and original building but it couldn't disguise the fact that the course was not much more than a rugged mountainside with eighteen flags randomly planted along its contours.

For the first hour in the sun, I felt as if I was staggering home from a party with a drunk on my back. At the sixth tee I stopped to make sure Ross hadn't climbed in beside his clubs and by the time we reached the ninth green my head was about to explode in the heat. I ran into the pro shop to find a hat. All they could offer me was a wide-brimmed safari number, which Ross suggested I douse in water before putting it on.

'An old trick from my days on the Safari golf tour,' he said.

This had a magical refreshing effect. I was able to concentrate on the golf.

Ross was playing with Stephen McAllister, one of his regular practice partners. They strolled round the course as if they'd played it all their lives. If they hit a bad shot, they simply reloaded and hit another straight down the flag. It looked so easy. Ross, who'd scarcely swung a golf club for six weeks, looked relaxed and confident. I dashed back to the hotel to tell Paul my news: Ross had made five birdies in practice.

He was lying by the pool watching a crowd of young women half-heartedly playing water polo.

'Five birdies?' He made a face. 'Noo bad.'

'Noo bad? It was bloody great,' I said.

This made him laugh. 'Come on, friend, it's only Tuesday. It's like playing football without goals.'

I knew it was the first tournament of the season but a tiny part of me thought we could still win. I told Paul.

He laughed even louder. 'Don't be ridil, ridicil. What's it you say?'

'Ridiculous?'

'That's it. Don't be ridiculous.'

A second practice round, over the Gary Player course, did little to diminish my excitement. Ross holed a nine-iron from 155 yards at the seventeenth. It was the first time he'd holed a full shot for years and as it went in he looked at the club as if it had just spoken to him. We finished the round. Smiling, we strode manfully towards the practice putting green.

I'd had an idea. During the winter I'd been flicking through the pages of a golf magazine when I'd come across a table of statistics that ranked PGA tour players according to their record of hitting greens in regulation (one shot to get on the green at a par-three, two shots at a par-four, and so on). It was a measure of a player's accuracy and the usual names were at the top of the list: Woosnam, Montgomerie, Olazábal, Drummond.

Drummond!

If this was true, Ross was the eleventh most accurate player in Europe. It didn't take a genius to work out how the eleventh most accurate golfer on tour from tee to green ended up as the 111th best money-earner on tour: it was bad putting, which was where my idea came in.

It took great courage even to bring the subject up as I was

way out of my depth. What insight could I give a professional who had been playing the game at the highest level for nineteen years? He had seen me play. He knew I swung a seven-iron with the same finesse as a Canadian fisherman clubbing baby seals. I would have been as well advising Margaret Thatcher on how she could triple unemployment.

We reached the practice putting green. 'Ross, I've got an idea.' He didn't flinch. 'Go on,' he said. 'I'm listening.'

I explained that I knew he was an awesome golfer but that his putting was letting him down 'What you have to do is hole forty four-foot putts in succession at the end of every day. It'll improve your technique, give you confidence over short putts and a sense of achievement to take to bed every night.'

He didn't display the slightest irritation at my presumption, at least not until we had been on the putting green for another forty minutes. He got as far as twenty putts in a row before missing one; then ten, five, one. He finally got up to twenty-nine.

Number thirty horseshoed round the hole. He stood up and rubbed his hands together. 'My finger is sore, you know,' he said.

I ignored him. He tried again. 'I've not got to hole forty of these in a row, have I?'

'It'll be good for you,' I said. 'Set yourself goals. Achieve. Let's go, positive thoughts.'

It was hardly Sigmund Freud but it was the best I could manage on a limited grasp of psychology and a low budget.

'Yeah, but what if I can't do forty putts? Anyway, it's too tough.'

'Just give it ten more minutes.'

He summoned up the determination from somewhere and rolled the next thirty-six straight in the middle.

I tried to put pressure on him – 'Thirty-seven, thirty-eight . . .' – but he rolled the next four in as well.

'Well done,' I said. I shook his hand. It was sodden.

Exhausted, he drifted off towards the hotel. I hung around. I wanted to soak up the atmosphere of big-time golf. I walked over to the eighteenth green and knew for sure I had come to the wrong tournament. There was no tented village, just a press tent about the size of a marquee that a middle-class couple would pitch in their back garden for their daughter's wedding. Two PGA officials were sitting in a smaller tent in the shadow of an oak tree. There were no grandstands, just a limp blue nylon rope round the circumference of the green. A group of children playing nearby added to the air of a gentle school sports day.

I double-checked the scoreboard. Ross's name was there, at the top of the second column of names on the right. We were paired with Michael Du Toit, a South African pro, first match off at six thirty a.m.

I woke at two o'clock in the morning. Paul was sitting up in bed playing his Gameboy.

'What's wrong?' I said. He was due on the tee ten minutes after me, at six forty a.m., and I suggested that perhaps this wasn't the best preparation.

'Caddy dreams,' he said. 'Early start. Never out of sleep, never in sleep, exasperation.'

He played his Gameboy until dawn. I drifted in and out of sleep, like a drunk on a train, trying my damndest to keep one eye on the clock.

Ross and I met in his hotel lobby at five thirty. He was well scrubbed, colour-coordinated and wilfully casual, as though he'd stepped from the pages of a Littlewoods' catalogue. 'How are you, faithful retainer?' he said cheerily.

'Feeling good,' I lied. I couldn't have been more nervous if he had been head to head with Greg Norman in the last round of the Open.

'Get the bag, Lawrence, will you, please,' he said.

He'd carried it from the room to the lift, left it at the lift door on the ground floor and walked across the reception area.

I paused for a second – couldn't he have carried his own bag from the lift? – then scampered off to fetch it. What else was he paying me for? He had asked me to fetch his bag. What was wrong with that? It meant that everything was for real and he was treating me like a proper caddy. Anyway, it was time I got used to menial tasks: my life was about to become full of them. Collect a bucket of golf balls at the range; check the time; wet one end of the towel used to clean his clubs; check the time; make sure the balls were marked with a red circle round the i of Titleist; put a piece of fruit and some mineral water in the bag; collect a piece of paper which detailed the pin positions on every hole for that day; check the time.

We were standing on the first tee at six twenty-three a.m., give or take five seconds. It was still twilight. Michael Du Toit shook Ross's hand and ignored me. His caddy Albert Mashaya, dressed in a pair of lime green shorts and faded blue T-shirt with the neck stretched down to his nipples, looked as if he'd dropped by on the way to the beach.

Our amateur partner was Joe Grove, a talkative Afrikaner with the physique of a telephone box. He ran a bank, loved rugby and had a golf handicap of three. He kept firearms and spent $20,000 a year watering his garden and hated playing off the forward tees. 'We're not bloody women after all, are we?' he said, when this last piece of news was broken to him. I hated him immediately.

The two pros collected their scorecard from the officials behind a desk at the side of the tee. We were ready. First Du Toit, then Ross. I handed Ross the driver and retreated to the bag.

The first shot of any tournament is the most important. It only counts as one on the scorecard but it sets the tone for the week. A feeling of dread rushed through me as I watched Ross take a practice swing. I was certain he was going to make a complete fool of himself. Mercifully, there were no spectators around. My mind was racing. What could I say to make him feel better about what was about to happen?

This was illogical. I'd spent the previous two days in slack-jawed admiration at the way he had been hitting the ball. So what? I started praying. Dear God, I will trade anything for one more good shot; my sex life, twenty years of a Labour government, the Clash re-forming with me on lead guitar, Celtic winning the European Cup.

I couldn't look. My eyes fixed on a blade of grass two inches from my left shoe until I heard the crack of ball against his metal-headed driver. I looked up. It was high, too high, and moving slightly left to right but it was in play. Only kidding, God. I skipped up the fairway after Ross.

'Good shot,' I said.

'It'll do,' he replied quietly. He seemed subdued. The confidence of the previous two days had disappeared. He holed a five-foot putt to par the first hole but a high, fading tee shot at the second left him with an impossible lie in the rough and he took a double bogey six. A birdie at the sixth helped but he was four over by the fifteenth.

Ross looked desolate. I walked ahead of him on the sixteenth fairway and struck up a conversation with Joe Grove. 'Nice day,' I said. It had turned into a balmy summer's morning. The sound of music, 'Young Girl' by Gary Puckett and the Union Gap, drifted on the breeze like smoke.

'Idyllic, Lawrence. Idyllic.'

He didn't want to talk but I pressed him. 'What do you reckon to Nelson Mandela, then? A great man, isn't he?' I said.

He melted. 'Lawrence. That man is a saint. Man, when you're in a room and he comes into it, oh, what a presence. You know, I worry so much about what will happen when he dies.'

His eyes had filled up. The conversation lasted less than two minutes but it made the trip to South Africa worthwhile. If a white, gun-toting, rugby-playing Boer like Joe Grove could be reduced to a jelly of admiration by a black South African president, I was sure I could learn to love Sun City.

We became best friends for the last two holes. Ross made another bogey but, perversely, cheered up. The three of us were walking down the final fairway discussing how attitudes had changed among white South Africans when Michael Du Toit hit his third shot into the lake in front of the green. We watched in disbelief as he sent his caddy into the water to find the ball.

Albert Mashaya looked as dumbfounded as the rest of us.

Ross three-putted the last green but I scarcely noticed. Albert was back on dry land. He hadn't found the ball, which was hardly surprising as the water was chest-deep and the colour of mud.

I went over to offer him a towel. 'He told me he is poor and can't afford to lose balls,' he said. 'I can't say no, I need the job.'

Ross's first round of seventy-eight was not the worst of the day. There were a handful of seventy-nines and ten scores in the eighties. Thomas Levet, a French pro, shot ninety. He was last seen heading towards the casino where, according to a caddy I spoke to afterwards, he tried to put 10,000 francs on himself to miss the half-way cut. This was a lie, but it was a fair indication of how brutal tour humour can be.

Ross and I held a post-mortem on the practice putting green and agreed that his prospects of being among the top sixty-five players who would make the cut were slim.

'What went wrong?' I said.

He leaned on his putter and looked guiltily at the ground, like a schoolboy who'd been hauled before the headmaster. He muttered something about worrying too much about a couple of holes where he needed a really accurate drive and being in a bad frame of mind when he woke up that morning. I wanted to ask him how anyone could know they had woken up in a bad frame of mind when they had only just woken up, but managed to stop myself.

'Who's knows what went wrong?' He shrugged. 'I just knobbed it round.'

(This is a golf professional's way of saying he played badly: it doesn't mean he hit the ball round the course with his penis but that he might as well have done.)

A second-round seventy-one, for a total of 149, wasn't good enough.

I was lying back on the grass outside the clubhouse when an official slapped a black magnetic strip on to the scoreboard: Final Cut 147. This was three over par. He'd missed by two shots. At least he had played well on the second day. And he finished with an eagle three after hitting his second shot to within twenty feet of the flag, a shot that gave me my first caddying triumph of the week.

He'd wanted to take a three-iron, I suggested a four-iron. I'd like to say I based this advice on a range of factors, wind direction, high altitude and the like, but I didn't, it was just a hunch. Three-iron had water written all over it.

He hesitated and then said, 'What the hell?' and hit it 223 yards exactly, slightly left of the flag.

'Good club,' he said. I walked off the green flushed with pride. We hadn't won the Dimension Data Pro-Am but, just for that thirty seconds, it felt as if we had. I couldn't wait for the next tournament to start, but first there was some unfinished business.

At the eleventh hole, Du Toit's ball had been lying behind a stone the size of a fifty-pence piece, which Ross had thought was embedded in the ground. They had fallen into an argument after the South African picked up the stone and threw it away. Technically, if the stone has been embedded, Du Toit had committed an offence punishable by a two-stroke penalty. It was arcane and stupid but the rules of golf are like that.

The incident was still troubling Ross when he walked off the final green. He had a fetish about playing by the rules. He asked me whether I thought he should report Du Toit to the tournament director.

What I knew about the rules of the European PGA Tour could be engraved in capital letters on the back of a fifty-pence piece. The alleged 'offence' seemed mind-bogglingly trivial, but then I thought of Albert towelling off his legs at the side of the final green the previous day.

'Oh, you must report him, Ross,' I said, with as much solemnity as I could muster. 'After all, rules are rules.'

Albert and I retreated to the shade of the clubhouse forecourt. We watched as the two players went off to solve the mystery of the embedded stone, a conundrum, I suspected, that would have stretched the combined might of Inspector Clouseau, Miss Marple and the NYPD, never mind an overworked PGA rules official. I was right. The case against Du Toit was not proven. He had the satisfaction of not being penalized and Ross had at least cleared his conscience. I found the two of them having a beer together, as if nothing had happened.

Eventually, it was time to go back to the hotel. I loaded the bag on to the courtesy car and Ross jumped in the front seat. He seemed happier than I imagined anyone could be after travelling eight thousand miles to miss the cut.

'What are we going to do now?' I asked.

It was still only Friday night. We were trapped in Sun City until Sunday afternoon. The weather was sub-tropical. There were casinos, bars, wild-game parks, a man-made surf beach and a building that staged a fake earthquake every hour on the hour, all within seven-iron distance. The Sun City topless dance troupe even sunbathed by our hotel swimming pool every afternoon.

'I suppose we'll find something,' Ross replied, gleefully rubbing his hands.

*

31

Too many people were trying to get on to the bus taking us to Johannesburg for the next tournament. One of the tour's travel agents came on board and said two caddies would have to give up their seats for players. Paul, who was sitting next to me, was one of the unlucky pair to be thrown off. I was indignant but he didn't seem bothered: there would be another bus in a couple of hours.

We rolled slowly down the hill towards the exit gates, out of the shadow of the hotel. I could see a small crowd of spectators following the last group of players along the closing holes. The Dimension Data Pro-Am was coming to a climax.

A caddy who had been sitting on the floor of the bus while we were waiting to leave was now occupying Paul's seat. 'I wonder who won the golf tournament,' I said to him.

'Who cares who won the fuckin' golf tournament?' he growled. 'It wasn't me.'

4. Buck's Fizz and Death Threats

Paul Ray, a morbid Londoner better known on tour as Saddam on account of his dark, bushy moustache and even blacker demeanour, looked suspiciously at the row of champagne glasses on a coffee table in the reception of a Johannesburg apartment block. Each was filled with a sickly orange liquid. 'What the fuckin'el is this?'

Martin Rowley overheard him and walked over towards the table. 'It's Buck's Fizz, you peasant. Champagne and orange juice, just what a caddy deserves at the end of a hard day's work,' he said, in the haughty accent I imagined he once used when slapping down socialist councillors.

'I know it's fuckin' Buck's Fizz, you stupid bastard,' Saddam hissed. 'It's just not exactly what we're used to, is it?'

Rowley glanced sideways at me. 'Not everyone treats us like this,' he confirmed. There was deep regret in his voice.

'Maybe they think we're the players,' I said.

A smiling receptionist, wearing a green, two-piece trouser suit with a badge on the lapel that said Jodie, interrupted, 'No, you are the caddies' group. Eleven rooms reserved, late arrival. The European Caddies' Tour Association.'

I corrected her. 'The European Tour Caddies' Association.'

'That's right,' she said, her smile tightening slightly. 'Delighted you made it. Did you have a nice journey?'

Rowley went off to register the group, while I guided Jodie through our two-hour circumlocutions of Johannesburg's northern suburbs in search of the apartments. I was just about to reach the part where we drove past a restaurant called Jimmy's Killer Prawns for the fourth time – it sounded tempting but we didn't stop for dinner – when Rowley called us all together.

I felt a familiar wave of exclusion washing towards me as he started handing out the room keys and pairing people off. The huddle was thinning out ominiously when he turned to me and said, 'I've put you in an apartment with Pat, Julian and Gazza.'

Most of the caddies were in the main buildings but we were given apartment thirty-four, in a terrace of prim, two-storey houses at the far end of a compound guarded by an electrified fence the height of a rugby goal. The other three raced out of the front door and through the security gates. I hung back. I was still a new boy and I didn't want to get into trouble for taking the best room. It had been raining heavily and an ankle-deep pool of water had formed outside our front door. We splashed our way through and took the muck inside.

The interior was like the home of a recently married couple. It had a compact-disc player, a video, a television, all just out of the box, and a kitchen that smelled of woodchip and paint, as though it had been fitted that afternoon. There were two bedrooms, Pat and Gazza in one, Julian and I in the other.

We unpacked, then sat down in front of the television and drank pot after pot of weak tea. It was a scene of genteel domesticity. I felt comfortable. Accepted. We talked for hours, about what had brought us out on tour, about caddying, golf and golfers.

Pat was Pat McSweeney, an ex-carpet fitter who'd come out on the tour for three weeks in 1991 and stayed out. He had five children, had been divorced and now lived in a council flat in Colchester with his girlfriend, Sheila. He caddied for Paul Curry, a solid, workmanlike English pro for whom he'd once fitted a carpet. They had been together for three years. I was amazed. 'We get on well about everything, except politics,' he said. 'I'm Labour, he's the biggest Tory ever. The thing about these players is they live on a different planet from us, nice hotels, big money, courtesy cars, all the rest of it. It's them and us, always remember that.'

Julian Phillips, 'Ferret', had been on the tour for even longer, nine years. He was called Ferret because everyone said he chased after women with great determination. He was single, good-looking, with sharply cut straw-coloured hair slightly thinning at the front. There wasn't a trace of a beer belly on his thirty-six-year-old body, unlike most of the other guys who'd been on the tour as long as he had. He had humorous eyes and a northern accent as flat as the base of an iron. He spoke in torrents. We were on our second pot of tea when I asked him why he kept so fit.

'You've got ta be professional, lak, take the job seriously, lak. The big players, lak the ones who'll make you real money, don't want to walk down fairway with a fat tramp carrying their bag, do they, lak . . .'

He stopped for breath and I asked him what he did when he wasn't caddying.

'Bog cleana',' McSweeney said.

'That's not right,' Phillips said. 'Don't listen to that twat – a do a bit of school care-taking lak.'

During the golf season, Phillips caddied for Miguel Angel Jimenez, a Spanish player on the fringes of the Ryder Cup team. He wasn't quite in the caddies' premier league, his player wasn't yet good enough, but everyone said he was getting there. He even had a sponsor, a company called Foam Techniques, which had given him a wardrobe full of clothes embroidered with its slogan: 'The Home of Foam – You Beauty'.

Whatever Foam Techniques paid him to display its name it got its money's worth. Phillips would have tried to sell foam to a man with two sponges for a backside. 'It's not just any old foam lak you get in settees lak it's the stuff they put in air-conditioning and fridges to stop it rattling,' he told me one day, unprompted, while we were standing on the range watching our respective players beating balls.

He was the same on the golf course, keen, enthusiastic, ambitious. He intended staying on tour for another three years, or as long as it took to make enough money to buy his own little hotel. And before he finished he wanted to caddy for one special player. He started to tell me about this ambition at the Moroccan Open, three weeks after that first night in Johannesburg.

'Don't tell me,' I interrupted. 'Seve.'

He looked surprised. ''Ow did you know?'

'You and a million others.'

He laughed heartily. 'But me and Golden Bollocks were meant for each other.'

Gary 'Gazza' Currie was quieter than the other two. He had come to Johannesburg to look for work. He had lost his job with Ronan Rafferty, a former Ryder Cup player who could still win over £150,000 a year and we spent much of our first night in Johannesburg trying to find him a player.

McSweeney and Phillips ran through a list. Currie answered each name with a firm no or a shake of the head, while everyone else offered an opinion on the player: 'I wouldn't work for him either, Gazza, he's a choker/a chopper/shit/kidding himself if he thinks he can making a living playing professional golf . . .'

Currie was one of the new breed of caddies. Twenty-five years old, highly articulate, presentable, a former university student who saw caddying as a career. He was choosy about whom he worked for. 'There are plenty of crap bags I could pick up but I don't want to do that. I've got used to a bit of cash and excitement with Rafferty and can't be bothered starting at the bottom again,' he explained.

The list of potential employers was petering out when Phillips's face lit up. 'What about Paul Lawrie? I 'ear 'e's looking for someone,' he said.

I'd met Lawrie in Sun City, where he and Ross had played a practice round together. He had only just kept his tour card at the end of the previous year but his career record was good. He hit the ball further than most people go on holiday, putted smoothly and carried himself with an upright, confident gait.

'Good player,' I volunteered. Currie's ears pricked up at this second opinion: a good player without a regular caddy was a rare beast. 'But is he going to make me money?' he said.

'Money. That's the only thing anyone on the tour cares about. It's disgusting,' McSweeney said. The others looked at him with expressions that went whizzing past incomprehension. He started laughing. 'Only joking, plonkers.'

It was my turn. I explained that I was caddying for Ross Drummond. The other three fell over each other in their haste to tell me that I wouldn't make much money doing that. Money wasn't my prime motivation, I said. I was living my dream of being a professional sportsman. I was Don Quixote, if they really wanted to know. I was writing a book. I knew I wouldn't actually be playing golf but I wanted to experience the romance, the pain, the moments of glory of professional golf and, anyway, how did they know I wouldn't make much money? Ross was a good player and on his day, who knows, he could win a tournament. In fact, he was bound to win a tournament. It was my destiny.

McSweeney almost choked on his tea. 'You must be a good writer,' he chuckled, ''cause if you think Ross Drummond is going to win a tournament you've got some imagination.'

The following morning the mood was ugly as fifteen caddies crammed into a minibus outside the apartments at seven thirty. We'd been ripped off – forty pounds for a fifteen-minute ride to Houghton Golf Club, the venue for the South African PGA Championship. Rowley, a hero the previous night for organizing a place to stay that was cheap, clean and had a British sports television channel, was cast in the role of profligate villain for hiring the most expensive taxi in southern Africa.

Poor Rowley. He'd already become a diminished figure from the confident, urbane man I'd met in Worcester. The other caddies liked him but they hid it well, and his role on tour was to organize everything and take abuse for everything. Not a terrific deal as deals go, I thought.

He hadn't been forgiven by the time we arrived at the corner of Second Avenue and Lloys Ellis, the main entrance to the course. We turned in off the street, only to find that the gates were blocked by a crush of at least fifty black caddies.

'Come on, Rowley, get a move on,' someone shouted from the back of the minibus.

Rowley snapped at the driver, 'Come on, mate, we're going to be late for the players.'

He rolled down his window and started negotiating with the security guards. The crowd had now gathered round the bus and were staring silently at us. I caught myself looking at a middle-aged man, maybe about fifty. He was wearing a limp grey suit, darkened and mottled by the morning thunderstorm. A big splashy raindrop fell from a tree on to his head as our eyes met. I smiled but his face stayed blank. He and the others were looking for work.

'Somebody wave some cash at them,' the caddy in the seat behind me said. So much for international caddy solidarity. We started to move forward through the gates, past the blue-suited security guards and a huge temporary sign which said, 'Welcome to the South African PGA Championship. No cameras, video recorders, tape recorders or firearms.' Firearms? At a golf tournament?

George Mosheshe was waiting for me on the steps of the

Houghton clubhouse, taking shelter under the wooden porch by the front door. He'd been allowed inside the perimeter fence because he could prove he already had a job, working for Stephen McAllister.

George and I had met in Sun City. We had spent an evening together in Lekoadi, a dirt-track village of corrugated-iron houses ten miles south of the gambling complex. He stayed there whenever there was a golf tournament, renting a room in a house. It didn't have electricity or running water but it was cheap – fifty rand, about ten pounds a week – and friendly. When he took me there, the stunned looks at the sight of a white man stepping over the threshold (a rare sight in Lekoadi), with a Scottish accent (even rarer), gave way immediately to smiles. Someone produced bottles of warm lager and we got drunk. George and I commiserated with each other about missing the cut in Sun City. He sang some township folk songs and I sang him 'Wonderwall' and 'You Wear It Well'. I promised him a pair of Nikes and an Adidas shirt. He told me his life story.

He'd been addicted to golf ever since he'd peered through the fence at his grandmother's house in Soweto and caught his first sight of the black sand greens at Mofolo Golf Club. He started caddying a couple of years later at an all-white club in Johannesburg for seventy-five cents a day. His girlfriend Elizabeth, a social worker in Cape Town, wanted him to find a decent job, something in marketing. There'd been a million excuses to pack it in over the years, most of them to do with the behaviour of South African golfers.

'A lot of them are bastards. They call you kaffir or nigger,' he said. 'Some of them will pay you five hundred rand and pay a white guy twelve hundred for the same job.'

Somehow, George had hung in. Being a caddy was the best way of becoming a pro: he could pick up good habits and swing tips. He had a handicap of six (about the same as a good club golfer in Britain) but with a bit of hard work he could get it down to scratch. He was almost thirty, old for an amateur with unfulfilled ambitions, but he'd heard of a black guy from Swaziland who'd turned pro when he was forty.

'My grandmother was right. She told me to take up golf. It's a spiritual game, not like the other games – you can't get hurt playing golf.'

It had been way past midnight when George roused a driver from a nearby house and persuaded him to take me back to Sun City. Drinking in the open air under a starry, charcoal sky had made me feel New Age, almost tearful. 'That's a beautiful story about your grandmother, George,' I said, climbing into my taxi.

'I suppose it is.' He was laughing. 'Pity she knew fuck all about golf.'

George smiled now and stretched out his hand as I walked up the clubhouse stairs. 'How's Grandma, George?' I said.

'Didn't I tell you? She died five years ago.'

He looked smarter than most of the other black caddies, in pristine white training shoes, black jeans and a mustard polo neck, which still had packing creases. McAllister was paying him a thousand rand a week, plus percentage, plus a carrier bag full of golf shirts.

'No golf today but plenty of sport.' He pointed at the circle of five caddies that had formed in the middle of the rhododendron garden. They had surrounded a tall, grey-haired pro and an argument was being conducted in low, teeth-clenched voices to avoid attracting the attention of the security guards.

'That guy isn't going to pay his caddy. Says he gave him the wrong club last week and it cost him the tournament,' George said. 'It's total shit. The guy hit a three-wood out of bounds, hit the same club to the middle of the fairway. Took eight – a quad-bogey.'

The sound of thunder sent most of the caddies running for shelter. Justice, George's friend, joined us under the porch. The golfer with whom he and the others had been arguing was an

American who regularly played the South African Tour. The player had a reputation for welshing on deals with caddies.

'Last year he tried to pay someone with two pairs of size fourteen shoes. The caddy was a friend of mine, he was size eight.'

'What'll happen?' I asked.

'They say they'll kill him,' he replied. I didn't know whether to take him seriously. His answer had been so casual: because he knew they didn't mean it, or because it was a normal occurrence? The sign outside the front gates suddenly began to make some sense.

Thankfully, the squabble blew itself out. The pro paid up and agreed to take on another caddy although by then it didn't matter: play had been called off for the day because of rain.

It was ten o'clock. Ross wasn't due to arrive at the course until noon. The guards opened the gates and the caddies who'd been waiting outside spilled into the car park. Reggie Samewehi was among them. We'd also met in Sun City, where he had caddied for Eamonn Darcy. He greeted me as if I was his brother and got straight down to business. 'I need a new bag, man. Darcy's too old, man, too weak.'

This was true. Darcy had played in the 1987 Ryder Cup but his best days were probably now behind him. He had a strange, sing-song swing, which the television commentators described as 'unorthodox' or 'individual'. The other caddies said it looked like an octopus falling out of the window – not to Darcy's face, of course.

'Hey, you know Rocca, ask him if I can work for him this week.'

It was true that Costantino Rocca, one of the favourites for the tournament, was looking for a caddy that week. Less true was Samewehi's belief that I knew him. I didn't know him at all.

'Well, to be honest, Reggie . . .'

'Come on, man, help me out.'

I lied, it was easier. 'I'll see if I can find him in the clubhouse.'

I made my way from the car park, past the first tee and the practice putting green, where three local caddies were sitting on the sodden grass. 'Fuckin' white caddies,' one spat. Another caddy, in a long grey coat and black wraparound sunglasses, was stabbing his finger into the chest of a course official, keeping time with his angry speech. 'There will be no tournament this week. We'll dig this place up.' He prodded the man's chest extra hard for emphasis. 'Get. That.'

As far as I could make out there wasn't a ban on black caddies in the clubhouse but it was clear that Mandela's influence hadn't quite reached this particular corner of old South Africa. There were only whites in the dining room, players and European caddies. Rowley was standing by the orange-juice cooler, deep in conversation. When he had finished, I tapped him on the arm. I'd been meaning to ask him about my eligibility for the Caddies' Association.

'You've got to be joking. You're supposed to be a caddy for fifteen tournaments. So far you've been a bag carrier for one,' he snapped, walking away.

'What's wrong with you?' I asked.

He stopped, exasperated. 'I've got a lot on my mind. I feel like David Owen and Cyrus Vance rolled into one.' He nodded towards the scattering of black caddies outside the clubhouse. 'They've been threatening me they'd get their knives out.'

'They wouldn't, would they?'

Rowley had spent much of the morning in negotiation with the head of the South African caddies' organization, whose members were complaining that too many of the European players had brought their own caddies. The Johannesburg tournament was one of the local caddies' biggest earning weeks of the year, particularly if they could get on a European player's bag (they paid better than South African pros). Those who worked at Houghton every day had to get a bag for the tournament, otherwise they wouldn't earn any money for the week.

Rowley said, 'The thing is they've turned up and they've told themselves in their own minds they'll be working. This week is their Christmas and birthday rolled into one. As far as they're concerned we've stolen their jobs. I've tried to explain things but the best I can do is tell them how to get organized and get better conditions for themselves.

'What worries me is that these guys don't put a value on life. They might think fuck it, let's get someone. A lot of our boys are shitting themselves.'

I looked down the length of the dining room. Julian Phillips was sitting at the nearest table beside Pat McSweeney and Andy Prodger, who had caddied Faldo to two Majors. At the next table, Andy Blaydon, a Rod Stewart lookalike who caddied for Richard Boxall, was sipping his usual early-morning beer. Richie Blair and David 'Magic' Johnstone were in the far corner, lighting up. There were others whom I hadn't met yet: Kevin Woodward, an ex-Rhodesian Army officer back on tour after a three-year break, Neil Wallace, a pro golfer trying to make a living as a caddy, Saddam, the Silver Fox, the Seagull, the Judge, and Janet, the only full-time female caddy on tour now that Fanny had gone to the States with Faldo. Some were eating, others chatting. There was a card school in one corner. Another table had gathered round to read a four-day-old copy of the *News of the World*. It could have been any works canteen in England. Our boys, and girl, seemed to be far from shitting themselves. They just looked bored at the prospect of a day sitting around doing nothing.

We were a long way from home. We'd spent good money getting here, taking jobs from people who needed them more than we did. And there was no golf. Ross wasn't even in the tournament yet, he was only fifth reserve. It needed four people to trip over and injure themselves in the next forty-eight hours for Ross to get a game. I was disappointed but my spirit remained intact.

. . . friend Sancho, all these storms and hurricanes are but arguments of the approaching calm, 'tis a maxim that nothing violent can last long . . .

I sat down at Ferret's table. 'What in God's name are we doing here?' someone asked him.

'I'll tell you what we're doing here, ya miserable twat.' He pointed towards a smiling figure in a denim jacket and jeans at the opposite end of the room.

'You see that guy over there that's Ricky lak. Three years ago 'e was going nowhere 'e'd just been sacked by Derrick Cooper and managed to pick up another bag. Ernie fookin' Els's bag now look at 'im he's fookin' minted. That's why we're here. We all want to be Ricky.'

When he had finished his speech, I offered to buy Ferret a big glass of orange juice. It was too early for beer but I had to say thanks in any way possible. It was good to know I wasn't on my own.

5. A Momentous Day!

Ross won his first cheque. Two thousand, three hundred and thirteen pounds. Joint thirty-first in the Catalan Open with nine others. I thought about a lap of honour round Bonmont-Terres Noves golf course but it just wasn't big enough to express my happiness.

When we came off the final green he went to the scorers' tent. I dashed straight to the scoreboard in front of the clubhouse and started counting: from the worst scores forward, then the best scores backwards, and finally the median scores outwards. They couldn't take it away from me: R. Drummond, thirty-first. And I was his caddy. I scoured newspapers, magazines and the Internet for days afterwards and could find no mention of this performance. It was all war in Bosnia and Tories in by-election setback and Venables must go and Mitterrand had a mistress.

I dumped the bag in the changing room. It had just gone one o'clock. There was no rush, the drive to Barcelona airport would take only two hours and the flight back to London wasn't until six o'clock. I stretched out on one of the wooden benches by the lockers and sucked in the heat. When we had teed off at half past eight that morning it had been freezing, literally, zero degrees. There were more woolly hats on show than you'd see on *Ski Sunday*. I had on four layers of clothing, leaving me immobile from the waist upward. Ross was well wrapped up, too. How anyone could swing a golf club wearing those clothes was beyond me – it must have been like having sex in a sleeping bag – but he did it to great effect.

I was just starting to thaw out when Ross walked into the locker room. Silently he started to empty his locker. I watched as he wrestled the golf bag into its flight case until it dawned on me that this was precisely the sort of thing he was paying me to do. I jumped up and joined in.

'Thanks,' he said.

The silence was like an itch. 'That was a good day,' I ventured.

'It's a start . . .' he said.

A *start!* From nowhere to one hundred and seventh in the Order of Merit. How much higher would it have been if that putt on the eighteenth green had dropped? God knows, it had deserved to. Or that one on the second, forty-five feet I know, but did you see it brush the hole? If only you hadn't double-bogied the third; if I'd hinted at a six-iron and not a seven-iron at the fifth the ball would never have come up so short. Sorry. That bogey on nine; and the three-putt on eleven. If only you had scored sixty-five on the first day instead of seventy-one, and you could have done, I've just proved it, you would have been second instead of thirty-first.

'Yes, but we made up a lot of ground today.'

This wasn't strictly accurate. We were thirty-fifth overnight, when the wind stopped play and left us with nine holes to play. Still, better to move up four places than down four places. To come out and shoot level par in conditions more akin to the north face of Ben Nevis than the northern Mediterranean had been a heroic effort. I told him so.

'You played great.'

'The tour hasn't started yet.'

The tour hasn't started yet! Did I dream that birdie on the first hole of the first day, or the three-iron across the lake at the short eighteenth in a hellish cross-wind? The five six-foot putts in a row to save par? Don't you remember, Ross, the six-iron to two feet at the sixteenth, when the spectator in the blue cagoule, the first we had seen all day, put down his packed lunch, stood up and applauded? Don't lie to me! I saw you punching the air when that putt hit the back of the hole on seven, leaped up and fell in.

'You've won two thousand-odd pounds,' I said.

'Less tax,' he replied, drily. Caddying I knew little about; Spanish tax law even less. I gave up and loaded the bags on to the bus.

The Corrective Lens. The rush of blood induced by the first cheque of the season must have steadily diminished over the years – after nineteen years it was hardly enough to flutter an eyelash, never mind the heart. So what if he'd won a couple of thousand pounds? It was hardly enough to cover his costs or the grinding slog of a winter week in Spain.

He had a point, if I'd bothered to look.

Bonmont-Terres Noves had to be one of the oddest places in the world at which to stage a golf tournament. It was March. The course was glued to the side of the Sierras, a natural staging post for the strong winter winds as they swept off the mountains towards the sea. It was in hibernation; the fairways a chilly grey-green colour, the greens the texture of Ryvita crispbread.

The nearest town of any size was Salou, a holiday resort twenty miles up the coast notable only for sporadic bouts of fighting between English and German tourists and one of the worst outbreaks of typhoid in mainland Europe since the Second World War. No one goes to Salou in March. They come by the bus load in summer but then only to have sex with strangers or to catch typhoid, not to play or watch golf.

It was hard to believe that the event had the backing of the Catalan tourist board. I was sure there was a marketing executive somewhere who could come up with a plausible explanation for all of this but what kind of message did it send to the outside world? 'Come to Catalonia, you'll never believe how cold it can get in March'? Or how about 'Bonmont-Terres Noves: If you think the golf course is bad you wouldn't believe the appalling standard of public hygiene just up the road in Salou.'

Perhaps that explained why the number of spectators never got above two hundred. In my innocence I'd imagined vast hordes trailing in our wake. Most of those who did turn up hung around the clubhouse café watching events on the live television link, although our friend in the cagoule stood by the sixteenth green for three days clapping all manner of shots, good, bad and mediocre, like a demented seal which had somehow got stuck up a mountain. I stopped to shake his hand when we went past, so certain was I that he was a kindred spirit.

The first round was completed by late on Thursday evening as normal, despite the Arctic temperatures. The second round was cancelled due to high winds, and early on Saturday morning a hand-written notice was pinned outside the locker room announcing that the event had been further reduced from fifty-four to thirty-six holes. This turned out to be lucky for Gary Currie, who had approached Paul Lawrie before leaving South Africa and asked for a job. Lawrie offered him a week's trial at the Catalan tournament.

Our two golfers played a practice round together before the tournament. Lawrie, who was tinkering with his swing, looked out of sorts. Ross played beautifully. I didn't know then that this was a bad sign. One of the immutable rules of human existence is that he who practises well will not win the golf tournament; it's up there with 'what goes up must come down' and $E=MC^2$.

Afterwards, Currie looked anxious. 'I was out there thinking, Have the guys given me a bum steer here or what? Everybody says he's a good player but how good?'

I shrugged. 'What are you worrying about? He's a great player.'

There was a pause pregnant enough to give birth to twins until he replied, 'Is he?'

It took only one round to find out how good. Lawrie went out and shot sixty-five on the first day to lead the field by one. When I met Currie in the clubhouse that afternoon he looked like a man who'd lost a five handicap golfer and found an Open Champion. 'We were six under par and we still weren't on the leaderboard,' he began, excitedly.

We were in fifty-second place at the end of the first round. I had to admit – a leaderboard big enough to accommodate us hadn't been built yet.

'. . . and then when they did put it up they spelled his name the wrong way . . .'

(After a few weeks on tour it dawned on me that scoreboard operators were not put on this planet to keep spectators informed but to keep the players' egos in check with their pitiful attempts at spelling names.)

'. . . never mind, hopefully we can stay up there.'

Currie needn't have worried. Lawrie, who'd learned to play golf on the east coast and knew how to handle the wind, went out for the second round in what looked to my untutored eye to be a hurricane and shot seventy to stay in the lead by one. This was a truly magnificent performance. He knew before going out that the tournament had been cut to thirty-six holes, that this was the last round, and yet still kept going under the pressure.

More disruption by the weather meant that half of the field still had to complete the last round the following morning but Lawrie left the course that night virtually certain of winning his first European PGA event. His nearest challengers had all finished and the closest of those still to finish, Englishman Peter Baker, was four shots back.

Winning the tournament didn't just mean a cheque for £50,000. There were other rewards: automatic entry to tour events for the next two years; win bonuses from club manufacturers and sponsors running to thousands of pounds; the extra bit of respect from your peers that comes with winning a tournament.

Not surprisingly, Lawrie couldn't sleep when he went back to his hotel. 'I phoned my wife four or five times. I watched it on Eurosport. I got up at two o'clock. Read a John Grisham book, had a shower at four. Got up again at five o'clock, had a walk about,' he told me later. I was a nervous wreck myself just re-living the experience over a cup of coffee.

The scene in Currie's hotel room that night was marginally less frenetic. When I got there he was stretched out on the bed with his hands behind his head, watching television and trying his best not to look like a millionaire. I swear I was even happier than he was. He was living proof that I was right – that dreams did come true.

I asked him what it felt like to be a winning caddy in your first week with a new player. It must have been quite a surprise, a fantasy even, almost like a fairy story.

'It's a fuckin' dream come true,' he said. 'The only problem is we haven't won yet and I can't go out and celebrate. If only we hadn't double-bogied the second last hole there wouldn't be any doubt.'

The only flaw in Lawrie's last round had come when he hit his tee shot into the water at a short par-three but he held his nerve. He holed an eight-foot putt on the last for a four and a one-stroke lead.

'We had the money spent before we got to the end of the round,' Currie confessed. 'He said he was thinking about buying a Porsche, I said I was thinking about paying off my overdraft.'

He said he was going to stay in that night to watch himself on the televised golf highlights. 'I'll need to go up to the course early tomorrow and watch the leaderboard, maybe put a few guys off their game.'

He didn't have to bother. Dawn broke to find that the hurricane in which Lawrie had played so well the previous day had subsided, but only to a gale. No one could catch him. As our bus wound its way down the hill from the clubhouse we could see him on the lawn being photographed with the trophy, an eighteen-inch bronze sculpture of quite unsurpassable ugliness. 'I couldn't imagine having that thing in my house for the year,' someone said. I would have gladly had it in my grotty flat: it might have come in handy for throwing at burglars.

The sight of a smiling Lawrie posing with his prize seemed to induce a feeling in Ross something similar to that which had been reinforced in me when I went to Currie's bedroom. 'The fifty-thousand-pound cheque will look good, not to mention the two-year exemption,' he said brightly, joining in the general banter.

Later, when the gentle rocking of the coach as it sped towards the airport had sent most people to sleep, Ross told me that the win, with sponsors' bonuses, could be worth £70,000 to Lawrie.

'Will it be as much as that?' I said, not looking up from my newspaper. I didn't care: it still didn't feel as much as £2,313.

6. Walkman

Seventy-nine in the first round of a tournament is one better than eighty but, as scores go, it's not a lot of fun for a caddy. It means a long, sorry trudge between the final green and the clubhouse. Somewhere along the way another caddy will ask, 'What'd you score?' You will check to see if your player is listening. If he is, you will quietly reply, 'No good,' and if he isn't it might be something like, 'He shot hundreds, the useless prat.' The news will spread quickly and everyone will avoid you for the rest of the afternoon in the belief that working for a man who scored seventy-nine is more contagious than hepatitis B.

There is also the embarrassment factor. It's not much fun hanging around with someone who has scored seventy-nine when the other caddies' players have shot sixty-nine. It's like having an ugly friend.

And then there are the financial drawbacks: a probable missed cut, no prize money and, hence, no percentage money, which left you with a bare wage for the week, which wouldn't pay for travel, hotel and beer, even. When this happens you pray your player will head straight for the airport and at least you can have the weekend off. But if you are unfortunate enough to work for a conscientious practiser – a habit once confined to Swedish players but one that has spread to all nationalities – a missed cut means two days on the range watching him beat golf balls until either his hands or your eye sockets bleed.

But I'm being selfish.

I'm sure shooting seventy-nine is no fun for the player either. He knows that later in the day he will have to phone his family with the bad news, then go out for dinner with other players, one of whom will almost certainly have shot sixty-five. They will have a one-minute conversation about this fantastic round, which is never quite detailed enough for the man who scored sixty-five and is fifty-five seconds too long for the one who didn't.

And he has to cope with the disloyalty of his caddy, who has, no doubt, been bad-mouthing him to anyone who will listen.

Some players will sulk for a couple of days after scoring seventy-nine. Others will go straight back to the clubhouse, start throwing shoes around and kick the nearest locker door. Ross shot a first round seventy-nine only once during the season, at the Moroccan Open. He did none of the above. He walked back to the locker room, started to change and, after five minutes, said calmly, 'How did I take so many shots?'

It so happened that I was able to tell him. I had the round on tape, all seventy-nine blows. 'I've got it all on tape. We can listen to it if you like,' I answered, immediately.

He gave me a look that shot way past incomprehension *en route* to the kind of pained expression the family pet has when it is locked out of the house in a rainstorm. There is a long list of things a caddy should never, ever say to a player and, though I didn't know it at the time, 'I've got your seventy-nine on tape, boss,' was right up there near the top.

If he'd had the energy, I'm sure Ross would have asked me what on earth I was doing walking around Royal Golf Dar Es Salam with a tape recorder surreptitiously strapped to my inside leg in the first place.

The answer was simple: I wanted to find out what a caddy really did.

This had been troubling me since my meeting with Martin Rowley. His quintessentially Marxist analysis of the relationship between a caddy and a player – 'He pays the wages, bugger lugs' – had been both accurate and enlightening. But he had been vague on the nuts and bolts of caddying, leaning more to the nineteenth-century anarchist school: 'You don't get a training manual with the caddy's bib, sunshine. Make it up as you go along.' This had been less than useless.

Ross was just as vague. I asked him on our first day together exactly what he wanted me to do. He shrugged an easy-going shrug. 'Let's just play it by ear.'

We muddled by for a few weeks. Sometimes I would read the line of putt, occasionally I was too embarrassed by my effort on the previous hole and shuffled off to the side of the green to tie a shoelace. Sometimes Ross was too stunned by the advice I'd given him on the previous green to ask me again. He rarely asked me what club he should hit. I couldn't fault him for this: he'd seen me play golf after all.

I didn't like this *laissez-faire* approach, it seemed too chaotic for a sport that was supposed to be so precise.

I watched other players to see what they expected from a caddy. Some wanted a cheerleader who constantly told them how good they were, others just wanted a bag carrier, or someone they could speak to, or someone who didn't speak, or someone who spoke but only when they were spoken to, or someone who spoke and who could make them speak when they didn't want to speak.

Then there were some players who wouldn't go to the toilet without taking advice from their caddy. There was a caddy called 'Edinburgh' Jimmy Rae who as far as I could see took every single decision for the player he worked for. He was a wizard on the greens and always made the right club selection.

Even on the few occasions he was wrong he was still right. 'Awa' ye go, ya fuckin' eejit, ye fuckin' hooked it,' I once heard him tell his employer after he had accused Edinburgh of choosing the wrong club.

I would have stuck a dagger in my chest to have been as good a caddy as Edinburgh but I couldn't quite hear myself telling Ross he was a fuckin' eejit.

At Sun City I spent an idle half-hour over a cool beer chatting with Nick Price about this whole caddying business. (How about that? Me and the second best golfer in the world, double Major winner and multi-millionaire, sitting down with beer to chew the fat about golf!) He looked exhausted although his red-rimmed eyes kicked into life when I told him what I was doing in South Africa.

'You caddy for Roscoe?'

I nodded, surprised that he'd remembered Ross. It must have been fifteen years.

'Man, what about the old days when we were out there making cuts and cheques together? What a great player.'

Ross had missed the cut by miles that morning and looked anything but a great player. I mumbled something that might have been mistaken for, 'Sure is.'

I could hardly get rid of Price once he started reminiscing. When he had first come to Europe, he drove to tournaments in a battered Ford Capri and pulled his own bag on a trolley. It wasn't long before he could afford to hire a caddy. When I last looked, he had earned $10 million in prize money. This made him the richest man I had ever shared a beer with. It also meant that he had paid out at least $500,000 to caddies over the years.

Presumably, he hadn't handed over that money for nothing. I was certain he was the man to explain to me what a caddy really did.

'That's a tough question,' he said suspiciously, as if I'd insulted him. Our friendly beer was careering towards an embarrassing silence. I was beginning to wish I'd never asked.

'Caddying isn't a difficult job but it's difficult to do well,' he said, eventually.

I prompted him. 'What made Squeaky so good?' Squeaky was Jeff Medlen, who'd worked for Price for six years. One of the game's best-known caddies, he died in 1997. 'Was it because he was reliable?'

I swear I saw the light-bulb being drawn in above his head.

'That's it! He was reliable.'

Perhaps it was his body language, the way he stood up, offered me his hand and said, 'I've got to go now,' but I got the impression our conversation was now at an end. The world's number two golfer dragged himself off to the press tent, clearly a troubled man.

I ordered another beer and pondered one of life's little absurdities: half a million dollars for being reliable. I made a mental note to ask for an application form the next time we met.

I couldn't find much in the way of serious academic research about the art of caddying, only one book in fact, *Carry Your Bag, Sir?* by David Stirk. Ross gave me a copy that had been gathering dust in a cupboard at his house, Drumrossie. I started reading it on a flight to Dubai.

In chapter one I discovered that the name caddy stems from the French word *cadet*, meaning the youngest son of the family. And, according to *Jamieson's Etymological Dictionary of the Scottish Language* (1840) in 1730 a Captain Burt described certain people in Edinburgh at that time as 'cawdys – useful blackguards who attend coffee houses and publick places to go on errands'. Not only that, but there was once a caddy called Daft Willie Gunn, who lived in a garret in Edinburgh and survived entirely on baps.

And then I fell asleep. I left the book behind on the plane, thus placing future passengers on the cusp of an aviation first – something to read that was more tedious than the in-flight magazine.

I decided to carry out my own academic research. Caddies as a breed are not overly given to self-analysis. There is always a bus to catch or a game of cards to finish. When I asked out loud in the locker room at the Catalan Open for someone to explain to me a caddy's *raison d'être* I got three 'fuck offs', one 'I don't like raisins' and a wet sock in the face. Then everybody went off to find their friends to tell them that the big clown, Drummond's caddy, was asking stupid questions again.

This might have been because I was still a newcomer. You weren't allowed to ask stupid questions until you had been on tour for fifteen years, won three tournaments and had been called by your first name by Fred Couples. Once this had happened you could do anything you liked.

The weeks rolled past and still I didn't have a clue.

Did it matter anyway? So what if I wandered through the season in blind ignorance? As long as Ross was happy and I didn't cost him any money or penalty shots. I asked him and he insisted, rather unenthusiastically I thought, that I was perfectly adequate.

I was about to settle for my lot when I met Andy Prodger.

I had first seen him in the clubhouse in Johannesburg. He had been wearing a white golf cap, which was three sizes too big, and a pair of huge, fish-bowl sunglasses. He had a Dick Van Dyke Cockney accent, which must have stuck out like a bright red Ferrari in Auchterarder where he now lived with his wife and a baby girl. You could spot him a mile off on the golf course, too. He hardly lifted his feet when he walked, and shuffled up the fairway after his player, looking for all the world like he was being pulled along on castors.

Prodger had been on the road for years. He had won a dozen tournaments. He'd caddied Faldo to two Majors, the 1987 Open and the 1989 Masters. Fred Couples dispensed with first names when he spoke to Prodger – he called him Prodge just like everyone else. Prodge was a gentle, modest man, generous to a fault. Best of all, he would talk to anyone on tour, no matter who they were. Even me.

We were finally introduced in the bar of the Hotel Estival in Tarragona. He had a yardage wheel in one hand and a bottle of beer in the other. I nominated him there and then as my mentor.

Prodge and I spent hours talking about golf and caddying, in clubhouses and flea-pit hotels, on buses, boats and planes. 'Pay attenshun to wat your player has to say and wat he does out on the golf course,' he would tell me. 'And remember, nevar waste a day. Every round is a learning experience.'

This explained why I had spent a night in my room at the Hotel Splendid after the first round of the Moroccan Open, listening to a five-hour recording of Ross and me at work while the rest of the European tour was out on the town.

As far as I am aware it is the only tape of its kind in existence.

There is no other player in the world who would have tolerated his caddy wandering around Royal Golf Dar Es Salam with a tape recorder strapped to his inside leg. There is no other caddy in the world who could have thought he might have learned something from the exercise.

I publish the transcript here in the hope that it will shed some light on the hitherto Masonic world of professional caddying. Like Richard Nixon, I reserved the right to erase the bits that made me look like a liar, a cheat and a crook.

Ross and I were not alone. That day there were four others in the group: Pierre Fulke, a Swedish pro, his caddy Lars Ugarph, French pro Antoine Lebouc and his caddy, a Moroccan called Mohammed who said nothing but did kneel down to pray beside the tenth tee. Lebouc scored 153 to miss the cut by miles, which just goes to show that Allah, like Jesus Christ, Buddha and the Church of Scientology, is no help when it comes to golf.

Hole One: 402 yards, bunkers left and right

Ross drove off last. His ball went left. He snaked his head to the right in the hope that the ball would notice him and follow suit. 'I think it's going to be OK,' he said.

'Where?' I pleaded.

'Just over the bunker on the left.'

'But I didn't know there was a bunker there.'

I shouldn't have said this. I detected a slight irritation in Ross's voice. 'You've got to remember each and every hole, bunkers and all. Go over it every night, try to think how we would play it.'

We made it over the bunker. Ross stood by his ball, frantically groping the right side of his head as though he'd just discovered his ear had fallen off. 'Damn. I've dropped my pencil.'

I flushed with pleasure – a chance to redeem myself. 'Don't panic, I've got one here.'

'Thanks,' he said. 'Two off red.'

'Two off the red. One three four.'

'One four five to the pin.'

(Technical note: the fairways at every tour event are painted with coloured spots, red, yellow, yellow star, red star, which allows the player to measure the exact distance of every shot to the flag. Here, the red spot was 134 yards from the front of the green, the flag eleven yards further on, making a shot of 145 yards.)

We waited while Fulke played from the right-hand rough. Ross started whistling. 'I wish I hadn't heard that song.'

'What is it?'

He looked up. 'Probably an eight-iron.'

'No, no. What's the song?'

'Sorry. 'I Am A Cider Drinker', by the Wurzels. It was on television.'

He hit an eight-iron straight at the flag.

'Oh, yeah, sexy,' I cooed.

'Thanks.'

The ball landed twenty feet short of the flag, a birdie chance, but the putt slid past the right-hand side of the hole. Ross walked to the next hole whistling 'I Am A Cider Drinker'. I sang 'Wonderwall' by Oasis.

Hole Two: 233 yards, par-three, bunkers left and right

Fulke had the honour and he was welcome to it. It was a tricky tee shot, long and into a crosswind. Club selection had to be spot-on.

Fulke hit his tee shot to six feet. I prayed Ross wouldn't ask me for advice.

'What do you think about the wind?'

That was easy. 'Right to left, against.'

'A four-iron?' he said.

I looked plaintively at Fulke's caddy, Lars, who took pity on me and signalled back, three fingers pointing to the ground: Fulke had hit a three-iron.

(Technical note: this is against the rules.)

I remembered hearing Prodger's voice in my head: 'Wha'eva you do, don't be a yes man.'

I thought it was a three-iron for sure. My face was reddening, Ross was waiting for an answer. 'Four-iron's fine,' I said.

He hit a bad shot, high and drifting to the right. It finished on the green but sixty feet from the flag. I slipped the club back into the bag. 'Don't worry, it's fine.'

'Maybe it should have been a three-iron,' he said.

We walked towards the green. 'That was definitely a three-iron,' I said.

Hole Three: 441 yards, dog-leg right, narrow green

Lars was first to the tee. When we got there he was wearing a clown's red nose.

'What's this?' I touched his nose. It fell off.

'It's a birdie nose.' He stuck it back on. 'I put it on when he makes a birdie. Pierre loves it. The first time I did it, he said, "Wooow, that feels good."'

I caught Fulke's unsmiling gaze. He looked like a man who had never said 'Wooow' in his life.

Ross made it to the green in two. Fulke drove into the trees, hacked out sideways, duffed his third, thinned a bunker shot into another bunker and slashed out to ten feet. It was terrifying to watch, especially when Ross was about to attempt to hole a tricky five-foot downhill putt for par. I tried to distract him.

'How would you like it if I became a personality caddy, like Lars?'

He shook his head. He was transfixed by Lars's nose. 'You see, Anthony would say that you put the red nose on if you had a bogey, try and change the pattern. It would make you smile, stop you being angry with yourself.'

I was confused. 'Anthony?'

'Anthony Robbins. *Awaken the Giant Within.*'

'Oh, I'd forgotten about him.'

'Well, he'd say it would be more effective if you put the nose on when you'd made an arse of things – that way it would cheer you up.'

Ross made his par. Fulke had a putt for seven, a triple bogey. Lars stood to the side of the green, his head bowed, wishing his nose away.

Hole Four: 405 yards, dog-leg left
Looking back from the tee, I saw Lars slipping the birdie nose into his trouser pocket. I grabbed Ross's sleeve. 'Look, look, the birdie nose is off.'

'So it is. It's off big-time.' He grinned. 'Do you think he'd wear it going down the last hole at the Open?'

Ross drove it long and straight.

'Very good, Ross,' I said. Have I always been this obsequious or had someone slipped a smarmy pill in my coffee that morning?

We trotted off up the fairway. 'I like the French boy's swing. He hits it a long way,' I said, filling the silence.

(Technical note: the batteries in the tape recorder started to go flat at this point – either that or Ross and I dropped some LSD somewhere on the fourth fairway.)

Ross said, 'Yes, it's nice. I think I'll need to take my sweatshirt off.'

'About a cup and a half,' I replied.

'Have you got another pencil? I lost mine when I took my sweatshirt off.'

'Go on, go on. Shit!'

'You'd better not take your sweatshirt off, Lawrence.'

'What a relief, sunshine on Leith.'

'But if you don't cover it in plastic sheeting it will rust.'

'Well-holed, Ross.'

I checked with the scorer afterwards. The putt was for par.

Hole Five: 579 yards, par-five, bunkers everywhere
I changed the batteries.

Things were going well – four pars, no big mistakes – but Ross seemed nervous. He stood over his tee shot longer than normal, twitching his shoulders and shuffling. I could hear his feet squelching in the sodden grass for what seemed like an age.

It was time to take his mind off golf. 'It looks as though we're going to get the best of the weather.'

This was a lie but it was the best I could manage, under the circumstances. I'd searched frantically but there was nothing around to inspire a sensible, distracting conversation. The fairways at Royal Golf Dar Es Salam were tightly lined with cork trees. The sky was a heavy, claustrophobic grey. There were no spectators. Which left the weather.

'That wind is getting up,' I said.

'No, it's not,' Ross said.

'You're right, it's not.'

He hit a good drive, followed by a terrible, duffed two-iron, which scuttled behind a tree. 'Oh, Roscoe,' he sighed.

I cut him off. 'I thought we agreed, none of this "Oh, Roscoe" business. Try and smile, like your mate Anthony Robbins says you should, or get a red nose and stick that on.'

'You're right.' He sighed again. 'But we had to get our drive past this tree.'

This had conversational potential. 'Are you sure these are cork trees?'

'Definite,' he said. 'Four off the red spot.'

'One hundred and nineteen to the pin. Take a wedge,' I said, forgetting to end my suggestion with my usual question mark. I quickly corrected myself. 'Wedge?'

'Wedge?'

'Wedge?' I was prepared to stand there all day, throwing one-word questions at him until he made the decision.

'Wedge it is,' he said eventually.

Wedge it shouldn't have been. He hit a good shot but the ball landed twenty yards short of the green. It bounced twice before stopping. 'Sorry. Fuck,' I said in perfect rhythm.

Ross didn't look at me. 'It was a nine-iron. That was my first thought,' he said flatly, handing me the club.

Hole Six: 442 yards, long and straight

We held an inquest going down the sixth fairway. Not that anyone had died on the fifth green, it just felt as though someone had. I'd cost him a shot. I couldn't have felt worse if I'd taken five hundred pounds from his wallet and set fire to it.

'Always take the first thought,' I said, meekly.

'That's right,' Ross said. 'That's how you express yourself.'

The look on his face suggested he would best express himself at that moment by knocking me out.

Thankfully, Fulke birdied the fifth hole and Lars had his red nose on. Fun was in the air again. Fulke hooked his drive into the trees.

Ross's tee shot landed safely in the centre of the fairway. We stood by his ball and we watched Fulke hack out. 'It can't help, seeing your caddy standing there with a stupid red nose on,' Ross said. I could only agree. As always.

Hole Seven: 422 yards, dog-leg right

Ross was beginning to lose confidence. He didn't drag his feet or drop his head but I could hear it in his voice. It had assumed the fake joviality of the doomed.

'Time to make some bird-dogs,' he said, unconvincingly.

(Technical note: bird-dog is pro-speak for a birdie.)

What he really meant was 'Time to make some bogeys.'

A pro never wants to drop a shot but once he decides something is about to go wrong an irresistible force takes control of his muscle functions and guides him towards his predestined misery. I'd only been on tour a few weeks but I could easily recognize the symptoms. I tried frantically to distract Ross, the desperation is etched in my voice on the tape, but it was like trying to catch a deluge in a paper cup.

'I don't like the way Fulke swings it.'

'Mmmm,' he said.

'His caddy said he's shortened his swing over the winter. This is a smelly pin position. It might rain . . .'

'Smelly. That's a good word.'

He hit his second shot on the green and we walked forward.

'You didn't fancy that in the air, did you?' I said. 'Ross. Ross? Are you listening to me?'

'Sorry. Yes. It's come down just fine.'

'It certainly did. My goodness, a crowd.'

A small temporary stand had been erected along the left-hand side of the seventh green. Nothing too optimistic, just three rows of twenty seats. Five seats were occupied. We walked on to the green, no one clapped. They probably sensed what was coming.

He three-putted for a bogey.

Hole Eight: 585 yards, par-five

We walked to the eighth tee in silence, past the eighteenth green, the scoreboard and the tented village. The latter was a sorry affair, comprising three empty marquees and a duty-free shop stacked from floor to ceiling with family-size Toblerone bars. I could hear two Moroccan caddies squabbling over a player by the clubhouse.

Antoine Lebouc was first to drive. A spectator took a photograph at the top of his backswing and his ball scuttled into the trees on the left. The Frenchman responded as if his first-born had been slaughtered, battering the hapless snapper with what I could only guess was the kind of abuse that would have made a Marseille sailor blush. Thankfully, he stopped short of rearranging his face with an eight-degree driver.

Somehow Ross managed to hit his drive down the middle. A heroic effort, in the circumstances. He was happy again, talkative.

'We ate in Pizza Hut last night.'

'Oh, did you? How was it?' I said, feigning interest.

'Not as good as the ones in Britain. We had some garlic bread and cheese and a couple of pizzas, which were OK. They filled a hole. You can't expect any culinary delights in Pizza Hut.'

'No, you can't, can you? The Pizza Huts back home really are something special, aren't they?'

Hole Nine: 172 yards, par-three with an island green

It started raining. Ross slipped on his green tartan waterproof top. It clashed horribly with the paisley shirt he was wearing.

'Not exactly matching, is it?' I said.

'It doesn't matter. You can only see the shirt collar,' he replied, running over to a tree by the side of the fairway.

I shouted after him, 'It's a twenty-year jail sentence in Morocco for pissing in public.'

He re-emerged two minutes later, pulling up his zip. The offending shirt collar had been tucked out of sight.

'Right then,' he said, briskly. 'Four-iron?'

I thought he needed a three-iron. 'Sure,' I said.

His shot landed on the green but fifty feet from the flag. He left the first putt short and asked me if I would 'take a look' at the second putt. I knew then that we were heading towards a score in the high seventies. Not because I was giving him advice but because he was asking for it. If he was confident with his putting he would have asked me to clean his ball and then gently ushered me off to the side of the green where I could do little damage to his score.

'Inside the right edge, give it a nice positive stroke,' I said.

He gave it a nice positive stroke, inside the right edge. It missed.

'Did you pull the putt?' I asked.

(Technical note: to be this tactless doesn't come naturally, I've worked at it for years.)

Hole Ten: 468 yards, par-four, uphill

A gilt-framed poster of King Hassan II had been mounted on a pallet by the tee. It was unprotected against the rain and had blown over earlier on. It was splattered with mud. The King looked miserable, but not as miserable as Ross and I.

A long silence ensued as we trudged up the fairway, broken only by the hiss of the wind and the squelch of damp socks.

Ross was first to speak. 'Is this my ball here? You're kidding.'

Unfortunately, it was.

Another bogey.

Hole Eleven: 430 yards, green surrounded by bunkers

Three bogeys in four holes. The round was now, officially, in a tailspin.

(Technical note: this is where a good caddy earns his money, first by judging whether his player wishes to speak and, if he does, engaging him in a light, distracting conversation on any subject but the fact that he has just had three bogeys.)

'So tell me, Ross, when was this course built?' I asked. I already knew the answer – 1972 – but so what?

Silence.

I tried again. 'Brilliant course, isn't it?'

This incessant, nervous babbling is a sacking offence as far as some players are concerned. Ross, an altogether more tolerant soul, merely changed the subject. 'Thirteen on to the yellow spot.'

'That makes it two hundred and eight to the front,' I said.

'Two-iron?'

'If you feel good with a two-iron, Ross, go with it.'

A two-iron wasn't enough. His ball took one bounce and skipped into a bunker at the front of the green. He flipped his third shot on to the green but missed the putt for par.

'They've cut the greens. They seem much faster than they were in practice,' I said, by way of consolation.

'No, they haven't,' he snapped back.

Hole Twelve: 529 yards, par-five

We walked up the fairway in silence until we reached his ball. It was lying wickedly in a divot. We both stared at it in disbelief: he'd hit a perfect drive.

Somehow, he dug it out and up the fairway with a six-iron. 'Did you see how that was lying?' he said.

'I did, I did. Everything is against us.'

Two shots later, one a long, arching putt across the green, and he had his first birdie of the day. He handed me the putter with a winning smile. 'Thank Christ.'

I couldn't restrain myself any further, 'Let's go, Roscoe. Come on, a couple more birdies. I've seen the scoreboard [a lie] and we're not out of this tournament yet [a big lie].'

Hole Thirteen: 386 yards, par-four

Ross had the umbrella. In professional golf, the player always gets the umbrella, the caddy has his waterproofs. I had forgotten my waterproofs. I was soaked, not that it bothered me. I was, as they say in the body-building world, pumped up.

'Let's go, two more birdies,' I said, loud enough to be heard over the dull thud of rain beating on the grass. 'Let's go, Roscoe, let's go, Roscoe.'

Ross hit his drive behind a tree, left of the fairway. He looked crestfallen. I felt wet all of a sudden.

'Let's get it up and down for par,' I said.

'Up and down from here, sure,' Ross replied, a little sarcastically, I thought.

He hit a wedge shot straight across the fairway. It landed in ankle-deep rough. He chipped up and two-putted for a bogey. He was now four over par and inconsolable. This didn't stop me trying. 'The ball must have hit something, or maybe it had a lump of mud stuck to it – it had a strange flight,' I said.

He cut me dead. 'It was absolute crap.'

Hole Fourteen: 191 yards, par-three, heavily bunkered

Ross threw a few strands of grass in the air. 'A hundred and ninety-one yards to the pin, wind helping.'

'Four-iron,' I shot back. Did I say that? I checked the tape. I did. And I said it again, this time with a little more indecision. 'I think it's a four-iron.'

He rattled around in the bag before grabbing a club. 'Five-iron.'

If I was honest, I would have to admit to a little tingle of satisfaction as I watched the ball sailing straight into the bunker protecting the front of the green. It *was* a four-iron.

Ross hung his head. He handed over the guilty club. I slipped it back into the bag. I thought about saying, 'Told you so,' but decided I wanted to live to see the next tee.

Hole Fifteen: 390 yards, short par-four

There had been an article in that morning's *Sun* newspaper in which an English pro called Mark Roe claimed he had once put a loaded shotgun in his mouth. 'I sat there for five minutes with the barrel in my mouth – no one could have any idea how bad I felt,' he told the *Sun*'s suicide-cases-who-lived-to-tell-the-tale correspondent.

Golfers and caddies, being such sensitive souls, thought this very amusing and immediately christened him 'Trigger'.

Funnily enough, I began to understand just how bad Roe had felt as I watched Ross's second shot at the fifteenth dive into the green-side bunker.

Neither of us had said anything since he told me off for singing while I was walking the fairway. It's difficult to make out from the tape what the song was but it was probably 'Wonderwall' again. Whatever it was, it annoyed the hell out of Ross. 'Will you shut it with that bloody song!'

I was still in a huff when he hit an exquisite bunker shot to within six inches of the flag. I didn't even say, 'Well done.'

Hole Sixteen: 426 yards, par-four, dog-leg left

Something strange happened during the short walk from the previous green. The morose Scottish voices on my tape had been replaced by those of a couple of teenagers squabbling in the school playground.

'Give us a bit of your banana, then,' one said.

'No chance. Why didn't you get one for yourself?' replied the other.

'I forgot to bring any,' the banana-less one said.

'Well, I'm sorry but you're not getting a bit,' said the smug one.

'Come on. Pul-ease.'

The smug one eventually gave in. 'OK, here's a bit.'

'No, no, keep it for yourself,' said the other. Pause. 'Oh, I see, I get the rotten bit of banana.'

'It's my banana, you're lucky to get that rotten piece.'

This cheerful banter was interrupted by the sound of Ross attempting to hit a six-iron to the green while a thunderstorm broke directly over his head.

'Damn! Jesus, I should've waited,' he said, as his shot went straight left.

'Well, why didn't you?' I said, as sensitively as ever.

We wandered off in search of the ball. It had nestled behind a tree-trunk on the left of the fairway. We sheltered there until the slap of rain against the leaves subsided to a pitter-patter.

'What score are we?' I asked. I was beginning to lose count. 'Five over.'

'Are we? I can't believe it, you've played so well.'

Even Ross thought this was stretching the truth a little. 'I've played OK,' he said. 'I've driven the ball well, I just haven't made enough birdies.'

Unperturbed, I said, 'Let's birdie the next hole, give yourself a chance to make the cut, maybe win the tournament.'

Hole Seventeen: 225 yards, par-three

Maybe win the tournament? What was I talking about? The scoreboard by the tee showed we were eight shots behind the leader.

The seventeenth at Royal Golf Dar Es Salam is quite possibly the hardest golf hole on earth: long, downwind, with a green the size of a kiddies' paddling pool. Ross glanced at his yardage book. 'Three off the yellow, two hundred and twenty yards to the pin. There's only one club for this shot.'

I took a wild guess. 'Two-iron.'

'Three-iron.'

He hit a poor tee shot, chipped his second into a bunker, flopped out on the green and two-putted for a double bogey. Ten shots behind the leader. Ross handed me the putter. 'Shit,' he said. 'I tried to be too cute. Another couple of inches and I was over the bunker.'

'That's right, a couple of inches,' I said, wearily. I was tired now. We both were.

Hole Eighteen: 555 yards, par-five

'Good drive.'

I wasn't crawling again. Honest. He hit a wonderful tee shot, the best of the day. I walked down the fairway with Lars. He was more depressed than me. The red nose had been in his pocket for the last eight holes and Fulke was in the trees again.

'Don't worry, Lars, there's always tomorrow,' I said.

'Is there?' he said, stomping off towards the forest again.

Ross knocked his second shot safely down the fairway. His third, a smooth nine-iron, landed within four feet of the flag. A certain birdie.

It felt grand to finish on a high note. I watched Ross stride after his ball. It was easy to understand why he put himself through the agony that sometimes comes with playing golf for a living. He looked so happy with the shot he'd just played, not just cheerful happy but isn't-it-brilliant-to-be-alive happy.

'There is a beautiful feeling, I had it there, when your arms and your body work together in perfect harmony, the feeling that the club gets right through the ball and past your body. Wonderful,' he said.

The putt, the certain birdie putt, missed. It didn't even touch the hole. I watched Fulke and Lebouc hole their putts. Ross stared at the grass. 'What are you thinking?' I whispered.

He smiled ruefully. 'I'm thinking what you're thinking.'

7. King Hassan and I

Rabat was a city of a thousand mysteries. The biggest one was how the newspaper kiosk at the railway station came to be selling copies of the *Sun* at five pounds a throw and the *Guardian* for 20p.

It was Friday rush hour. Thousands, make that zillions, of weary Moroccans were making their way home through the evening bedlam. Dusty, oven hot, heads down, eye contact banned, body contact unavoidable. I had nowhere to go and time to waste so I spent ten minutes trying to point out to the kiosk's proprietor the absurdity of his pricing strategy. My French is not so much broken as powdered. Try as I might I could find no translation for 'quality broadsheet', 'tabloid', 'an excellent window on the world' and 'not fit to wipe your arse with'.

I bought a three-day-old copy of the *Guardian* and the *Messenger of Morocco*, an English-language newspaper that led its front page with the frankly irresistible headline 'Reconsideration of Daniel Defoe's *Moll Flanders*'. Inside, it carried a verbatim report of a speech by Prince Charles across three pages.

I was meandering along Boulevard Hussain, reading the *Messenger*, when I felt someone tugging at my sleeve. I turned round. A young Moroccan man, aged twenty or thereabouts, was standing behind me with his arms outstretched.

'No, thanks,' I said, instinctively.

My guide book said, 'Avoid conversations in the street with strangers, they will only be trying to sell you drugs.'

Not that I have a problem with drugs. It's dried goat's manure masquerading as drugs I really object to and this guy had 'goat's manure for sale' stamped on his forehead. He had a four-day beard, lank hair and pock-marked skin. He was wearing a pair of black jeans held together by city grime and a USA World Cup '94 T-shirt which he'd no doubt stolen from the last American backpacker he'd murdered. He looked both terrifying and terrible.

He grinned disarmingly. 'Excuse me, can you tell me what empathy means? And cynical?'

The European Union recently commissioned a top-secret investigation into the worldwide cannabis trade, the results of which I happen to have in front of me. Morocco is Europe's biggest supplier of hash. Though why it took a top-secret inquiry to find this out when all they had to do was ask any British adult under the age of fifty is baffling. The figures would blow your mind, so to speak. Morocco's cannabis industry earns £5 billion annually. It is the country's biggest employer and produces a thousand tonnes of the drug every single year.

That is a lot of weed and it requires a great deal of ingenuity to sell it all. This guy was clearly the man for the job. What an opening sales line!

I had to laugh. 'No, thanks,' I said. 'I don't want any drugs today, thank you.'

'And anti-disestablishmentarianism, is that the longest word in the English dictionary?' he shouted after me.

I walked away but he followed me through the crowds for about a hundred yards, begging me to talk to him. Eventually, I was forced to stop and explain that anti-disestablishmentarianism was indeed the longest word in the dictionary, and that empathy was not what I was feeling at that precise moment, cynical was.

'How interesting,' he replied. 'Do you want to go for a cup of coffee? I'm a student, I want to improve my English.'

Why the hell not? I thought. I had planned on going back to my five-pounds-a-night twin room at the less-than-aptly named Hotel Splendid to watch the cockroaches mating but decided to save that treat until bedtime. In any case, if I stayed out I wouldn't have to listen to the tszing-tzsing of Spanish Paul's Walkman all night.

My new friend and I dived out of the rush hour and into Café Gascoigne, a three-table outfit just off the main drag. He said his name was Said, though I suspect he made that up. He also said that he was one of seventeen children, the offspring of a farmer who now worked in Marrakesh in a Turkish bath, which absolutely refused entry to Western homosexuals. I was absolutely certain he made that up.

But I felt safe: there were enough people at the other tables to wipe up the blood when the time came for Said to slit my throat.

The funny thing is, he didn't. He didn't even try to sell me drugs. We chatted for half an hour and drank cup after cup of thick, syrupy coffee. To my astonishment, he gave every impression of being a student trying to improve his English.

I explained I was in Rabat for the Moroccan Open golf tournament, caddying for Ross Drummond, the world's 438th best golfer. He looked utterly bemused. He'd never heard of the Moroccan Open golf tournament.

'Seve Ballesteros is playing, the famous Seve Ballesteros,' I said. 'So is Ian Woosnam and Sam Torrance. It started yesterday, out at Royal Golf Dar Es Salam, about ten kilometres away.'

A flicker of recognition registered on Said's face. It could have been politeness. 'Oh, yes, Dar Es Salam,' he said slowly. 'Poor people like me aren't allowed there. If I went up there they would arrest me.'

I was prepared to believe this.

Royal Golf Dar Es Salam was about as hospitable as Jupiter. I was almost arrested the day we arrived. Most of the caddies had their passports taken off them when we landed at Rabat airport, with the promise they would be returned promptly once we got to the golf club. As a first-time visitor to Morocco, I made the ludicrous mistake of believing this would actually happen.

By nightfall it was becoming clear that it might not. About twenty caddies had gathered in the reception area, growing ever more agitated. It is illegal for a hotel-owner in Rabat to rent a room to a foreigner without a passport. The luggage was piled high on the clubhouse steps and a night on the locker room's stone floor beckoned. I was appointed (more self-appointed, really) to try to sort everything out with the beautiful, black-eyed receptionist who appeared to be in charge. For convenience, I'll call her Hell's Bitch.

'I am not your dog,' she shouted, picking up a phone which I assumed was straight through to the local police station.

'But. We only want our passports.'

'Woof. Woof. Is that what you want me to say?'

'I beg your pardon?'

'WOOOF!'

At that moment a thick-set man in a light grey suit appeared with a large brown envelope stuffed with passports. I seized mine and gleefully vanished into the night. Hell's Bitch hadn't had enough time to rouse the local *gendarmerie*. She looked devastated to see me depart with a cheery smile but made up for her disappointment by barking whenever she saw me come into the clubhouse during the tournament.

Said and I got along famously. He asked if I wanted to meet up the following night. He and some friends planned to have a few beers on the town.

I said yes. Ross had missed the cut. Our flight wasn't due to leave until Sunday night. I had two whole days to waste and there was a limit to the amount of fun you could have stamping on cockroaches just before they reached the peak of sexual excitement.

I don't know what it is like to lounge in the back of a long white limousine with three sexy supermodels. I would imagine it's a bit like making up a four-ball with three professional golfers. It sounds like a great idea but when you get down to it you feel ugly and inadequate and you want get out of there as quickly as possible. That's how I felt as Ross and I teed up the following morning.

We were playing a four-ball on Royal Golf Dar Es Salam's second course against two pros who had also missed the cut – a Mancunian called Craig Cassells and an American called Jason Widener.

Ross arranged the match to cheer me up.

He'd played brilliantly in the second round but still needed a hole-in-one at the last to make the cut. When we got to the tee the rain was so heavy it looked like fog. I could just about see the scoreboard by the green. He was sixteen shots off the lead. He made par, a heroic effort in the circumstances.

We caught the bus back to the clubhouse and dashed into the locker room. It was deserted but for two players lying stretched out on the massage tables. The bag was soaked through. I dropped it on the floor and sat down on the bench. I felt as though I'd been sitting in a bath all morning.

Then, without warning, I felt my eyes fill with tears. This was daft, I hadn't cried since Margaret Thatcher won the '87 election. Had I forgotten I was Don Quixote?

. . . thereupon he got up with much ado and clapped the left hand before his mouth so that the rest of his loose teeth might not drop out.

Ross could see I was in distress.

76

'We just couldn't get going, could we?' he said, sympathetically.

'No.'

He took off his wet shirt. 'Feel like slitting your wrists?'

'Just about,' I said, bending over to hide my face.

'Well, don't worry, you'll get used to it.'

Craig Cassells had a heavenly swing and a hellish temperament. Widener was once the top-ranked junior in the US but he was still waiting to make his first cheque of the season. Neither were household names but, in the understated vocabulary that pros use when talking about each other, both could play a bit.

I had two drives on the first hole and neither reached the ladies' tee. I stone-cold missed my third effort. Ross, in the overstated way that pros have when confronted with a hopeless amateur, invited me to play from the middle of the fairway. That didn't work either.

It took six holes before I hit my first proper golf shot, a forty-foot breaking putt for a half. I then proceeded to play like a man possessed for the next two holes, including a two-iron to within six feet of the flag at the eighth, which drew admiring gasps from three schoolkids sitting on a bench by the tee and a grudging, 'Great shot,' from Cassells. There is something magical about hearing a pro describe your shot as 'great', like Albert Roux admiring your cheese on toast or Errol Flynn seeing you in the shower and gasping, 'My god, that's huge.'

Ross and I scrambled to victory on the last hole. The missed cut and the tears of the previous day were forgotten, by me at least. We skipped back gleefully to the clubhouse to claim our prize of two bottles of warm beer and a potentially lethal chicken sandwich.

The place was packed, mostly with middle-aged men, and women wearing heavy ball-gowns and even heavier make-up. A television set in the corner was showing the golf. No one was watching. There was only a handful of people out on the course itself. The tournament was more of a social event, like Royal Ascot. Someone said if a bomb exploded over by the Coke machine at that precise moment it would have killed six cabinet ministers, three generals, the heir to the throne, the Moroccan amateur golf champion and every top-class hooker in North Africa.

In fact, the only Moroccan socialite missing was the one at the top.

King Hassan II of Morocco, or Amir al-Moumineen, descendant of the prophet Mohammed, is a golf fanatic, reputedly a seven-handicapper. He is best remembered in Britain as the only man ever to make our own dear Queen lose her temper in public when he turned up ten minutes late to meet her during a state visit to Morocco because he was playing golf.

It is not known which course His Majesty was playing at the time, he has so many. Twenty-three at the last count.

Morocco has spent a fortune over the last ten years, building world-class golf courses in keeping with Hassan's world-class preoccupation with the game. There is the Dunes at Agadir, Marrakesh Royal, Ouarzazate Royal, El Jadida Royal, Mohammedia Royal, Anfa Royal, Ben Slimane Royal and a nine-holer at Fez, where the first tee is on the battlements of the royal palace. The Moroccan Open is usually held at the best of the lot: Royal Golf Agadir is a magnificent course built inside the grounds of yet another royal palace. The story is that it is only ever played by the King, his sons and the occasional four-ball of five-star generals. It has bunkers near the tees in case any of them gets bored and wants to play it back-to-front. Every year, the players turn up and find the pins in the same positions as they were on the last day of the previous year's tournament. Alas, it was waterlogged this year and the tournament had been moved to Royal Golf Dar Es Salam, reported to be the monarch's second favourite course.

The King was unable to attend because of business commitments but had clearly left orders that no expense be spared.

The prize fund was £350,000, and the hospitality of the order usually dished out by doting grandmothers when the grandson brings his first girlfriend to visit. The course was better prepared than just about any I'd ever seen. There was even a super-efficient practice range staffed by locals in hard hats who stood at the other end and collected any golf balls that didn't whack them on the head. A privilege for which they were paid 50p an hour.

Ross and I hung around the clubhouse for an hour. We ate fulsomely and lived to tell the tale. Afterwards, I went to the press tent where I was presented with a magnificent leather folder stuffed with a pile of glossy magazines about Morocco, a pen, a key-ring and gold-embossed invitations to three cocktail parties. I even went along to one, where I struck up a conversation with a very helpful young lady from the press centre about the shortage of 'ordinary' Moroccans about the place.

'Well, it costs nothing to get in,' she said.

'But the only people I've seen are Moroccan jet-setters, ex-pat civil engineers and bored diplomats,' I said.

'I can assure you everyone is welcome.'

'So why aren't they here? Perhaps it's the guys at the gate with the guns.'

'Or perhaps people just don't like golf,' she replied huffily, and flounced off.

What was the use of spending all this money on golf when, apparently, no one in Morocco was interested?

Tourism, I hear you say.

But that's just daft. Have you ever heard anyone say, 'I want a golf holiday, I'll go to Morocco'? Of course not. They might say, 'I want to get my hands on a lot of cheap drugs, I'll go to Morocco', but a golf holiday? I don't think so. If you want a golf holiday you go to Scotland or Florida or Spain, not Morocco.

Rabat was an interesting and lively city but there were holes in the roads and beggars on the streets. The public buses looked as if they had been bought second-hand from the makers of the *Mad Max* movies. Fewer golf courses and the authorities could have shipped in some shiny red Routemasters. Better still, they could have built new sewers or created jobs for people killing rats.

Two things struck me as I stood there amongst polite Rabat society, sipping my wine: (a) I was a complete hypocrite and would never be able to forgive myself if I didn't immediately dash out on to the street and give all my money to the first poor person I met; and (b) of all of the dumb, shabby and utterly obscene sporting events I had ever witnessed, the Moroccan Open had to be the worst yet.

It stayed in the top spot for four days, then I went to Dubai for the Dubai Desert Classic.

Frankly, King Hassan II was an amateur compared to His Highness Sheikh Mohammed bin Rashid Al Maktoum, Crown Prince of Dubai, Minister of Defence of the United Arab Emirates and founder of the Emirates Golf Club.

It takes a vivid imagination to build a two-hundred-acre golf course in the middle of the desert and Sheikh Mohammed appeared to have one of those. He said he had got the idea for the Emirates after visiting the eighteen-hole lay-out in the middle of Doncaster racecourse. I have seen both and can confirm any similarities begin and end with the description 'golf course'.

Doncaster, it has to be said, will never stage an Open Championship.

Emirates was a golfing and engineering marvel. There was an aerial photograph of the course in the clubhouse that made it look like a solitary green chess square on a giant, sand-coloured board. The clubhouse itself was a stunning construction of glass and white tile in the shape of five Bedouin tents. There was a small pencil drawing of the founder just inside the front door, by far the most modest detail in a cathedral of marble floors, sweeping chrome stairwells and vast shimmering chandeliers.

The total cost? Sixty million pounds, give or take the odd shekel. The strangest thing was that the Sheikh was hardly a golf fanatic. He had his own concrete Bedouin tent by the eighth green, which lay empty from year to year. He was not unique among his countrymen in this indifference. Presumably, the locals had cottoned on to the idea that golf in 120°F heat was not the ideal way to spend one's leisure time. I was assured that the Emirates Golf Club had fifty Arab members, though I never saw one in all the time I was there.

Yet the Minister of Defence had thought it a good idea to spend upwards of a million pounds on staging a golf tournament. Why?

One day Dubai's oil reserves will run out and it will have to make its way in the world as a holiday resort and sports playground for the rich. It was important to establish the brand name. To that end the Sheikh hosted an annual Dubai Desert Tennis/Snooker/Cricket/Soccer/Table Tennis Classic. The cost of these events gets bigger every year. The inaugural Dubai Classic horse race had a first prize of £4 million. It all made sound economic sense.

But £65 million. On a golf course?

Try as I might to stir up a little local unrest at all this extravagance, I could find no one who thought that the Minister of Defence spending £65 million on a golf course was a bad idea, though I did a little vox-pop in the street outside our hotel and came across one gentleman who thought the cash would have been better spent on nuclear bombs to annihilate Israel. Everyone else was dashing off to the Dubai Shopping Festival to spend even more money and didn't have time to speak.

I expect the citizens of Dubai are just too rich to bother about trifling amounts like £65 million. Most probably thought it wasn't enough to spend on a golf course – 'Oh, Rashid, why don't we have gold dust in the bunkers instead of sand?' – and that's their privilege. But sometimes I'd just like to stop the world and get off.

To be honest, I had found just as much indifference in Morocco. Not only did no one know that the King had spent a fortune on golf courses, no one cared.

Said showed up late for our meeting the next night. He was drunk and looked even worse than the previous day. I had hoped he would bring along a bunch of lively, good-looking students, and they would sweep me off to Rabat's hippest nightclub for wild dancing. Instead, he came into the bar with a short, weaselly man in a battered blue suit. 'Meet Raul,' he slurred.

Raul had small nimble hands and eyes that were busily counting the cash in my back pocket the moment we sat down.

I hailed the waiter and ordered three beers. They were served with undisguised contempt and a bill twice as big as it should have been. I didn't feel like complaining. I was the token foreigner in a packed and smoky back-street dive, accompanied by two regulars who clearly hadn't settled their bar tab in months.

I tried to cover up my nerves by wittering on about my eighteen holes with the pros and my trip to the cocktail party. My two drinking partners stared blankly at the wall, waiting for the effect of the drugs they'd just taken – I suspected heroin – to kick in. Bored, I talked about the King and his golf.

Raul kicked me on the shin. 'Don't talk about the King like that. You never know who's listening,' he hissed.

I'd forgotten. Criticizing the King is punishable by up to twenty years' jail in Morocco – that's why its newspapers had front-page headlines like 'A Reconsideration of Daniel Defoe's *Moll Flanders*' and not 'King Plays Golf While Economy Collapses'.

The night out took its expected sinister turn when Said leaned over the table and said, 'I need help, my friend.'

I checked for an exit.

'You see, I'm a poor student and I need books. Normally I have plenty of money but not just now.'

I struck a deal. I thought it wise. I agreed to give him a hundred dirhams (about eight pounds) in exchange for a short interview about his feelings towards an imaginary monarch who spent a great deal of money on golf tournaments when the social and economic fibre of his homeland was crumbling.

Said grasped the part of the deal that involved me giving him money but I don't think he quite understood his half of the bargain. In fact, he genuinely seemed to think the Moroccan Open was a terrific idea – it would put Morocco in the news, attract tourists to the country, he insisted.

And the more tourists there were, the more chance he would have of selling some drugs. He hadn't met an American, French or British tourist for ages, which was why he had been reduced to mugging golf caddies for money.

8. 'Belgrano'

There are two ways a caddy can travel from tournament to tournament. Occasionally, it happens like this . . .

Emirates Airlines had been voted Best Airline to the Middle East for the last eight years by *Executive Travel* magazine. And Best Long-haul Airline, with the best in-flight entertainment, the best in-flight food, in-flight magazine, most hostesses with kissable scarlet lips and stewards who combine the servility of the Queen's butler with the butchness of the traffic cop from *Village People* . . . There's more but I won't go on except to say that the eleven o'clock flight from Gatwick to Dubai promised to be the closest encounter with luxury I would have all season.

At £540 a return ticket it had better have been.

In truth, I shouldn't really have been going anywhere near Dubai. I couldn't afford it. Like all of the other caddies who worked for – how can I put this? – players who had got their season off to a slow start, I should have stayed at home for the week. Ross even suggested that I take a week off, he would somehow struggle by with a local caddy. I couldn't bear the thought of someone else carrying my bag so I went anyway.

As I was saying, I made my way to the departure gate, gurgling with excitement.

For ten glorious hours I was treated like a sheikh. Like a golf professional, even. I ate until the buttons popped on my jeans and drank myself to sleep on free alcohol. When I woke up, I drank some more and watched John Travolta in *Get Shorty*. I ogled the hostesses for a while, drank some more, ate again, then read a fascinating article in the in-flight magazine about the rampant corruption within the ruling dynasties of the Middle East. Actually, I fell asleep after my second meal and suspect I may have dreamt that last bit.

The last hour of the journey I spent in a feeble attempt to impress the woman sitting next to me by telling her I was a golf professional. (Don't think less of me for this: there is not a caddy in the world who has not done it in pursuit of sexual gratification.)

Joyce James, for that was her name, was fulsome of lips and even more so in the chest department. I fancied her rotten. She was from Lincoln but had left five years ago to become a hostess in a Dubai nightclub. Her life was 'interesting', though the local men were pawing and sexually repressed. They made up for this, though, with their generosity. I noticed her watch, a Cartier, and her bracelet, gold and thick as a toilet chain. I knew then that she was out of my league but ventured on nevertheless. Of course, I skirted round issues of identity until I was completely sure she knew nothing about golf.

'My name is Freddie Couples, actually,' I finally revealed.

'Go on.' She giggled. 'No one's called Freddie Couples.'

'Honest. That's who I am.'

She looked at me with just a hint of interest, a flutter of the eyelash. 'Who?'

I saw my chance. 'Why don't you come along to the tournament? Tell them at the gate you're Fred Couples's personal guest and that he has reserved you the seat beside the Sheikh Mohammed bin Rashid Al Maktoum.' I'd plucked the name from the page of the in-flight magazine lying open in front of me.

'Freddie Couples, you say?'

'That's right. C-O-U-P-L-E-S. US Masters Champion 1992.'

The landing lights went on shortly afterwards. We glided smoothly on to the Tarmac. The airline crew waved goodbye with tears in their eyes. We were then ushered through Immigration with a degree of ease and courtesy normally reserved for visiting heads of state. The last time I spoke to Joyce was at the baggage carousel, just after she looked over my shoulder and saw the name on my passport. 'Fred Couples, my arse,' she said, throwing her Louis Vuitton hold-all on to a trolley and walking off.

I watched her go with supreme indifference. What was one tiny setback at the end of such a luxurious day? I collected my bag and wandered outside. The taxi drivers wouldn't leave the airport for less than twenty pounds. The city centre would cost thirty-five. I hailed a courtesy bus for the Dubai Hilton. 'Name of player, sir?' the driver said.

'Couples. Fred Couples.'

. . . but mostly it happens like this . . .

'Brian, where the fuck is the Belgrano?'

Brian McFeat, the conspicuously proud owner of a six-year-old Talbot camper van known to everyone on tour as the Belgrano, went quiet at the other end of the telephone.

'Brian. Are you still fucking there?'

'Dover,' a voice whispered. It sounded terrified.

'Where?'

'Dover,' McFeat said, this time more confidently. 'It'll be in Dover by now. What a fuck-up.'

Blood vessels popped in my forehead. 'No, Brian, it is an extraordinary fuck-up.'

I'd booked a three-week round trip on McFeat's camper van, London–Cannes–Valencia–Bergamo–London. It was by far the cheapest way to travel on tour unless you hitch-hiked. He was vague about the price but assured me that whatever he charged it wouldn't have got me to the end of the runway on Emirates Airlines.

I eagerly snapped up the offer. This proved to be a monumental mistake, which I will explain later. But first, my excuse.

Travelling with McFeat gave me the chance to meet the European tour's contingent of Argentinian caddies. There were half a dozen, all in their mid-twenties. Every March they arrived from Buenos Aires with nothing more than a small suitcase, short hair and a waterproof suit. They went home again in October with a small suitcase, a waterproof suit, long hair, a beard and a pile of money in eighteen different currencies. They travelled from tournament to tournament in McFeat's camper van. They were a friendly enough bunch but quiet and insular.

In the welcoming, not to mention hilarious, way that the British caddies have, they had christened their South American comrades the Corned-beef Inspectors. In that vein McFeat's camper was known as the Belgrano – after the Argentinian battleship sunk by the Royal Navy during the Falklands War with the loss of 288 lives.

I was desperate to know more about the Corned-beef Inspectors. What was it about their lives back home that made them come to Europe? What was it like living out of a suitcase for six months of the year? Did they ever get homesick? Did they have wives and children? Did they mind being called the Corned-beef Inspectors? These were interesting, unanswered questions and with the Belgrano in Dover, waiting to board the nine o'clock ferry to France, they seemed destined to remain so.

'What the fuck is it doing in Dover when it's supposed to meet me at Milton Keynes Central? You were meant to call and arrange a time to pick me up,' I screamed at McFeat.

There had been a change of plan. His mother was sick. He had stayed at home and put someone else in charge of the Belgrano.

'I'm sorry I just forgot to let you know.'

I wasn't falling for the sick-mother routine. 'Oh, you're sorry.

Well, that's all right, then. So how am I supposed to get to Cannes? Swim?'

Tour life had resumed its hurtful normality after Dubai. Nick Faldo had won the US Masters again. Ross had only just made the cut at the Portuguese Open. He had decided not to play in the Madeira Island Open. Ian Woosnam was leading the Order of Merit with £226,820 and sevenpence, 150 places and £223,947 ahead of Ross.

This depressing statistic appeared to leave Ross unmoved. He'd started to reread his Anthony Robbins book and had acquired an air of evangelical optimism. 'Things will start happening in Cannes,' he promised, and I believed him. Cannes would be Week Zero, a fresh start to the season for both of us. He would make some money and I would become a better caddy.

I slammed the phone down on McFeat with the thought that the great rebirth had got off to an unpromising start.

There was one seat left on an afternoon flight to Milan. The travel agent could smell my desperation down the telephone so the ticket cost a fortune, £250. I paid up. I had to. Ross was expecting me to be on the first tee at Royal Mougins golf club at noon the following day. He would not have appreciated having to pull a trolley round one of Europe's hillier courses.

Remarkably, the trip passed off fairly smoothly. The flight from London took off on time, landed on schedule and didn't crash in between. I took a bus to the city centre and was sitting in Milan's splendid Gothic railway station by tea-time. I spent a happy hour in the station bar, drinking Perroni and wondering why the shop across the forecourt was called Free when it charged thirty-five pounds for the acrylic tartan bonnets in its window.

The train to the French Riviera was a relic from Mussolini's days, with a top speed of seven miles per hour. It limped through the mountains to Genoa then freewheeled along the coast, through towns with wonderfully romantic names like Varazze, Finale Ligure, Imperia, Diano Marina and Ventimiglia, before finally creeping into Cannes at three a.m.

The Cannes Television Festival had started the previous day and all the respectable hotels were full. Eventually, I stumbled upon a back-street dump called the Little Royal Palace. Needless to say it was neither palatial nor royal but it had space. The night porter showed me to a converted pantry masquerading as a fifty-pound-a-night single room. I dropped my bag on the floor and leaped towards the bed. I was asleep by the time I landed.

In the morning I took a taxi to the course. The Belgrano was parked on a bare patch of land between the Cimetière du Grand Vallon and the tenth tee. The door was locked and the curtains drawn.

Two other campers were parked alongside. A brand new Fiat model, Stephenson's Rocket, which was owned by a Scouse caddy called, funnily enough, Stephenson. The other was custom-built and looked like the bastard offspring of a two-berth caravan and a Ford Transit. This belonged to a wild-haired caddy, about sixty years old, whom I knew only as Lovely Les. The cemetery had a fresh-water supply and there were enough trees around to provide cover for an *al fresco* toilet.

This was the caddy village.

It was smaller than usual. Most weeks, there was a circle of a dozen or so tents hidden away in a corner of the course. The attractions of Cannes, cheap apartments and a topless beach, had persuaded half of the village regulars to stay in the town. The others had found a cheap caravan site further up the valley. No one knew where the Argentinians had got to.

I ought to have read the signals in this eagerness in the others to abandon the caddy village. Incomprehensibly, I was still hopeful that my berth on the Belgrano would be empty. I decided to come back later and walked up the hill to the club-house. Ross was already there, getting ready for a practice round.

Royal Mougins was a typical new golf course, built for people with more money than sense. Membership cost £30,000, plus £3,000 annual fees. For this, and I'm reading from the glossy brochure here, members were informed that they 'will find a pro-shop selling clothing and golfing equipment'.

What a bargain! Thirty-three thousand quid and you get to buy your own golf balls. The colossally sickening thing was that people had actually signed up. Beautiful, rich, healthy people. They were wandering around the clubhouse dressed like dum-mies in Ralph Lauren's shop window with members' badges proudly pinned to their shirts. Idiots.

The course itself was built on a tiny patch of land half-way up a valley and felt more cramped than an office lift at closing time. It was cut in two by a road and had electricity pylons scattered across its fairways, like skinny giants escaping a fire. Some of the holes were silly enough to have been designed by Walt Disney. Ross said he liked it but played in practice as if he hated it.

At dusk, I walked back to the cemetery.

The Belgrano was bathed in a warm golden light. I felt a little tingle of pleasure. Camper vans had always struck me as the most romantic of vehicles. I knew they looked stupid and middle-aged but, ask yourself, how could anyone resist something which combined the freedom of the highway and home comforts on a single axle?

Andy Prodger was standing on the steps in his shorts and T-shirt. 'You've finally arrived.' He smiled. 'Come on in, we've kept a bed for you.'

I climbed on board and immediately knew I'd got it all wrong about camper vans. It smelt strongly of old food, leaking calor gas and chemical toilets. Thank God there were only three of us, Prodge, me and a caddy called Keith who was lying stretched out on the seats by the rear window smoking a roll-up.

I'd never met Keith before. He caught me staring at a set of false teeth lying by his ashtray next to six used golf balls.

'They're my little Christmas bonus. I sell them at the end of the year.' He grinned, showing off a splendid black gap along his lower gum. 'The golf balls, I mean.'

My heart sank. I'd already written the headline for my world-exclusive sport story – *Caddy in False Teeth Pay Shock!*

'Oh, Ross gives me his old golf balls as well,' I said, shaking Keith's hand. 'I have to buy my own false teeth, though.'

It was quickly established that I would be sleeping on the kitchen table, beside the chemical toilet, the rubbish bag and a fridge that wasn't quite working properly. It also turned out that Prodger had acute bronchitis and Keith snored like a revving Harley Davidson.

I finally got to sleep at about two a.m. I woke up at six when Keith stumbled out into the early-morning sun with a handful of tissues. He came back ten minutes later and announced in a loud voice he'd had a shit in the trees at the back of the ninth green – anything overhit could well find a plugged lie. A caddy is never off-duty so I roused myself and made a note in my yardage book.

As it turned out, I needn't have bothered. Ross hit a fine approach shot to the ninth hole. I remember it perfectly. It was one of the few fine shots in a terrible round of seventy-seven.

He followed this with seventy-six in the second round, though this could have been an eighty if a rules official hadn't intervened to save me from a four-shot penalty – a European Tour record for a caddy, I was reliably informed. I didn't begin to understand what was going on but it seemed that I had touched Ross's ball when I shouldn't have. For some reason, possibly sympathy, the penalty wasn't imposed in this instance.

We comfortably missed the cut, finishing 137th in a field of 150.

I spent the weekend battling against cabin fever, Prodge's bronchitis germs, Keith's pungent fags and manic depression. At least I had a decent view of a cemetery. The alternative was a shopping trip to Cannes, an unaffordable taxi ride away. Or if I got really, really desperate I had the option of wandering up to the course and watching some golf. (On second thoughts, this wasn't an option. A proper caddy would rather die than be discovered watching golf in his spare time.)

I got really, really, really desperate around six o'clock on Sunday afternoon. I wandered up to the eighteenth green in time to see Clark Ingram carrying the winning bag up the last hole.

I'd met Clark earlier in the week. Cannes was his first tournament. He'd only picked up a bag the day before it started, chasing down the first fairway after a young Scottish golfer called Raymond Russell who was pulling a trolley. And there he was, winning in his first week – the very thing Ross had spent a career trying to do and I dreamt about constantly. There were caddies who'd been on tour ten years and never come close to winning.

You couldn't hope to meet a kindlier, more generous man than Clark Ingram but, frankly, where the fuck was he when we were all missing cuts in Sun City, Morocco, and sleeping four to a single room in a Dubai brothel? I thought about hanging around for the prize-giving but, being a sad and bitter individual, thought, Sod it, and went back to the Belgrano.

Keith had a good week too. His man came third. He spent the first five hours of the journey to Valencia working out his share of the cheque and how to spend it (£1,575 and lots of alcohol, since you ask). The remaining ten hours he spent in a hugely satisfied and noisy sleep. I wanted to throw him overboard.

The good news was that I couldn't stay in the Belgrano once we got there. McFeat was back, his mother well again.

We arrived at seven in the morning. I danced out into the grey Spanish dawn, a thousand hotel rooms at my mercy. I plumped for number 471 at the Hotel Londres, a windowless cell that stank of diesel oil. The bedsheets were sprinkled liberally with someone else's pubic hair. It was brilliant.

Ross tied forty-ninth in Valencia. He won £2,330 and moved up a dizzying eight places in the Order of Merit. We retired to the clubhouse for a beer after the final round. He seemed so happy I didn't have the heart to tell him I'd just lost thirty pounds betting on him to win our three-ball. If I had, he would have said for the thousandth time, 'Never tell me when you bet money on me with the other caddies, it makes me nervous.'

The Belgrano was parked at the clubhouse gates. We weren't due to leave for Bergamo for another half-hour but McFeat was desperate to go. Stephenson's Rocket and Lovely Les's were loaded up and ready to rock. Engines were not exactly being revved but the smell of a Camper Van Grand Prix hung heavily in the air.

'Would you look at the state of that lot,' McFeat said, nodding in the direction of his two competitors. 'They're charging eighty quid a head and getting to Bergamo by the bloody country roads. Can you believe it?'

He had a point. Lovely Les's was a mobile public-hygiene offence – a sea of bodies smelling strongly of a municipal dump. The Rocket was cleaner but just as packed. The Belgrano seemed luxurious by comparison. McFeat was always meticulously turned out in his black Levi's, tan boots and tartan workshirt. Not a man, I thought by his appearance, to take to the highway in a disorderly, not to mention unsafe, manner. I handed over my seventy-pound fare and grabbed a seat.

We left Valencia seven seconds ahead of schedule, already in the bronze medal position.

There were nine of us on board, four up front, one in the

cubby-hole above the driver's cabin, and four in a space at the back of the van about the size of a cellar dungeon. I pointed out that this might not be legal. McFeat promised we would be in Bergamo in sixteen hours and suggested, in a manner I suspect wouldn't have found favour with *Executive Travel* magazine, that I might want 'to go to fucking sleep and stop [my] moaning'.

At least I had at last got the chance to meet the Corned-beef Inspectors.

A few of them had started coming to Europe in the late 1980s when a handful of Argentinian pros – Romero, Coceres, De Vicenzo – were making enough money to afford to bring caddies. Most of them now worked for younger Spanish or Italian pros. In winter they caddied on the South American golf tour. Their bags were kept in the Belgrano's toilet and, no, they didn't mind being called Corned-beef Inspectors by a bunch of thick Englishmen. Now, this might not seem like a lot of information to you but it took me three hours of ludicrous mistranslations, hand signals and facial contortions to collect.

Eventually, we all agreed it was time to shut up and go to sleep. I stretched out on the makeshift bed I was sharing with Stephen, a rookie caddy from Cordoba. His head was at the opposite end of the bed and his feet were three inches from my nose. Clearly he had had a sweatier, more exhausting day on the course than me and was asleep in seconds. I slipped into a restless dream in which I found myself trapped in a kipper-smoking factory.

I was woken by the sound of metallic banging. I checked my watch, it was one a.m. Through the windscreen I could see McFeat silhouetted against the white light of a service station. He was heckling someone I'd never seen before, a tall man wearing blue overalls and a quizzical expression. It didn't register that we had broken down until McFeat climbed back into the driver's seat and started pounding the wheel with the palms of his hands.

By then everyone was awake. We all got off and started pushing the Belgrano to and fro across the vast forecourt for a while. This had no mechanical effect but provided some unexpected entertainment for the ranks of watching truck drivers as they ate their plates of horse stew. We climbed back on board and sat silently as she was winched on to the back of the rescue truck.

It was four a.m. when we finally pulled up at a garage somewhere in southern France. It was pitch dark outside. Silent. Except for the bloodthirsty barking of the two Alsatian guard dogs and the sound of their paws scratching the Belgrano's paintwork.

'We'll just kip here for the night and they can fix us up in the morning,' McFeat announced, to general dismay.

'What? The nine of us in here all night?' someone said. 'But we all need the toilet.'

McFeat snapped, 'Well, you can go out there and have a piss if you like.'

The smell in the morning was indescribable so I won't even try to describe it. Let's just say it was bad.

Daylight brought a host of questions. Where were we? Could we go outside for a pee now? Does anyone know the French for 'Can I have an alternator for an H-reg Talbot camper van, please?'

We left McFeat to sort out the mess and walked into the village. We were in Corbières, a sleepy little hamlet by a canal. We found a café that was open and scrambled together enough loose change for one cup of coffee between two and a croissant between three. We sat there for two hours, long enough to make sure that McFeat had done all the hard work. When we got back to the garage the Belgrano was purring like a cat having its belly rubbed.

The spectacular drive along the French Riviera, through the foothills of the Alps to Bergamo, almost made up for the misery of everything that had gone before. The five guys in the front kept up a running commentary on tunnels we were about to enter and the spectacular sea-cliffs over which we could drive with the merest turn of the steering wheel. In the back we read trashy Argentinian tabloids with names like *Flash* and *Shock!*, sang along to a loop tape of soft rock anthems and generally had a fun time.

A blinking fluorescent sign for the Banco Popolare de Bergamo by the side of the motorway announced that we'd arrived at our destination. McFeat pulled off at the next exit then got lost for twenty minutes. To everyone's amazement, he somehow stumbled across the city centre and parked opposite the bus station. It was just before ten p.m., thirty hours after we had left Valencia, half a day later than promised. I calculated our average speed – 29.4 miles per hour.

I didn't bother stopping to say thanks as I grabbed my bag and left. (If this seems a little graceless I suggest you get eight friends, load them into a Transit van and drive round central London for a day and half, then see how you feel at the end of it all.)

It was pouring with rain and the streets were black and gleaming. Bergamo was supposed to be one of Italy's richest cities yet it had fewer hotels than Moss Side. There were a couple of cheap places near the red-light district but the rooms had been claimed by caddies who'd had the good sense not to travel on the Belgrano.

I wandered around for an hour before a golden glow of light attracted me to a discreet but obviously grand establishment in an alley by the railway station. I burst through the door like a thirsty man running the last few yards to an oasis. The proprietor, a stout man with slicked hair, was standing in the reception area. I could see row upon row of room keys dangling on the board behind him. Did he have a room for the week?

I may have lost something in the translation but I'm sure he said, 'I'm sorry, sir, we don't have anything left except the Prince Regent's Suite, with *en suite* bathroom, four-poster bed, television, personal masseuse and a fluffy white towelling bathrobe – four hundred thousand lire a night.'

It sounded ideal but was twenty times more than I could afford.

'No thanks,' I said, with as much dignity as I could muster with a fat raindrop hanging off the end of my nose. 'I'm looking for something more luxurious.'

9. Early Exits

The sun rose the next morning and I fell deeply in love with Bergamo. It lasted five days. Long enough to miss another cut. Long enough for this romantic Italian beauty spot, with its Venetian arches and cute coffee bars, to threaten the very thing that had brought me on tour in the first place. I should have known it was coming, this lack of faith: I had seen the signs at other tournaments, such as:

Cannes
We missed the cut in the morning. In the afternoon we caught a taxi to the hilltop village of Mougins and grabbed a table at a street café. We got talking about money. It didn't take John Maynard Keynes to work out that Ross was spending more than he was earning but I thought I'd ask anyway.

'Correct,' he said darkly, draining his glass. 'The finances are not good.'

A sentimental ballad was playing on the café's jukebox, 'Love Me For a Reason' by the Osmonds.

'Another beer, Ross?'

He grimaced. 'I know I played really bad today but, fuck it, there's so much money out here to win. I know that something's going to happen for me, I know I'm going to start playing well.' He looked out towards the valley. If he really strained he would

98

have been able to see the golf course. 'It's just that Cannes would have been a perfect place for a fresh start: just forget everything that's happened so far.'

I bought two more beers anyway. We sat there for another twenty minutes. I volunteered to take a pay cut — anything to break the silence. Ross shook his head. 'It hasn't come to that.'

On the walk back to Ross's hotel we saw a pensioner cleaning the outside walls of his cottage with a compressed air hose. Ross cheered up. 'I've got one of those things at home — best hundred quid I've ever spent. It'll clean anything.'

'That's what you could do if you lost your tour card — Ross Drummond's Power Cleaning Service. What do you think?'

'I think I don't like this talk about me missing my card, Lawrence.'

Dubai

Missed cut. For the first time during a tournament we admitted to each other that Ross wasn't going to win it. It wasn't as if he was in contention at the time or on the leaderboard even. He was tied for 105th place in a field of 133.

We were on the practice putting green, preparing to go out for the second round. I asked him to predict a winner. This was one of my favoured pre-round conversation topics. He would always say, 'Me,' and on cue I would say something daft like, 'That's right, you're the man.' We would both laugh and go to the first tee.

I knew something was up this time when Ross leaned on his putter and gave the question some serious thought.

'I don't know,' he said. 'Probably Colin Montgomerie. I was chatting to him earlier on, he's in the lead and feeling good. Yeah, Monty'll win it.'

This really troubled me. I could handle the other caddies making jokes about my seemingly misplaced optimism but when my own man was undermining me in such a thoughtful, deadly (and accurate – Montgomerie won) fashion it was time for a rethink. Did I really want to caddy for someone like that?

The next morning I spoke to Andy Prodger at breakfast. It was a half-hearted post-mortem. To be perfectly honest, I was more interested in the Russian prostitute sitting at the table opposite us. Our hotel was full of working girls but she was spectacularly beautiful. Marianne Faithfull, *circa* 1968, with an appetite. She cleared two plates of food, one heaped with frankfurter sausages and beans, the other with mixed fruit salad. She finished off with a coffee and a very smelly fag. It was love, sadly unrequited.

'So anyway, Prodge, as I was saying, he's stopped believing he can win. I'm getting worried.'

Prodger scratched his grey hair. 'It's 'im that should be panicking, 'e might not keep 'is card.'

'I can't tell him that, can I?'

'Noooooo. You should 'ave some idea of 'ow 'e's going to get 'is act togeva. Then when you've got that worked out – tell 'im.'

That was easy. 'He needs to stop putting like a man with Parkinson's disease.'

'Well, ask 'im what he was doing in the tournaments when 'e was putting well. Faldo kept three-putting in the third round at the Masters and 'e said to me, "What am I doing wrong, Prodge?" and I said, "You ain't aggressive enough wiv the putts, Nick." 'E changed 'is putter, took twenty-four putts in the last round and won it.'

'Brilliant. That's what I'll do.'

'You gotta tell 'im nicely, mind. Faldo told me to fuck off a few times when I suggested things. Tell 'im you're trying to be constructive. In a nice way.'

Aroeira

One week later. Ross and I met up on the putting green at the Portuguese Open. I asked him to remember the tournaments at which he had putted well. He said he'd never putted well. I said he had been on the European Tour for almost twenty years, he must have putted well sometimes.

He looked offended. 'I suppose I putted well at the Cannes Open last year.'

'I'm only trying to be constructive, Ross.'

We spent the rest of the day working on a new putting stroke and arrived at an uncomfortable hunch-backed stance, with his palms facing each other and the ball not more than the length of my pocket-sized red notebook from the big toe of the left foot. We were the last to leave the course.

'You'll laugh when I tell you this but I've got a strain in my thumb,' he said, when we were waiting for a car.

I laughed. We both did. I thought it was the perfect moment to give him a copy of an article I had clipped from the *Guardian* about an American golfer, Paul Goydos, who'd just won his first US Tour event after fifteen years of trying. 'Read it when you go to bed and when you brush your teeth in the morning – this could be you,' the cut-price psychiatrist inside me said.

After eight holes he was nine shots behind the leader. I could see the leaderboard by the side of the green as we walked up the centre of the ninth fairway. We turned sharp right into the trees where his ball was lying. Ross cleared away a few pine needles while I did some reconnaissance.

There was a gap between two pines directly in front of us, big enough to steer a bicycle through. I could just about see the top of the flag if I stood on tiptoes. Ross gathered himself, wiped the sweat off his hands.

'I think I can get a two-iron through there.'

He made a perfect swing, perfect contact. The ball disappeared as though it had been spirited away by a magician. The crunch of distressed tree bark. Four soft bounces on the mossy ground and it reappeared in exactly the same spot, again as if by magic.

I have never, ever wanted to laugh so much in my life. It was that bad. I couldn't bring myself to look at Ross but could sense his utter despair.

He birdied the next five straight – the most consecutive birdies during a single round of his career, stats fans – but even he had to admit that a couple of his putts had been missing the hole when they bounced off a lump in the green and somehow fell in. He ended the first round in forty-fifth place. And the world drew back from the brink of despair.

Ross finished the week in sixty-fifth place. He won £540. This was £452.79 less than he needed to cover his costs for the week. This wasn't a guess. I knew exactly how much he'd lost because he showed me his cash book when we got back to the hotel after a melancholy night out in Lisbon.

This was the first time we had shared a hotel room. A caddy and his player hardly ever stay together outside emergencies. Nor do they eat together often. It's mostly to do with money – we caddies can't afford the restaurants or the hotels the players use – but some players choose to treat their caddies like a feudal landlord dealing with an errant gamekeeper. Not Ross, thankfully, though we weren't friends – at least not in the way I understood *friends*. I would never have checked into a hotel room with a friend dreading the moment that I took my hot, stinking shoes off or fell into a loud, grunting sleep for fear of offending him.

We had spent so much time together yet we hardly knew each other. We talked a lot, but about golf, the weather, the goings-on in the caddies' digs – nothing serious, nothing personal. I had to guess about all of that. What was he like? I guessed that he got down on himself too much, but that was his way of coping with disappointment. He always bounced back and never held a grudge, against me or his fate. He was tougher than I'd imagined – that was what had kept him out on tour after nineteen years. He was naturally conservative, though why had he taken on someone like me – an amateur – as a caddy? I guessed there was a part of him, like there was a part of me, that was reckless, that believed in miracles. He just didn't like to admit this to himself.

What did he think of me? I'm guessing again – somewhere between bemusement and amusement. He was prepared to indulge me.

. . . and then he discovered an inn which, in spite of all he could say, Don Quixote was pleas'd to mistake for a castle. Sancho swore bloodily that it was an inn. Their dispute lasted so long, that before they could decide it they reach'd the Inn-door, where Sancho went straight in, without troubling himself any further about the matter . . .

By a stroke of immense bad luck we picked Lisbon's most expensive fish restaurant in which to eat. I couldn't really afford it and, as it turned out, neither could he.

I worked it out. He had spent £6,300 and 37 pence so far in the season and he'd won £2,853: a loss of £3,447 and 37 pence. Greg Norman or Nick Faldo would probably have spent more on a cashmere sweater but it was a lot of money to a player like Ross, who didn't have any million-dollar sponsorship deals or club contracts to fall back on. He was skint, or if not skint then poorer than I ever imagined a professional golfer could be.

He put the cashbook back in his suitcase.

'Not good, is it?' I sympathized.

He stretched out on his bed. 'To be honest, I'm getting to the end of my tether.'

'Don't worry, something good'll happen. You're still a good golfer, better than most I've seen this year.'

'So what? It's been the same for nineteen years, believe me. I can honestly say that over the last few years there has hardly been a round where I haven't come off at the end of it thinking I could have done better.'

He turned over and went to sleep. I couldn't remember ever

feeling so depressed. But, as I was saying, that was before Bergamo.

A tour pro usually knows when he's playing badly but in case he doesn't he gets paired with one of the local pros who have been invited to play in the local tournament. It's almost like a nudge in the ribs to say, 'Hey, if you're not careful you could end up like this guy.'

The routine was always the same. He would go to the first tee. The starter would shout the players' names or announce them over a fuzzy public-address system. It didn't matter either way. Hardly anyone would be watching or listening. Up would step his playing partner, the local hero. Everyone would shake hands. The local hero would hit his tee shot. To the untutored eye his swing would look enviable but the tour pro would have its fatal flaw identified in seconds. Sometimes the local hero's first shot would go straight, sometimes not. The only guarantee was that he had absolutely no chance of breaking eighty.

It happened to Ross at Bergamo, the Italian Open, where he was drawn to play against a club professional from Rome.

Gianluca Pietrobono was the thinnest man I have ever seen. He was three-dimensional but only just, with a long body, short legs and stick arms. Everything about him was thin, in fact. He was certainly no oil painting but it was his swing I'll never forget.

It had all the usual stuff, back and through the ball, but was preceded by a spectacular pre-shot routine. This started with a waggle, then a twitch of the head, another waggle, a fast waggle, a twitch of the arms followed by a super-fast waggle, head twitch, slow waggle taking club to waist height. It ended on the sixteenth waggle, after every part of his anatomy had twitched at least once.

I timed it. Thirty-five seconds – long enough for Michael Johnson to get four-fifths of the way to a four-hundred-metres

Olympic gold. Or an innocent on-looker, his playing partner, say, to be reduced to a mental case. I felt sorry for Gianluca. I wanted to grab the club and hit the ball for him but it would have been against the rules. Did he break eighty? Of course he didn't. I'll never know how Ross survived the experience.

Mind you, I don't blame Gianluca for what happened in Bergamo. Only God or someone with a grudge against Scottish golfers with eager caddies could have devised the week Ross and I experienced.

As usual, I had had a really good feeling the day before the tournament started. I always felt good on Wednesdays but this was different, Ross had finished forty-ninth the week before, he played brilliantly in practice and putted superbly. Best of all, he gave me the morning off. I spent it exploring what I thought at the time to be the most wonderful place I had ever visited. (Of course, I now know Bergamo is an absolute dump and if I ever see it again it will be too soon.)

First off, I took the funicular railway to the upper city. I felt obliged. It was supposed to be the one of the most important architectural sites in Europe, capturing all the elegance and style of seven hundred years of northern Italian history. (Can you tell I read that in a guidebook?) Its centrepiece was the fifteenth-century church of Santa Maria Maggiore, the interior of which was said by those who knew about this kind of thing both to shimmer like a casket of jewels and put Milan's Duomo to shame. I'm not really a churchy person but I thought I'd better have a look. It was shut, thank God.

With that I hared off down the hill to lower Bergamo. I had really wanted to go there all along. It had buildings too, chunky greystone terraces redolent of the fascist era, and wide, elegant avenues. More important than that, it had cafés and lively, gorgeous young people and shops, row after row of them, all selling fantastically expensive clothes.

I bought an English newspaper and went to a café where I

had a foaming cappuccino and a lump of the most artery-clogging cake on display.

Refreshed, I had a look round the shops. I even went into one, just to satisfy my curiosity. It was like stepping into a NASA laboratory, all white light and breathlessness. Its entire stock consisted of fourteen exquisite leather handbags. There were four assistants. How could the owner pay the electricity bills, the rates, four staff and feed his family on the proceeds of fourteen handbags? A very good question, one I would have asked but for the fact that the gentleman in question arrived while I was browsing. He looked extremely well connected in a family kind of way, if you get my drift, so I left without a word.

Its architectural and retail splendour aside, there are three things you should know about Bergamo: (a) Pope John XXIII was born there; (b) it once had a gay sauna called Caesar's Bath that was shut down after objections about the activities in its, ahem, 'dark room'; and (c) it was the centre of Italian resistance to fascism during the Second World War.

No doubt the Bergamese held wild street parties to mark the anniversary of all three – they looked like the sort of crowd that jumped gratefully on any old excuse for a knees-up – but that day it was the turn of the Resistance movement.

I arrived at the main square, Piazza Vittorio Veneto, in time to catch the parade. There were teenagers wearing Che Guevara T-shirts, kids on roller skates, businessmen in sharp suits carrying red flags, pensioners and stoned hippies. A school orchestra on the other side of the square was murdering something by Mozart but it didn't matter. It was a wonderful sight and sound. The Italians may not know much about economics but they certainly know how to stage a public holiday. What do we Britons do on public holidays? We spend the day at the Lakeside Shopping Centre or the DIY store. Sickening, isn't it?

Stirred with revolutionary vigour, I caught the bus to the golf course. I spent the afternoon watching Ross hit balls on the range and bitching quietly to the Ferret about a caddy's lot.

'We're butlers, that's what we are,' he said, calming me down. 'They could carry their own bags to the bus or fetch their own balls but that wouldn't look good. We're here to make them look good.'

I carried the bag to the bus while Ross nabbed two seats.

'Five hundred thousand prize money this week – we need to make top ten,' I said, on the drive back to the city.

'Definitely. We'll do it,' he said, flatly.

'How come you never look me in the eye when you say things like that?'

He shifted round on his seat until his face was six inches from mine. 'I am going to do it this week.'

And he did. For twelve holes.

The first day was washed out. I spent the time hanging around the alpine-style clubhouse. Like everything else in Bergamo, it was the last word in understated elegance, with polished hardwood floors and sofas the size of ocean-going yachts. The caddies gathered round the open fire in the centre of the main-lounge fireplace, gossiping and making paper aeroplanes out of the 'no caddies allowed' signs someone had stuck everywhere. Did they really expect us to stand outside collecting pocketfuls of rain?

Ross teed off the next morning at just after eight o'clock.

Once he'd got over the initial shock of Gianluca's pre-shot routine he played wonderfully. He drained a twenty-footer on the first for a birdie, bogied the third and birdied the fourth.

I'll admit I'd adjusted my expectations since Dubai. I still expected him to win, of course, but not every week. To be honest, after missing so many cuts I would happily have sold my nephew into child slavery just to see the name Drummond on a leaderboard.

He holed another putt for birdie on the seventh to go to two under par. There was a leaderboard behind the next tee, not a big one admittedly but one with enough space for four names:

Evans	-4
Sjöland	-3
Mouland	-3
Orr	-1

I glanced at it and in that instant I knew exactly how Scott felt when he arrived at the South Pole and discovered someone else had got there first. The name Drummond wasn't on it! I can't tell you how disappointed I was. I wanted to spend the next ten minutes punching the scoreboard operator's stupid, incompetent face into pulp but with the slow-play rules being what they are we had to press on.

It was too late by the time we got to the next leaderboard. Ross was still on two under par but there were half a dozen players at three under or better.

And then a biblical thunderstorm started. Thick black sheets of rain, lightning, then hailstones. The siren blared, calling play to a halt, and we ran back to the clubhouse. We sat around for an hour, staring miserably through misty windows and getting irritable.

'Lawrence, would you mind standing in the queue over there and getting me a ham sandwich?'

'What am I in this outfit, Ross? A butler?'

I don't know why I said this. It was probably the sight of all those Red Flags in Bergamo. He had queued up countless times to buy me coffee and sandwiches. Anyway, I should have known by now: proper tour caddies don't tell their players to stop treating them like a butler unless they're looking for the sack.

That was our first falling-out. Or, at least, I thought we had fallen out and I went into a huff.

Finally the rain stopped. We trudged back out through the mud to finish the round. Ross was mature enough not to let a dispute over a sandwich queue annoy him, but it couldn't have been much fun trying to play golf in the ever-present shadow of his caddy's petted lip. He hit his first shot straight into a ditch on the right and took a double bogey. He birdied the next but bogied three of the last four. He finished the day in seventy-fourth place. I could have cried at the injustice of it all. He'd played the best golf of the season so far.

I couldn't sleep that night for thinking how he might have performed if the rain hadn't come when it did.

What if? The caddy's motto.

I had that part of the job off pat. What if it hadn't rained? What if that putt had dropped? What if all seventy-three players in front of us withdrew because of the flu? What if I looked like Kevin Costner in *Tin Cup* instead of Wilfred Brambell in *Steptoe and Son* would a golf groupie sleep with me?

I don't suppose he would have won the Italian Open if it hadn't rained but he had been playing well enough to finish in the top ten. A decent cheque would have made the cashbook read less like a Stephen King horror story. But it did rain and he shot seventy-three.

It rained the next day as well and he shot seventy-five. Eleven birdies and we still missed the cut. I couldn't believe it. Ross slumped on a bench in the locker room.

'Take me home in a wheelbarrow,' he said.

We decided to take the plane instead. The travel agent said a bus was leaving the clubhouse for Milan airport.

'Shit, I've left my bag at the hotel. Have you brought yours, Ross?'

'Sure,' he said, mockingly. 'You'd have been really impressed if I pitched up this morning with my suitcase. I never do that and you shouldn't either.'

'But we'll miss the bus,' I wailed. And so we did.

We took a taxi to the airport. It cost seventy-five pounds. Ross spent most of the time with his head buried in the British

Airways worldwide timetable trying to work out if he would arrive at Heathrow in time for a Glasgow connection. I bid a silent good riddance to Bergamo and watched the flat Milanese landscape scroll past. It was a bleak journey. There was a line in the next day's newspaper about it, '. . . and there was also an early exit at the Italian Open for Prestwick's Ross Drummond'.

10. The Ballmark Kid, Elvis and Frank Sinatra

The Ballmark Kid tipped himself out of his car and waddled towards the practice putting green at Dunbar Golf Club. He didn't exactly look like a golfing legend: short and unathletic, with a belly the size and shape of a rhino's backside. He was wearing a crumpled pink polo shirt underneath a red and blue Argyle jumper, shiny navy slacks and golf spats that looked as though they'd just done a shift on a building site. His hair had been carefully positioned to hide his baldness, a conceit that lasted ten seconds in the sea breeze. His moustache was on loan from a Mexican police captain.

I watched him through the window while I ate my breakfast in the clubhouse's mixed lounge. He disappeared into a white Portakabin for ten minutes. When he reappeared he was in friendly discussion with a gentleman wearing a blazer and red armband – a rules official. They ended their chat with a hearty laugh and shook hands.

If I'd seen Princess Diana french-kiss Prince Charles I wouldn't have been more surprised than I was to witness this touching little scene.

I drained the dregs from my coffee cup, dropped a 10p tip on the table and walked out into the sunshine, ready to introduce myself to the most notorious cheat in modern professional golf. I was shaking with excitement.

Tom Watson started it. Not cheating, heaven forbid. He got me interested in cheating at golf.

Not that I cheat at golf, you understand. Well, not if you don't count my bad shots, which I don't. In fact, as far as I'm concerned, I have never cheated at golf in my life, not even when I forgot to count an air shot in an especially tight match at Ballybunion Golf Club, Co. Kerry, last year with my good friend Huw Owen. Nor do I consider the hundreds of incorrectly replaced ball markers (we're talking millimetres here), grounded clubs in bunkers and unrecorded shanks over the years as anything other than confirmation that I maintain a relaxed, flexible approach when it comes to dealing with the injustices of a stupid game. There are millions of amateur golfers like me.

When challenged I refer all pedants to Dan Jenkins's pithy verdict on the rules of the game: they are dumber than carrots.

Tom Watson thinks differently.

Just after the season had started the great champion was quoted as having said in a lengthy harangue about cheating in the professional game, 'We all know who they [the cheats] are.' I knew for a fact that he is an honorary member of Ballybunion so I had a quick read through it to check if my name was in there. It wasn't, thankfully. No names were mentioned, for the very good reason that even Tom Watson knows you can't run around accusing people of cheating at golf: it's like saying they sell heroin at school gates.

You may think this is overstating the case but it's true. I once spent a week reporting on a libel action brought by a man accused of dropping a ball down his trouser leg during a club competition, a slur so grievous he thought it worthy of spending £200,000 on expensive barristers to prove it wasn't true. The jury ruled against him on a legal technicality that no one but the expensive barristers, the judge and the man from the *Harvard Law Review* understood, though it specifically asked the judge to tell the alleged cheat that it did not believe he had done the deed.

It struck me, reading Watson's comments, that if one of the world's best golfers doesn't have the guts to name names, then one of the world's worst golfers should. It would give me something to do during the season besides caddying and might lend a veneer of investigative journalism to an otherwise frivolous expedition.

I didn't actually buy myself a police hat and lie-detector machine but I did maintain a wary eye for cheats. To no avail.

Ross, needless to say, was lilywhite in the rules department. His idea of cheating was turning up in the morning wearing trousers and a shirt that didn't colour-coordinate, which he never did. He didn't do any of the ball-and-trouser-leg stuff either.

I did see plenty of pros having a piss on the finest golf courses in the world, I saw one smoking a joint in the woods, I heard them swearing, I saw them calling penalty shots on themselves which would have earned a medal from Mother Teresa, I saw them throwing clubs at trees, on motorways, in ponds. But not once did I see anyone roll a ball down their trouser leg or take a black marker pen to their scorecard, cross out a five and put a four next to it.

This isn't to say that cheating doesn't happen in professional golf. It does. Or so I was told.

I spent the evening in a Hamburg bar with a crowd of caddies as they identified every cheat in the world's top hundred. I'd like to pass on the names here but, forgive me, I'm a coward when it comes to standing up in court without any hard facts.

There was a legion of stories in the locker room, like the one about an Open Champion who was supposed to have lost his ball coming down the stretch only for his caddy to roll a spare ball down his trousers. Another featured a legendary figure who pulled his caddy aside after winning a tournament and warned him that 'no one must ever know' that he had asked a mate for a swing tip during the winning round – because as the whole world surely knows this is contrary to rule 4a, sub-section 3c, clause IV (i) of the rules and would have resulted in immediate disqualification.

These stories were repeated *ad nauseam* with the hushed reverence Christians reserve for the New Testament. I didn't know if any were true. Did it matter to professional golfers anyway? Only as much as life itself.

Here's a golf tip. If you ever find yourself trapped at a party with a boring pro golfer, accuse him of cheating. He will never talk to you again.

Sixteen years ago Gary Player was accused by Tom Watson of illegally removing a weed from behind his ball at a tournament in Arizona. To this day their relationship is, as they say in the popular press, strained. Greg Norman won't speak to an American player called Mark McCumber after accusing him of tapping down a spike mark during a tournament round.

Tapping down a whole spike mark!

As crimes go, this is hardly in the Al Capone class. I only mention America's most notorious gangster because he, too, cheated at golf. His caddy, an Irishman called Tim Sullivan, used to keep a couple of extra balls in his pocket and drop them if Big Al lost one in the rough. And you thought his biggest crime was to murder people like the rest of us swat flies.

I don't know if Capone was ever accused of laundering his scorecard to make sure he made the cut but the tour pros Vijay Singh and Joakim Tumba were.

Both denied any wrong-doing, of course. Everybody does.

Tumba was banned for five years. Scion of one of Sweden's most famous sporting families, he spent a fortune in trying to clear his name. The European Tour sent his scorecard to Scotland Yard's forensics department. It took about three seconds to prove that it had been doctored. (Funny that, how the police solved that particular mystery pretty quickly and yet took sixteen years to discover that the Birmingham Six's confessions had been doctored by West Midlands detectives.) These days, Tumba spends his time playing in 'long driving' competitions, still insisting that he was the victim of a misunderstanding and getting ready for a comeback.

Singh claimed he was framed by the son of an Indonesian VIP but was banned for two years. He found work as a club pro in Borneo before easing his way back into the professional game. Fully rehabilitated, he is now one of the best players in the world.

There were no Indonesian VIPs around to blame when the Ballmark Kid was accused of cheating. No misunderstanding or dispute over a scorecard at some obscure tournament. His alleged crime was that of moving his ball marker twenty feet nearer the hole during the qualifying round for the 1985 Open Championship. As the locker room sages said, why didn't he rape the Queen Mother on her birthday and have done with it?

I stretched my hand out to shake the hand that was alleged to have committed the infamous act.

'How are you doing? Are you looking for a caddy today?'

'No, I've got this,' Ballmark said, pointing at an electric cart loaded with a bag of Lee Trevino SuperMex blades (*circa* 1972). Somehow I knew he wouldn't be playing Big Bertha graphites.

'Do you mind if I walk round with you, then?'

'Nothing in the rules against it, is there?'

I believed him. Almost everyone else connected with the European Tour would have looked in the rule book to double-check.

Ballmark had always denied cheating at the Open. He spent £10,000 on lawyers fighting the case but it was his word against everyone else who had seen him play that day: his two playing partners and four caddies.

His problem was that there had been other 'misunderstand-ings' in the past. He'd been disqualified twice as an amateur, once for incorrectly placing a ball marker and once over a scorecard dispute. Later, he was 'given permission to withdraw' from a tournament in Portugal after his playing partner accused him of dropping a second ball in the rough.

After the incident at the Open, Ballmark was banned from professional golf for twenty years. He was reinstated as an amateur six years later and made his competitive comeback in 1993. The early days of his rehabilitation were not easy: some-times his entry fees were returned – though technically eligible, he was in fact 'unacceptable'. However, as time has gone on, some in the world of golf have been prepared to let bygones be bygones. In 1996, for instance, he came within a hair's breadth of a recall to the Scottish team.

Match 18 was either the tie of the first round of that year's Scottish Amateur Championship or, as Ballmark's girlfriend Jean described it while we were walking towards Dunbar's picturesque white starter's hut, 'a bit of a fix'.

Certainly, the Scottish Golf Union's computer had been unkind when it paired him against Euan Little, the best young player in the country. 'Even *it* wants to make sure ma man disnae win the tournament,' Jean said, *sotto voce*, as we reached the tee.

Ballmark tucked in his shirt and lit another fag.

Little took a few practice swings. He was the physiological opposite of the older man, handsome, lean, supple, happy, not bald – do I have to go on?

Ballmark hacked up a cupful of phlegm.

Little's swing was as sweet and smooth as honey. There was a glint in his eye that said, 'World, I'm going to rip your throat out.' He had a bag full of hi-tech golf equipment which would have knocked a sizeable hole in the defence budget. Not that any of this did him any good. He was three down after eight holes and walking back to the clubhouse, a beaten man, after the sixteenth.

'What a fuckin' brilliant golfer,' he said, shaking his head in disbelief.

It must have come as a bit of a shock to be beaten by someone with the physical prowess of his grandad but, to be honest, he never stood a chance as soon as his opponent ripped his first drive straight down the fairway.

Ballmark didn't have a golf swing in the traditional sense – he couldn't get his arms round his belly or above his head – but more of a primordial swipe generated by two Popeye forearms. It went awry only once, when he hit his drive on to the beach at the fourteenth hole. He shambled over to the ball and smashed it back towards the flag. Everything in his way, stones, sand, seaweed, driftwood, disappeared like a small town caught in the path of a tornado.

When he got back to the clubhouse he was taken straight to the press tent. He sat down, confronted by eight journalists, and forced a smile. He knew what was coming. He always knew what was coming.

In the way that journalists do, they asked a couple of gentle openers.

How old was he?

'Thirty-nine,' he said, grinning. 'Still a big kid.'

Did he think he had a chance to win the tournament?

'It'll take a good player to beat me.'

What about this whole cheating business?

The grin left Ballmark's face as quickly as snow on a coal fire. Jean started muttering obscenities. Ten seconds later the press conference came to an end.

'Why do people want to talk about something that happened eleven years ago?' Ballmark said, disappearing through the door and into the daylight. Jean followed him out but not before shooting us all a withering look.

I left them for ten minutes, then followed them into the mixed lounge. I bought them a drink. He had a Coke, she had a double Bacardi. We got talking.

The only time I've ever spent much time in the company of someone accused of a terrible wrong-doing was when I interviewed a man in Durham jail who said he'd been framed for the murder of his wife. He had bad breath and a crazy stare. Not only had he murdered his wife, I am certain he would have murdered me, given half a chance.

Ballmark was much nicer than that. He was very shy. His was a sad story. I half remembered bits of it from the back pages of the newspapers I'd read when I was growing up.

He had started playing golf with a couple of cut-down clubs when he was three years old, took it up seriously when he was seven and was winning adult golf tournaments when he was nine. He was a one-handicapper at fourteen and, as a boy in Scotland, won every tournament there was to win.

'My dad wanted to put five hundred pounds on me to win the Open Championship before I was twenty-five but the book-makers wouldn't take the bet because they thought I'd do it,' he said.

Jean nodded proudly and said, apropos of nothing, 'They just don't want to believe ma wee man here has got so much talent.'

Ballmark was given honorary membership of Dunbar – his home club – after he won the European section of the Andy Williams World Junior Championships in 1972. This meant he had to meet Andy, who was kind enough not to sing to him. 'It was in San Diego. He talked to me for a while then introduced me to Elvis Presley, who was hanging around at the golf club.'

'You met the King?' I said, 'Fucking hell! What was he like? What did you say to him?'

'Not much, really – how's things, Elvis? That was about it.'

Ballmark turned professional when he was seventeen. He'd

won everything he could at amateur level. He won nothing of any note as a professional.

'I almost won the Welsh Classic, mind you,' he said, wistfully. 'I played with Greg Norman in the last round. The crowd was only interested in what he was doing and once he'd hit his shot that was it – the noise was so distracting. He didn't out-drive me, though.

'My ambition was to be the best golfer in the world. I liked the tour for one year and hated it for the next ten. It got so bad that I wouldn't practise. I'd stay in my hotel until the tournament was ready to start, then go to the course and peg it up.'

Euan Little came over to our table. He was leaving and wanted to wish Ballmark good luck in the rest of the tournament. Jean insisted on showing me the huge silver trophy Ballmark had won at the district championship a couple of weeks before. It was perched on a shelf by the bar. 'Lovely, isn't it? That showed them all.'

We wandered back to the table. Little had gone. Ballmark was staring morosely at his Coke. I suggested we go outside into the sunshine. Scotland's east coast enjoys such days once a decade and it seemed a shame to waste it in a haze of cigarette smoke and ceaseless bar chatter.

We sat on a wooden bench under the clubhouse window. We had a clear view of Dunbar, a quarter of a mile along the coast. Ballmark had been born and raised there, the heir-apparent to a butcher's shop. It's an ugly, thrawn little place, its high street lined with empty shop fronts. Golf must have seemed a great escape for a teenager faced with a lifetime of serving boiling beef to little old ladies in woollen hats.

Ballmark seemed more relaxed outside, away from the dis-approving looks of the people around us. Dunbar is a typical east-coast town, Presbyterian and golf crazy. It need hardly be said that the locals didn't appreciate his contribution to local history. I'd only been in the place five minutes and already I felt as if I was the best friend he had. He'd almost started to relax in my company.

'I'm sorry to bring this up, I know it's embarrassing and you might not want to talk about it and, believe me, I'd understand. But that business back in eighty-five. What happened?'

I had to ask. Ross had given me the week off and I'd spent a whole day of it in Dunbar. For that kind of sacrifice I was entitled to ask the Lord Mayor if he'd slept with any farmyard animals recently.

Jean's cheeks reddened. 'Don't be so cheeky.'

Ballmark put his hand on her shoulder. 'It's all right,' he said. He looked at me. 'I never cheated in the British Open. I swear it.'

For the next half-hour he took me through the infamous round.

It had been blowing a gale that day. He had been drawn in a group with an English guy called Middleton and an American.

He had played well. He was four over after thirteen holes, a good score in such bad weather.

'The fourteenth was three hundred and forty yards, downwind left to right. I hit a two-iron to fifteen feet. The other two had gone through the green. I marked my ball and walked off the green. The American guy . . .'

(I looked up the American's name afterwards. Alvin Odom Jnr. You may have heard of him but only if you were a close relative. He shot eighty-three that day.)

'Anyway, he chips up and then walks on the green and says my ball was nearer the hole, twenty feet or something like that.'

I said twenty feet was too far a distance to make a mistake about.

'The way I see it, he approached the green from a different angle the second time and his eyes deceived him,' Ballmark said, steadily.

A rules official was called. 'He gave me the option of replacing my ball. I said, how could I replace it when I hadn't moved it? He said you can play the last four holes and we'd talk about it at the end of the round. I played another couple of holes and then thought 'Fuck it' – the car park was next to the green. I threw the clubs in the boot of my car and left.

'I hid for two or three days. My mum and dad had to put an advert in the paper telling me to get in touch.'

Retribution was swift. The PGA held a disciplinary meeting within a month. Evidence was taken from the rules official, the other two players and four caddies, including one who had been working for Ballmark but who had walked off after nine holes.

His punishment was the harshest in the history of the game.

'Mike Tyson got less for rape,' Ballmark said.

As far as I could see, Tyson got a lot less: five years in a state penitentiary alongside some of Ohio's hardest criminals. Ballmark has had to spend a lifetime in disgrace in Dunbar.

He tried to overturn the ban. He still has the papers, boxes of them, in a cupboard at home.

'In the end I just thought, fuck it. Do you know how much a barrister costs? I'd do as well to put all my money in that bunker over there and let the next guy to come along steal it.'

He didn't pick up a golf club for four years. He ran a pub for a while, worked in the family butcher's, then dabbled in property deals. He said he was now officially unemployed and his life consisted of playing golf or socializing with his girlfriend and his family. It all sounded as far as you could possibly get from Elvis and Andy Williams and San Diego.

We sat on the bench for a while longer, drinking in the wholesome, healthy atmosphere of a scorching day by the Scottish coast. But mostly drinking lager. It was with a light head and heavy legs I got up to leave. I told him he would win the tournament. (He lost, naturally.) I liked him. I didn't believe all that bollocks about Alvin Odom Jnr's eyes deceiving him, of course, but, so what? Everyone deserves a second chance. Or even a third, fourth and fifth one.

A few weeks later I found myself in a McDonald's in Glasgow, sitting opposite a chubby, red-faced man with his foot in plaster. He told me his name but said if I printed it he would 'see me, all right'.

'Frank,' he said, menacingly. 'Call me Frank Sinatra.'

I met Frank when Ross played in the Scottish PGA Championship near Edinburgh. It had been a hellish week, like playing golf in a chest freezer. Ross finished seventeenth when he'd hoped to make the top five. I was shivering by the scoreboard at the end of the second day, getting ready to go home, when one of the other caddies pointed at Frank. 'See that guy over there, he worked for the Ballmark Kid when he cheated in the Open.'

Frank used to caddy on the European Tour but left after an incident with a South African caddy. I say incident, it was more an act of unforgivable brutality. The South African had teased him in a bar and called him a wanker in Afrikaans. Frank crept into his room that night and smacked him over the head with a chair while he was sleeping. He was banned for five years. He had no regrets.

Frank had never talked about the Ballmark, not even when a reporter offered him £1,000 or the *Sun* printed a picture of Ballmark with the plea, 'Did you caddy for this man? Please call this number.'

'Where I'm frae, a grass is a grass,' he explained. 'The guys just wouldnae understand what it was all aboot. As far as they wur concerned, if ye talked to the paper ye would hae been grassing somebody up.'

He only agreed to talk to me after a glowing reference from some of the other caddies – and then only on condition that he got to use a false name.

Two Big Macs, two fries, two Cokes, two apple pies. I paid. We sat down in a corner as far away as possible from the other customers.

Frank said he had picked up Ballmark's bag in the carpark the day before the Open Qualifying. 'I didnae want the job. I'd heard about his reputation, the things he'd been done fur as an amateur, but I needed the cash. I knew the guy would pay me. Everything started off OK, except he was three over after two holes. He hit his approach shot to the third well short.

'I was walking towards the putting green thinking, Shit, we're in three-putt territory here, because he was that far away from the hole. We went through the green to find the other two balls and when I went back to clean his ball it was only fifteen foot from the hole. I thought this was odd – would I have been thinking possible three-putt if the ball had landed fifteen foot away?'

Frank claimed there were other strange incidents, on the fourth hole, the seventh and the ninth. He described them in the written evidence he gave to the PGA investigation.

He decided he'd had enough after nine holes. 'The green was right next to the clubhouse. I told him I was going to the toilet, I dumped the bag on the tenth tee and never went back.'

I've condensed Frank's story. He went on for an hour and he grew increasingly agitated, tearful with rage almost. Eventually, he got up to leave.

'I've done some daft things in my time, been in Barlinnie Prison and that,' he said, shaking his head. 'But I wid never cheat at golf. What's the point?'

I watched him disappear into the black Glasgow night and sat back down in a sombre mood. He'd left me with much to ponder. I drank another coffee and thought about Tom Watson and his unnamed cheats, about Elvis and Ballmark and all that wasted talent, but most of all I thought about the sheer madness of anyone who laughed about smashing a guy over the head with a chair while they were asleep but could cry with rage at someone who may or may not have moved a golf ball a couple of feet.

11. The Giant is Awake

The first time I saw Nick Faldo in the flesh he was driving into the car park at the Oxfordshire Golf Club at the wheel of a shiny new Jaguar.

The car was a gift from his sponsors. I knew this because five minutes earlier I'd been reading a newspaper article about the new Masters Champion's finances. Jaguar had given him a new model and £1 million. Then there was £8 million from a golf-club company, £3 million for playing one brand of golf balls, another £1 million appearance money and £3.5 million to design seven golf courses. Negotiations with God plc were continuing but Faldo's manager said he hoped to close a £2 million deal that would secure his client's agreement to breathe oxygen for the next five years.

'Nick has seen his world go mad,' Mr Manager said.

He wasn't the only one. Was it just me or had the sponsorship business lost all sense of proportion? Faldo was good – OK, brilliant – but did anyone really need to give him eight million for using a particular brand of golf clubs? He couldn't play golf without clubs, after all. Or golf balls. And I was fairly certain the planet could survive without another seven golf courses. It struck me, reading this article, that if life had any semblance of justice then Nick should have been able to struggle by on, say, £10 million. The other millions could then have been shared out among other less glamorous pros like, and I'll pluck out a name at random here, Ross Drummond.

He didn't have any sponsorship deals. Not one. I may have been biased but I thought this was ridiculous. Faldo was only – only! – two shots a round better than he was. Anyway, even I could get a sponsorship deal.

Not long after I saw Faldo at the car park, Martin Rowley wandered into the caddyshack and asked if anyone wanted two acrylic golf shirts. They cost fifteen pounds each in the shops and came in two colours, mauve or pink. They were mine on condition that I wore a visor with the maker's name on it during the tournament. I was tempted. If I ever bought a cornfield at least I'd have something for the scarecrow to wear. On the other hand, acrylic gave me nipple rash. I needed clean shirts but I hated visors. Mauve was just about OK, pink was unacceptable. Did Nick, I wondered, agonize this much over his knitwear contracts or did he leave it all to his manager?

'Can I think about it, Rowley?'

'Course you can, mate. But not too long, they're going like hot cakes.'

To be honest, golf-shirt sponsorship was not my biggest worry as I sat there, chewing a cold bacon roll. There was also the small matter of how Ross was going to make some money, or even make the cut.

The Benson and Hedges International Open was about to start and the bare facts were these. He was in 152nd place in the Order of Merit. He had earned £5,000 and spent twice as much. He'd had one of his worst starts to a season. Ever. There were players below us in the money list, but no one I'd ever heard of. He was swinging well but putting like a dog. His morale was not so much low as subterranean, a danger-ous mixture of self-pity and fatalism. In short, he was rock bottom.

I was down there with him. The days of turning up at a

tournament thinking we were going to win, I'd decided, were over. In any case, the B&H was not an event for indulging in fantasy. It had the strongest field of the year so far. If we were going to win we would have to beat every member of Europe's Ryder Cup team. The on-course bookmaker had Ross at 250–1 to win but I still couldn't bring myself to bet on him.

It was time to get tough.

And so it was that Ross and I stood on the practice green outside the Oxfordshire's clubhouse, our faces drawn by the cold, and started to squabble. It began when I asked how he was feeling. This made him very suspicious.

'Fine. Why?'

'Good, because we've really got to pull the finger out this week.'

This made him very annoyed. 'You don't need to tell me that.'

'I'm just saying, that's all. Sorry.'

'Yes, but you saying something like that just gets me on edge. It's like a big wave of panic comes over me. You don't have to say things like that.'

'Fine.'

'I just want to play like I played in practice, stand up there and play golf.'

'Fine.'

'I've been worrying about all sorts of things – what's the cut?, the standard's really high, oh, God, I'm going to make a bad shot here.'

'Fine, Ross.'

'And you saying that kind of thing doesn't help.'

'Sorry.'

'Fine. Well, this week is going to be different. I mean it.'

One of us always made a short speech on this optimistic theme at the start of a new tournament – it had degenerated into a mere passing reference since the Churchillian efforts at the start of the season. I was better at it than Ross, who could never take it seriously. This time there was no weary obligation in his voice, no hesitation or embarrassment. It may have been the weather but his face was cold and hard-set and blue.

And I know I always say this, but he really did play beautifully in the first round. He was two under playing the twelfth and just short of the green. I handed him a pitching wedge but he put it back in the bag and took a sand wedge. It was a simple shot and he fluffed it.

'Do one thing for me,' he said, as we walked to the next tee. 'Don't say pitching wedge for every shot near the green, that was never a pitching wedge. That was a fucking sand wedge shot.'

He finished the round one over par.

'Same old shit,' he moaned, when he came out of the scorer's tent.

The next morning I arrived at the course early. The Oxfordshire was another modern monstrosity, built at vast expense on a patch of featureless farmland. It was frequented only by people idiotic enough to pay more to join a golf club than most would contemplate spending on a small house. Caddies were not allowed inside the main clubhouse so I had no firm picture of what the interior was like. I suspected there were wagon wheels tacked to the wall, shelves filled with Capo-dimonte ornaments and fluffy white throw-rugs everywhere. Certainly, from the outside it looked like a scrap-dealer's dream home, right down to the miniature Big Ben clock-face on the fake chimney.

I breakfasted in the caddyshack. A couple of caddies at the next table were talking disapprovingly about Joey Jones, a Scouse caddy who had apparently served a writ on Seve Ballesteros on the practice range for alleged breach of contract. It had all happened a couple of hours earlier but already the story had developed into the script for an Ealing comedy. As far as I could make out it ended up with Joey running after Seve, trying to hit him on the arm with the writ, and Seve shooing him away like he was a leper.

Joey had been threatening to do this for months. I'd spoken to him about it in Portugal, not long after he'd seen a lawyer, and he told me his side of the story.

Seve had asked Joey to caddy for him a couple of years back. The deal was £400 a week, 7 per cent of all prize cheques, plus whatever Joey could get in sponsorship. Ballesteros's bag is to caddies what the post of British Foreign Secretary is to ambitious politicians. Neither holds the power it once did but, God, the prestige is irresistible. No one turns the job down.

It was a big day for Joey and his story appeared in the local paper. Unfortunately he had lasted only a few weeks.

I'd asked him if he knew what he'd done wrong.

'Fuck knows,' he'd replied. 'Seve promised me the job for the whole year and I lasted six tournaments. We even won one of them but I was still out on my ear, no explanation or warning. He said I was a good caddy but he wanted to take someone else.'

Seve told the press he'd been nice to Joey, that he'd treated him as well as other players treated their caddies.

Joey's lawyer told him he'd be a test case. Most of the other caddies thought he was a head case. People got sacked all the time and thought nothing of it. Every week someone would pitch up at the course with the news that they had lost their job for turning up late or smelling of drink or falling out with the player's wife or putting the 52-degree wedge instead of the 48-degree wedge in the bag or looking scruffy.

Friedrick von Hayek, the godfather of Thatcherism, would have loved the tour. It was the free market on steroids, a flexible labour market. I guessed Joey had simply got fed up with being flexible.

When I got there Ross was waiting at the range. He hadn't been able to find a spot to practise. The place was teeming with golf-ball salesmen, wives, managers, agents, shaft experts, swing teachers, psychologists – the full complement of hangers-on, someone said. Even Faldo had been banished to the far corner beside the tea wagon.

We had to wait ten minutes for a space. I spent the time trying to scrounge free advice from a passing golf guru. Was there something I could do or say to Ross that would help him win the tournament? 'Hit him over the head with a spade and when he wakes up tell him he's Nick Faldo.' He sniggered. I contemplated driving my fist into his smug face but then Ross asked me to fetch some balls. We were due to tee off in forty-five minutes. I handed him the bucket of balls and he tipped the contents on to the wet grass. 'Let's get down to business,' he said.

Faldo was in the group five holes in front of us. The entire population of Oxfordshire seemed to be following him round.

Seven people at the tee watched Ross sky his first shot of the day into a right-hand bunker, hack out straight left on to a bank covered with a thick down of mustard-coloured grass, hack a sand wedge on to the green and two-putt for a bogey. There was a wagon selling food by the eleventh green. The spectators making their way back to Faldo's group with steaming cups of coffee might have seen Ross hole a twenty-footer for a birdie, had they bothered to stop.

The wind picked up speed and it started to rain. Faster and heavier by the second.

The twelfth tee was the highest point on the back nine and exposed to the worst of the weather. No one was mad enough to watch golf from up there, even for Faldo. We played the hole accompanied only by the wind. Ross drove to the middle of the fairway, torpedoed a three-wood short of the green, chipped up and holed the putt. A simple par, but he did it with such ease and grace, while all across the golf course people scampered for cover. Waste paper zipped across the sky like crazy starlings.

Rain as solid and black as coal bounced off our heads. Together we watched the others finish the hole, arms folded, saying nothing but smiling faintly, and just then everything felt so right.

Looking back, I think that this was the moment Ross Drummond, talented but under-achieving golfer of this ilk, like some crackpot experiment simmering away for far too long in a school laboratory, finally reached critical mass.

It might only have been my imagination but he always looked different after that one golf hole. A bit taller, with less-rounded shoulders. Maybe he realized then that he wasn't such a bad golfer, after all. Or that he actually liked the feeling of making an awesome par when nature demanded he make a double bogey and that the only way to repeat this feeling was to do the same thing again and again and again.

He scored sixty-nine. In a gale. The fourth best score of the day. As long as I live I will never know how the other three managed to better it.

I don't remember much after the twelfth hole, except that he told me he had bought a cassette tape at the motorway travel lodge where he was staying. He was standing in the queue for his key when he spotted it in a box on the reception desk.

'You'll never guess what it was. Tony Robbins.'

'Tony who?'

'Anthony Robbins, you know, awaken the giant and all that.'

'Oh, him. I thought we'd given up on him months ago.'

'Nah, he's the man.'

He'd bought it for £2.99 and dashed straight out to his car and played it.

'You should hear his voice, it's as though it's through a synthesiser. He sounds like God, SHAPE YOUR OWN DESTINY . . .'

He laughed. I laughed. It felt good to have something to laugh about on a Friday. Fridays were usually for packing bags and making arrangements to meet next Tuesday for practice.

The wind and rain subsided for a while on the back nine then returned, blacker and sharper than before, as we played the last hole. Through the murk I could see a handful of wan figures huddled together on the first tee – players and caddies getting ready to start their round. Ross grinned. 'Good weather,' he shouted over to his French playing partner, Fabrice Tarnaud.

Tarnaud shouted back, in a voice as rich and romantic as Paris itself, 'Beautiful.' He raised his right hand to the black clouds, 'Can we have more of this lovely wet shit for the rest of the day, *s'il vous plaît?*'

Ross finished with a regulation par-four.

He strode purposefully through the smattering of people gathered around the clubhouse and on towards the scorer's tent by the eighteenth green. I scuttled along behind him. The bag bounced excitedly on my shoulder.

I stopped by the scoreboard to check the other scores. I looked around for another caddy. 'Sixty-nine,' I planned to say, when the inevitable question came, 'It could have been better but only if it'd rained champagne.' Frustratingly, no one was around. I unburdened my excitement on an elderly man holding a sodden *Daily Telegraph* over his head who thanked me for the information and asked how Faldo had got on.

Ten minutes later Ross was ushered into the press tent to give his first press conference of the season. It was more of quick chat by the photocopier, actually. A handful of journalists wandered over to listen to what he had to say. And why not? The helicopter bringing lunch from the kitchens of Le Gavroche wasn't due for another hour. A quick burst of honest work must have been a pleasant change for them all.

'OK, Ross, explain yourself,' one said. He struck me as being slightly less reverential than he might have been towards, say, Greg Norman. Not that Ross seemed to mind. His relations with the golf correspondents were friendly but disengaged. He couldn't remember the last time he'd been summoned to the press tent.

Ross batted back the questions as assuredly as he'd played. 'You played well?'

'Pretty good, apart from one brainstorm.'

'You've missed a lot of cuts?'

'We all miss cuts. It's a long season.'

'How much harder is it when the wind blows?'

'Fifty per cent.'

The huddle of reporters started to thin out until only the *Guardian*'s estimable David Davies remained. 'It must help, having a good caddy,' he said, in an outstanding display of loyalty to a work colleague.

Amazingly, Ross took him seriously. 'It helps having someone there to keep your spirits up.'

The press conference finished, Ross decided he'd had enough for the day. We walked back to his car. I threw the clubs in the boot, waved him goodbye and walked back towards the golf course. It was far too early to go home and there had to be at least four thousand people out there who hadn't heard my big news.

I started off in the tented village. I noticed the bookmakers had cut Ross's odds to 50–1. Then over to the caddyshack, back to the practice range, the scoreboard by the clubhouse, back to the tented village for a quick peek through the bookie's window (still 50–1) and then out to the course. It was hard work but worth it. By dusk, I must have told a hundred people that Ross had scored 'sixty-nine, though it could have been better'.

I decided a last look at the eighteenth green would be a fitting way to end such a momentous day. I took the path from the tented village, down a dip, past the frozen rose garden and back up towards the clubhouse entrance. As I crested the hill I caught my first sight of the huge scoreboard by the final green and there,

in black letters big enough to be seen from a passing 747, I saw
something I had begun to doubt I'd ever see:

JIMENEZ	138
WOOSNAM	142
FALDO	143
MONTGOMERIE	140
LANGER	140
DRUMMOND	142

That took care of the thousands I'd missed. It was time to go
home.

We were paired in the third round with Howard Clark, a Ryder
Cup player. I was nervous anyway but this terrified me. Off the
course, he was every mother's delight – polite, witty, tidy hair,
matching shirt and slacks – but when he picked up a golf club
he became possessed by all kinds of demons.

'Be careful what you do today, make sure you stand in the
right places. No noises,' Ross murmured in my direction, as
Clark prowled the front of the tee.

I scolded him with as much professional pride as I could
muster. 'What do you take me for – an amateur?'

Fortunately he didn't have time to answer, it was his shot.

It was another filthy day. A huge bank of black cloud, sullen
and unspent, moved in above our heads as if to bestow the
occasion with due solemnity. A tiny huddle of spectators gathered by the tee in the darkness, like a funeral party.

Ross pulled out his driver. I could hardly watch him hit.
Nervous giggles bubbled inside me like boiling water. Somehow
I squeezed them out in a daffy, silent grin. Both players made it
to the centre of the fairway. From there they made pars.

Clark was remarkably cheery, although this only lasted to the
next green where he lipped a six-foot birdie putt. Ross holed
his to go to three under par for the tournament.

We were both in high spirits now, chattering away about what we'd done the previous night. The big news was I'd spent it at home watching television. Ross and his wife, Claire, had had a Chinese meal then gone to the hotel and slept restlessly while the couple upstairs dismantled their bed, made lots of ooooohing and aaaahing noises, then reassembled their bed again while screaming intermittently. We agreed that people in hotels got up to the strangest things.

Ross birdied the fourth, a tricky par-five. He parred the fifth and sixth to stay at four under par.

The seventh was downwind and downhill, 491 yards, another par-five. We were on in two shots, a driver out of the screws and a cutty three-iron that dribbled on to the front edge of the green.

We walked after the ball. The scoreboard behind the green was no bigger than a bedroom door and it only came into focus when we were fifty yards from the green: Jimenez −5, Drummond −4, and then a list of other names, Faldo, Montgomerie, Langer, I didn't take them all in.

Ross had left himself with a double-breaking, downhill putt about the length of Nick Faldo's Jaguar. It was a lag putt − knock it near enough the cup to make sure you holed the second − but if he holed it he would go into the lead. I didn't mention this to him. He might have started hyperventilating. After all, I was.

He took ages over the ball. I couldn't bear it and looked away. Faldo was a couple of holes in front of us and had stolen the meagre gallery we had had on the first tee. We were left with the scoreboard operator, an elderly couple who didn't have the energy left to move and a gorgeous woman sheltering under a long waterproof coat and emerald baseball cap. I was thinking that perhaps she might find a tournament leader's caddy interest-ing and attractive when a rustle of applause interrupted my gawping. He'd holed it.

Ross handed me the putter and strode off towards the next tee.

'Nice putt,' a steward said.

'Thank you,' he replied, calmly.

We were leading the tournament. I wanted to scream at the top of my voice 'Fuck me! We're leading, Ross.' On second thoughts, that might only have encouraged him to cold top his next shot into the lake to the right of the fairway. Besides, we were now live on national television and, as everyone knows, you can't swear on *Grandstand*: it's a national institution.

I stood at the back of the eighth tee transfixed by the camera's red light and wearing a deranged grin. I don't know how sad your teenage years were but mine were very sad indeed. Every Saturday I would sit in front of the television and watch *Grandstand* with trainspotterish fervour, from Football Focus to the teleprinter. I even sat through the water-skiing from Reading. I loved *Grandstand*. To appear on it live was to be ushered into Sigourney Weaver's bedroom – exciting, yes, but terrifying in an oh-my-God-what-do-I-do-now way. I could hear Peter Alliss's commentary: '. . . and there's the leader Drummond, and there's his happy caddy. Nice to see Ross employing a Care in the Community patient. Well, it gets the poor chaps out, you know . . .'

Ross led for an hour, until the eleventh hole. He pushed his tee shot into the lake that ran the right-hand length of the fairway. It might have stayed above ground but for a devilish kick off one of the grass moguls placed around driving distance by a psychopathic course designer. Cursing, he dropped another ball. An angry three-iron, wedge and two putts later he was walking to the twelfth after a bogey six. He was back in the bunch at five under par.

'I told you we should've brought the remote control Titleist,' I said. This made him laugh.

We usually held a minute's silence for bogeys, punctuated

only by the occasional swear word or a grunt pertaining to the identity of the club with which he intended to beat the ball from the next tee. Maybe, just maybe, conversation would be restored half-way down the next fairway. This time, however, he was chattering away on the next tee, as relaxed as I'd ever seen him.

'I've just got to accept the good with the bad,' he said, brightly. It was like caddying for a different player.

He parred the next five holes.

The seventeenth is the Oxfordshire's signature hole. From an elevated back tee in the next county, a player has to hit a career drive just to reach the fairway. If he succeeded and was lucky enough not to bounce into the Sahara-sized bunker on the right, he had a choice for his second shot: down a single-file strip of land masquerading as a fairway on the right, or across a life-size model of Lake Ontario on the left to another fairway. From there, he had a simple third shot to an undulating green where he could easily spend the rest of his life sword-fencing the ball into the cup. It cost £500,000 to build and was a remarkable tribute to what mankind can achieve on hallucinogenic drugs and an unlimited budget.

The only consolation was that caddies can take a short-cut from the sixteenth green, avoiding the long hike back to the tee. I handed Ross his driver, a compass and a packed lunch, and made my way through the spectators to the edge of the water. I got talking to a marshal. We stopped to watch Ross's tee shot land in the middle of the fairway.

'Faldo's drive landed just about there,' the marshal said approvingly. 'If it was me I'd play my next shot that way but no one's done it today.'

He pointed across the lake and as he did so I was overcome by a curious sensation, an inner sense of well-being and confidence born, I suspect, of a heady day spent on the leaderboard.

'Come on, Ross, you've got to go this way.' I pointed across the lake. 'Don't laugh, you can do it.'

He rubbed his moustache. 'Where do you want me to hit it?'

'Just over there.' I waved vaguely in the direction of the left-hand fairway.

'And what club is it?'

'Seven-iron.'

This was a guess.

'Six- or seven-iron?'

'Six-iron, that's right.'

The Greeks have a word for this kind of behaviour: *hubristikos*. The British have two: criminal negligence.

The shot never looked like getting over. It clattered into the lake's rocky bank, bounced seventy feet in the air and landed on the fairway. On *Grandstand* Peter Alliss said, 'Well, well, goodness me, he'll probably walk over the water now.' Clark, who'd been a little quiet since taking seven at the tenth hole, shouted over, 'Just as you planned it.'

Ross and I were too horrified to talk at first, until I started giggling. 'Good shot.'

He handed me the club and walked away. 'You can laugh now.'

I chased after him. 'It was his idea,' I said, pointing at the steward, but he didn't hear me.

Somehow, he parred the hole. He horseshoed a putt on the last for a bogey five to finish four under par, level with Faldo but behind Montgomerie, Woosnam and a couple of others.

Afterwards, I stood on the grassy bank by the green, thinking I'd never tire of seeing the name Drummond in foot-high letters. They'd even spelled his name correctly. I saw Faldo's caddy, Fanny Sunesson, wearily picking her way through the crowd on her way back to the range. I felt a tap on my shoulder. Ross sighed, lifted his hat and pushed the sodden hair off his brow. He looked like he'd stood on the Devil's tail.

'I think I'm playing with Faldo tomorrow.'

12. Now's the Day,
Now's the Hour

A cheerful voice answered the telephone at the PGA office. 'Drummond? Hang on . . . Here we are, Jimenez. One fifty-four p.m.'

My heart sank. Miguel Angel Jimenez. Spain's third best golfer and a name for every household thesaurus: file under disappointment, tantalization and blighted hopes. Faldo was paired in the group after us.

Ross said he was disappointed too, but his easy grin when we met on Sunday suggested otherwise.

'No Faldo, eh?'

'Yeah. Shame.'

'What would you have said to him?'

'I would have shaken his hand and said it's nice to meet you, the last time I played you I beat you – nineteen seventy-five, the amateur home internationals, Scotland against England. And you know what, Nick, I'm going to beat you again.'

'You wouldn't say that.'

He laughed. 'On second thoughts, maybe not.'

Jimenez was on the range when we got there. I grabbed a spot between Woosnam's caddy and Andy Prodger. Faldo was at the other end, immaculate in black trousers, blue sweater and matching bobble hat. A huge crowd huddled behind the crash barrier to watch him hit balls and complain about the weather.

The forecast was 'warmer – but windier than yesterday'. Fifty per cent right. It was freezing and still blowing a gale. I had on four layers – vest, lucky white T-shirt, sweatshirt and lucky blue waterproof – but still had goose-bumps on my arms. The massive scoreboard by the last green was swaying in the gale like a drunk and had been abandoned. The operators had been sent indoors before someone was smacked on the head by a giant-sized DRUMMOND.

I had to content myself with the measly, shrunken scoreboard by the clubhouse. Ross's name had been reduced to a less dangerous size but it was still thrilling, listening to his letters rattle and flap in the wind.

He was seventh. If the tournament had been called off because of bad weather right then he would have won £21,000. Without hitting a shot! But we weren't playing for the money, we were playing to win. Weren't we? Prodger told me about the notice at the ball-dispensing machine – *'The tournament director will take all necessary steps to ensure play will be completed tonight'* – so I didn't have to tangle with that little dilemma for long. It was to be broadcast live on television. We would play in an earthquake if necessary.

'Get him to practise 'is winter shots,' Prodger whispered, as he walked past on his way to the first tee.

The range was virtually empty. Only the top ten. No need playfully to eke out a space in the line of players hitting shots or to queue for balls. No camaraderie, just a quick 'good morning' and down to work. Like a science lab.

I watched Faldo, then Montgomerie and Torrance. Finally, my gaze fell on Woosnam beside us hitting three-irons towards the red flag at the bottom of the hill with mesmeric accuracy. Poetry. None of that complicated Ezra Pound stuff but a simple, rhythmic smack up the ball's backside. Just enough to make a mortal golfer weep with envy. It was time to go. I picked up the bag and pulled my hat a bit tighter.

It hardly seemed possible but Jimenez's caddy was even more disappointed not to be drawn with Faldo than I was.

No offence, Ferret said, but a round with Faldo would have been good for his sponsors, the Home of Foam. That and the added lustre when he went out clubbing in Rochdale. 'If you're on the telly playing golf with Faldo, a bit of glamour rubs off, dun't it?'

I nodded. 'And if Ross was playing with Faldo the crowd would keep the wind off the greens. At least then he could putt without the ball wobbling around.'

'That's right. It would.'

Our two players, oblivious to the disappointment surrounding them, seemed happy enough in each other's company.

Ross started with four pars.

The short fifth was playing downwind to a shallow green across a pond. He couldn't bring himself to aim for the green, far less for a terrifying pin, cut four yards over the water on the right-hand corner. After four practice swings, though it seemed like forty, he hit his tee shot towards the left-hand gallery. It landed thirty yards from the flag, buried in ankle-deep rough.

'Bad luck,' I lied. It was a rank bad shot.

'No. I wimped it.'

He took three to get down from the rough. It crossed my mind on the way to the next tee that he was about to shoot eighty-one and finish fiftieth. I racked my brain for something caddyish to say. Something inspirational.

'Come on, Ross, come on.'

He parred the next but bogied the seventh. He was still on the leaderboard at two under par.

He stood over his second shot on the eighth for an age, whispering softly, trying to convince himself. 'It's a nine-iron yardage so it's a nine-iron.' I could stand it no longer.

'It's an eight.'

'Sorry, Lawrence?'

'An eight-iron.'

I had to say something, to rise to the occasion. We were on live television, for God's sake. It felt like a lifetime of recklessness in three words.

'The wind has changed, take an eight-iron.'

'You're sure?'

'I'm sure.'

At least, I had been sure, but that was five seconds ago, before I started thinking about how much money I was about to cost him. I handed him the club and stood to the side, mentally composing the apology I was about to make.

I couldn't bear to watch so I stared at the head-covers. Blue wool with a white M for Mizuno. They could have done with a wash. Applause rustled back on the wind. He was on, long and left and far from perfect, but on the fucking green, dear God.

'Good club,' he said. Or I think he did. I wasn't listening, I was waving at the crowd. I felt like Superman – or a proper caddy, even.

He birdied the tenth. Three under par, two shots off the lead.

A dropped shot at the twelfth scarcely mattered, everybody was dropping shots. We were going to win. The superstars had fallen away. Montgomerie had kicked the sand in a bunker for a two-shot penalty. Woosnam got fed up in the wind and slipped back. Faldo triple-bogied the eighth and doubled the ninth.

We met the Masters Champion on the bridge over the lake to the eleventh tee. He said hello but I ignored him. Well, I was busy, wasn't I?

Jimenez hit a six-iron at the thirteenth. The ball ballooned into the grey sky. I lost sight of it until it landed just over the water on the grassy bank at the front of the green. It took one bounce forward to safety.

'Six-iron?' Ross asked.

I couldn't answer. It was just too important.

Ross walked to the front of the tee, plucked some grass and threw it up in the air. A couple of blades tickled my face on the way past. It was still blowing a gale.

'Six-iron? Lawrence?'

There is a way of suggesting a club to a player without actually saying anything. It is ideal for the caddy who is too cowardly to give voice to an opinion when the pressure is on or to take responsibility for a mistake, while ensuring he is ideally placed to take the credit if the decision turns out to be correct.

I gave the golf bag a shake. The five-iron drifted to one side, until its number stamp screamed at him, 'Take me, take me.' He looked at it, then walked away again. Plucked some more grass. He checked the numbers, 134 yards to the flag. He took the five-iron.

Jimenez looked in my direction and nodded. 'Good.' It was the only thing he said to me all day, all season in fact.

He made a wonderful swing, slow and rhythmic. The ball soared straight over the flag and into the bunker beyond. Even now, months later, I need only close my eyes to see it cut through the wind like tracer fire in a night-time battle.

One club too much, at least.

I walked off the tee in front of him, my hand outstretched behind me like a relay runner. I had to get the club back but I didn't want to look at him.

'It's OK, it's OK,' I shouted over my shoulder.

'Plugged in the fucking bunker,' he shouted back. 'That's just fucking perfect.'

In the distance I could see featureless faces, like a row of red balloons, craning to see where it had gone, oooohing and aaahing. People were shaking their heads when I got there.

It was far from OK. A fleck of white balata gleamed in the heavy goo like a bald man caught in quicksand. I'd left him with an impossible shot back in the direction of the water, plugged lie, downhill, downwind, with the grain of the grass.

'A four will do us,' I said, handing him the sand wedge. I would have taken a six.

He played a brave shot and holed an eight-footer for a bogey. I could have hugged him.

'Brilliant.'

'I thought I was gone there,' he said.

Walking to the next tee it occurred to me that I'd just cost him his chance to join Trevino, Weiskopf, Norman, Langer and Ballesteros as a winner of the Benson and Hedges International Open.

Ferret leaned over and whispered, 'Pity, that. A birdie there and you might have won it, mate.'

A wave of guilt washed over me and settled like a sea mist. It blurred my memory of the next four holes. I do recall that Ross parred every one. If anything he was more animated than ever, cajoling me on through the head wind as my legs got heavier. I remember he offered to carry the bag. He abandoned a lifetime's obedience to the code of modest gestures and punched the air when he holed a snaking downhill putt on the sixteenth for par.

By the time we reached the eighteenth it was as though he'd forgotten my mistake at the thirteenth. He seemed to have forgotten everything that had happened in the previous three months. Sun City, Morocco, Portugal, Cannes, Bergamo – all washed away in one glorious afternoon.

He hit a career three-wood on to the last green and we were home. Two under par.

My mind slowed from its troubled sprint and savoured the long, looping walk up the hill into the natural bowl of the final green. I heard the public address system booming down, and into my head wandered a terrifying thought: '. . . a round of applause, please, for Ross Drummond, finishing today in the top ten for the first time this season, no thanks, of course, to his caddy who in case you haven't heard suggested a five-iron a few holes back when a six-iron might have given his man the tournament. Speak to the Ferret, Jimenez's caddy, over there, he'll fill you in on the details . . .'

When we finished, Claire Drummond was standing by the press tent. We hugged. 'I told you he was good enough.'

'You didn't have to tell me,' she said, beaming.

Ross stepped out of the scorer's hut. 'Well, that'll pay the mortgage,' he laughed.

He had finished the round in seventh place. All six players ahead of him were still on the course. With any luck they would be blown away in the gale.

I threw the clubs in the boot of the car and dashed back to the press tent. Faldo had shot eighty, Woosnam, eighty-two, Langer, seventy-nine, Torrance, seventy-seven. I sat in front of the television to watch the others finish, silently willing every iron shot mis-hit and every putt missed. This, of course, is a complete perversion of everything the Royal and Ancient game stands for. I felt awful for all of five minutes, right up to the moment the sixth-placed man lipped out from four feet on the last to earn Ross an extra £5,000.

The weather got even worse. Ross ended up finishing fourth. From £21,000 to £32,320 in an hour. £11,320 in an hour! Not even the chairman of a privatized utility made that kind of money. Personally, I would have turned down the cash if they had let me go back to the thirteenth and have that tee shot again. I wasn't so sure about Ross, though.

13. Mr Magic

I never met Mitsubishi Tommy, the only caddy ever to steal a European Tour courtesy car in the all-important pursuit of saving money. His legend lived on in caddyshack stories of the day he borrowed a £10,000 Mitsubishi to nip down to Salzburg railway station, only to drive it all the way to the next tournament in Stuttgart, park in the carpark and hand the keys in to the PGA office. He was banned *sine die* and went home to Liverpool to sell insurance. (Don't say you haven't been warned.)

I like to think we were displaying a little of the Mitsubishi Tommy spirit when we ripped off the ferry company by buying a £1 'booze cruise' day return instead of the £150 ticket the booking clerk insisted we would need for a week-long trip to the Continent.

And so it was that Andy Prodger, Kevin Woodward and I arrived on French soil in high spirits, refreshed and looking forward to the long drive to the Tournament Players' Championship in Hamburg. There was always an unofficial contest between some caddies to make the cheapest journey to any European Tour event and at 33p-a-head we were ready to accept the plaudits of our peers when we got there.

The drive north was long and mostly tedious. No doubt a map would have got us there quicker and bringing some foreign currency would have allowed us to eat. But that would have required a modicum of forward thinking. Instead, we drove aimlessly across the Low Countries and starved.

Kevin and I spent the first half of the journey squabbling, mostly about politics. (Here's a travel tip for the liberally inclined: never spend fifteen hours in a car with an ex-Rhodesian Army officer.) Prodger sat in the back with his hands over his ears, wincing every time I veered towards an on-coming HGV while trying to make my point. It was with huge relief that he steered the conversation towards a less controversial, though much more important, topic than the moral corruption wrought by decades of white rule in southern Africa: I needed to find a player to caddy for at the Austrian Open later in the season.

Ross had announced he was taking that week off.

He'd had weeks off before and I'd gratefully seized the chance to spend the time at home, exploring the world of cuisine beyond the ham-and-cheese sandwich. I felt that the time was now right to stretch my legs, so to speak. I'd had a top-ten finish as a caddy and there was bound to be a player out there gullible enough to give me a job.

Most caddies worked when their regular player had the week off. They couldn't afford to do otherwise. Great care was taken when it came to selecting a player. Ideally, he would be someone who could win the tournament or finish top ten. Failing that, it was important that he missed the cut. That way the caddy could be home on Friday night with enough cash to pay the bills and see him through a weekend's drinking.

I considered Kevin and Prodger to be absolute masters at the art of picking up good bags on the off-chance, Kevin because he once picked up Paul Azinger's bag for the week and came second in the Open Championship, Prodger because he once got Faldo's bag for the week and stayed with him to win two major championships.

We haggled and bickered across northern Germany. It was finally established that I was looking for a player who was happy, but not weird-happy, had masses of talent but not so much he wouldn't employ a dud caddy like me, a positive thinker but someone who didn't demand high fives every ten minutes or very much else from his caddy other than turning up on time and carrying the bag. Most of all, he must pay well and miss the cut. Greg Norman on a bad week would have been perfect.

Prodger thought this was a bit demanding. 'How about Darcy?'

Eamonn Darcy took a different caddy every few months, partly by choice but mostly because no one could take too much of his particular brand of humour. If a caddy gave Darcy the wrong club for a shot and it flew the green he would say things like, 'It's not your fault, it's mine for employing you.'

I shook my head.

'How about a Swede?'

'They practise too much.' I knew a handful of caddies who worked for Swedes and they always seemed to be queuing up for practice balls.

Kevin chipped in. 'A Spaniard?'

'I still can't forgive them for Franco. And, anyway, what would we talk about?'

Prodger said one of his friends had just finished working for an Australian pro called Mike Clayton. Kevin screwed up his face. 'You don't want to go with him. He's a nice guy but on the course he's like a punk rocker.' I liked the sound of this Clayton character but then Kevin piped up again, 'I know just the man for you . . .'

I never got to discover who the man for me was because just then Hamburg came into view. It was a spectacular sight as we crossed the Elbe. Below us the port was bathed in the sheer white light by which the night shift worked. A silver moon glimmered on the river. It looked deep and mysterious rather than mud brown. Tiny figures wandered along the dockside. In my mind I imagined them to be prostitutes, pimps and Singaporean sailors. Hamburg by night looked ripe with adventure. Unfortunately, the tournament was twenty miles further north in a godforsaken dump called Gut Kaden.

We drove on in search of a hotel near the golf course. It was now two a.m., fifteen hours since we'd left Dover. We were becoming desperate. I spotted a sign for the 'QuickStop Lodge – Truckers welcome, hot and cold water, tarts to order' (I may have translated that last part wrong but it certainly looked like that sort of place) and turned off the motorway. There were no signs of life, though the car park was full. I rang the door bell for what seemed like an hour until a light went on. I could see a female figure silhouetted through the frosted glass.

'Can you help us? We need a place for the night,' I said.

She answered in English. 'Go away.'

'But you are a hotel, aren't you?'

'Fuck off. Don't you know what time it is?' The light snapped off. It was very late and to the suspicious eye we must have looked like three axe murderers but this was devastatingly inhospitable. I felt like crying.

We toyed with the idea of following the signs to Nippleburg, which could have been a highly amusing detour in a *Carry On Caddy*ing sort of way, but we decided a drive back to Hamburg was the safest bet. We found a hotel by the airport which was so delighted to have our custom that it let us have a room for only £149, exactly the amount we had conned out of the ferry company.

Gut Kaden Golf Club was as ugly as it sounded. Owned by Deutsche Bank, it looked as if it had fallen into the company's hands by way of a bad debt and was kept grudgingly. The lay-out was flat and dull. Its greens were scruffy, the rough patchy and the membership list, pinned on the noticeboard in the converted barn that served as the clubhouse, short. Germany has been a hotbed of many things over the years, extremism mostly, but never golf.

I was sitting on the wooden bench outside the locker room when Ross arrived.

'Committee meeting,' he said sharply, pointing towards the café in the tented village. 'Let's have a coffee. I want a word.'

I'll be honest, I thought it was the sack. Whatever magical formula we'd discovered at the Oxfordshire had disappeared when we'd travelled sixty miles south to Wentworth for the PGA Championship. He had missed the cut again. Easily. We'd played the last few holes in virtual silence. What's more, I'd point blank refused to hang around to watch him practise his chipping. It was raining and, besides, he'd been giving Anthony Robbins too much credit for what happened at the Oxfordshire and not enough to me. Sure, Ross hit all the shots but did I ever turn up late to carry the bag? Of course not. And where was Mr Awaken-the-Giant-Within when buckets of balls had to be collected or someone had to queue for cups of tea? Without wishing to linger too long in Barbara Cartland country, I would have to say I felt hurt and under-appreciated.

We sat down with our coffee.

'I'm thinking about working with Jos.'

'Jos? The guru guy?'

'That's right, Jos.' Ross blushed. 'I think I should be working with someone on that side of the game. What do you think?'

Every golfer in the world seemed to be 'working with someone on that side of the game'. Gurus were standard issue. Faldo couldn't button his shirt without guidance from David Leadbetter. Seve had a Mac O'Grady, an American ex-pro, part genius, part crackpot, who had him burying his bad memories in the Arizona desert. (I ask you!) Every week on the range I would trip over qualified psychologists and decrepit teaching pros with drink-ravaged strawberry noses, who were now trading under the description 'guru'.

It struck me that if you laid every golf guru in the world from head to toe it would make the world safer and less expensive for gullible golf professionals. I met one player – I won't mention his name as I'm sure there are laws protecting the identity of the insane – who on the advice of a guru climbed inside the body of the late Tony Lema when he got to the first tee, jumped into Nick Faldo's torso for iron shots and Ben Crenshaw's hands for putting. And he *still* couldn't make a cut. He spent his weekends at home trying to climb into Greg Norman's wallet so that he could pay his mortgage.

Jos was Jos Vanstiphout, a Belgian with a Californian vocabulary for whom 'Pleased to meet you' was always 'Ho, my friend', a handshake was a street-wise arm-wrestling grip and anyone who skipped the queue at the bar 'a filthy motherfucker'. He was a former pop star. Remember the Mayfair Set's 1973 Brazilian hit single, 'Jerimia'? Don't worry, I didn't either.

Life for Jos had been a downhill run after the demise of the Mayfair Set. (How could it have been anything else, pop-pickers?) He told me that he had gone from music to a job with the Chamber of Commerce, then a newspaper marketing man. He took up golf, discovered he had an aptitude for the game and got down to a seven-handicap. Finally, he went to California in search of his own guru and found W. Timothy Gallwey, the creator of a brand of sporting psychobabble called the Inner Game. From that day his life changed.

You may have heard of Gallwey. His book *The Inner Game of Golf* has sold millions, though why I'll never know. I once bought a copy of it on impulse. I took it home, had a quick flick through its pages and threw it in a box where it lay untouched for five years. I often wondered what strange urge had persuaded me to spend money on a book with chapter headings like 'A Critique of the Do-Instruction', 'The Essence of Experiential Learning' and 'Humming Your Swing'.

It dawned on me, as Ross waited patiently for my verdict on Jos Vanstiphout, that there was only one way to find out.

We drank up our coffee and walked into the brilliant sunshine of the Gut Kaden morning. 'I think it would be a terrific idea if you worked with Jos,' I said. 'Who knows? It could have been the difference between fourth place at the Oxfordshire and winning.'

When I arrived early the next morning Ross and Jos were already practising. I could see them through the iridescent mist as I walked towards the range, Ross's tall, rangy silhouette and Jos, a foot shorter, shoulder-length hair, blowing a jet of cigarette smoke into the fresh air.

'Morning,' I said. Ross nodded sheepishly.

The first time I had ever seen Jos we were on a bus from the hotel in Italy to the golf course. It was six a.m. He was chewing a thick salami sausage and listening to the Beatles on a portable compact-disc player. Since then we'd nodded on passing a few times but had never been properly introduced.

'My friend,' he said, presenting his upturned hand. We arm-wrestled briefly and he went back to work.

He looked exhausted close up, his face stretched and battered like weathered varnish. What joy it was to have been the young and sexy lead singer in the Mayfair Set, I thought to myself, but Jesus Christ he was paying for it now in wrinkles.

I made myself busy, cleaning clubs, fetching balls, eavesdropping as best I could on what was clearly a private client–guru conversation. It appeared that Jos had Ross playing an imaginary golf course. He would describe a hole – say a 554-yard par-five, bunkers left and right, big tree straight ahead – and Ross would hit a shot.

Occasionally, Jos would snap, 'How was that?'

Ross would stop, look down the length of the range, as barren and featureless a piece of land as you could hope to come across this side of a nuclear winter, and say something like, 'Not too bad. At least I missed the tree at the front of the green.' Every once in a while he would flash me a secret grimace, like a man looking for a way to escape a blind date.

This went on for an hour. Phase two was a soliloquy from Jos that revolved around the phrases 'one ball', 'smile, focus' and 'self one, self two'.

I may have picked this up wrong but it seemed that Ross, contrary to appearances, was not one but two people, Mr Self One and Mr Self Two. The former was his destructive personality, the brat who lived in his head and constantly complained about the terrible shots he hit. The latter was his subconscious, a long-haired hippie type who hung out in his belly, smoking dope and generally going with the flow. No prizes for guessing which guy Jos preferred.

The four of us had lunch in the canteen. I snatched a whispered conversation with the two of Ross while Jos bought coffee.

'I'm not so sure about this, you know,' he said. 'It's just a bit embarrassing standing there with this guy you hardly know asking you all these personal questions.'

'It's too late now,' I replied – maliciously, I regret to say.

Ross spent the afternoon putting with his eyes closed while Jos yakked away. 'In America they call me Mr Magic but it's not me who's magic, it's you. Putt like this tomorrow and miracles will happen.'

I lounged around in the sunshine, gossiping with the other caddies and players. It had not gone unnoticed that Ross was putting with his eyes shut or that he had found himself a guru.

'What's this guy like?' one of the younger pros asked.

'A bloody genius.' I laughed. 'Possibly.'

Someone else chipped in, 'Bollocks. You don't need all that shite. Just get up there and hit the bloody thing.'

I had some sympathy with this view but as the days passed I found much to admire about Jos: his complete lack of cynicism and limitless enthusiasm, his ability to stay up until two a.m. and still be first on the range every morning, his commitment to the Drummond cause, the way he insisted we stop and smell the flowers. By the weekend, I was hooked on the Inner Game of Golf. Brainwashed, even. I trawled the practice range, bars and canteens in search of anyone who would listen to me explain the difference between Self One and Self Two. There were few takers. That was one of the snags of becoming a fully fledged guru's disciple – most people thought I was mad.

There were other drawbacks, too. Such as Jos standing by the first tee with his thumbs up, insisting that Ross was 'one hot baby'. This was clearly not true and, worse, would have been deeply embarrassing if another caddy had heard it and spread it around.

Worryingly, Ross's moods started to swing back and forth like the door of a western saloon again. One minute he was whistling a jaunty version of 'The Bare Necessities', the next he looked fit to explode just because he missed a putt. Jos blamed Mr Self One for this and promised to 'kill the motherfucker'.

'Believe me, my friend, I see this beautiful man standing in front of me. Ross has so much ability but he is not using it because of this Self One guy. He is my beautiful challenge.'

Still, when Friday afternoon came he made the cut again, the second time in three weeks. Only by a shot, mind, but playing at the weekend was threatening to become a habit.

With this cheerful thought, I left Mr Magic and Mr Beautiful Challenge double-checking the scoreboard and went to the locker room for a shower. I was drying off when Bernhard Langer and his caddy Peter Coleman came in. They barely spoke. Langer changed his shoes and left. Coleman waited until the door banged shut then smiled ruefully.

I didn't know Coleman but had heard all about him. He was a caddying legend. He had been with Langer for fifteen years. They had won over thirty tournaments together. The previous week they had missed the cut for the first time in sixty-eight events – four years, thirty-six top-ten finishes, 272 rounds, 18,961

,hots, 499 under par, with a stroke average of 69.70. Langer's career winnings were over £5 million. No wonder Coleman was smiling. It was the rueful bit I couldn't work out.

'He's got the yips again.'

I nodded sympathetically and carried on dressing. I'd read about Langer's putting problems in that morning's newspaper. It was front-page news in Hamburg.

'Bad luck.'

'It's the fourth time now. He can hit the hardest shot in the world and can't hole a four-footer. It's not as if I can sit him down and say, "Bernhard, you've got the yips", can I?'

'Can't you?'

He stopped tending his tight grey perm and looked at me, puzzled, trying to place this strange caddy who thought you could just walk up to Bernhard Langer and tell him he was a terrible putter.

'You can't say that sort of thing to your player. It's too negative.'

'Of course not.' I realized my mistake. 'Have you tried a psychologist or something?'

'The thing about Bernhard is he thinks too much, he's too strong up there.' He tapped his head. 'Too brainy, you know.'

I put on my shoes and walked through to the toilet. 'Listen,' I shouted over the cubicle. 'Try this. Me, you, Bernhard – we're all two people. There's this guy in your head and another one in your belly.'

I finished, zipped myself up and pushed open the locker-room door. 'As I was saying, one of these guys is called Self One . . .'

When I looked up Coleman was gone.

When we finished the third round Jos was standing by the final green. 'Come here, come here,' he whispered, as I struggled to take off my bib. His voice was straining with excitement. 'You'll never guess what happened this morning.'

To be perfectly honest, I wasn't in the mood. Ross had shot a respectable seventy-one but seventeen pars and one birdie hadn't exactly been a roller-coaster of excitement. I wanted to get back to the hotel, have a bath, catch a train to Hamburg and throw myself into a night of unimaginable debauchery. Anything to escape Gut Kaden.

I found it hard to believe that anyone within a twenty-five mile radius, even Jos, could find something to get this excited about, especially on a damp Saturday morning. We stopped under the shade of the main grandstand. Jos spoke slowly, enunciating every word as if he was in shock. 'I worked with Seve Ballesteros this morning.'

I would have been more impressed if he'd revealed himself as Lord Lucan or got engaged to Cindy Crawford but not by much. We danced a jig of delight back to the clubhouse. The ex-lead singer of the Mayfair Set had given a golf lesson to Seve Ballesteros, possibly the most naturally gifted golfer ever!

Thoughts of Hamburg were abandoned as Jos and I retired to the bar to celebrate. We watched his new disciple's day unfold on the television. He told the story at least five times of how they had met in the physiotherapy unit that morning. Seve asked if he was Jos, what he did on tour, who did he work with and what was the Inner Game of Golf? Finally – *magically!* – he had asked Jos to spend fifteen minutes with him on the putting green before he went out to play his round.

'He thought I was going to brainwash him. I said, "Seve, you don't have to worry, I'm not going to change a single thing about you." We did some blind putting. I had to touch his face with my hand – he jumped. After that we got on fine.'

The afternoon rolled on and on and Seve kept scoring birdies. He played the last hole in par for a sixty-six, his best score for nigh on two seasons.

'This is a present for everything that I have done in my life,' Jos said, surveying the scoreboard afterwards. He poked himself hard in the chest. 'Me. I'm Mr Nobody.' He was almost weeping with joy and it was hard to deny him this moment of triumph. Hard but not impossible.

'Hang on. Didn't you say you were Mr Magic?'

14. The Sweat-box

Jos and I must have looked like two first-formers limbering up for a playground fight, with him as the school bully and me as the snivelling punch bag. He pushed me in the chest. 'Feel the balance – can you feel the balance?' I fell over. The black-haired secretary in the PGA office stared disapprovingly as I rolled around on her precious practice green for a few seconds.

I got back on my feet. Jos circled me, speaking in the kind of slow, hypnotic voice found only on the twenty-minute prologue you get when you telephone a 50p-a-minute sex line on the office phone (I'm guessing here, honest).

'Can you feel the balance, my friend? Feel the grass beneath your feet. Isn't it beautiful? Isn't the grass beautiful? Close your eyes. Can you feel the balance?'

A week had passed since Hamburg. Jos and I were confirmed best friends, bound together by our unwavering belief in the Inner Game of Golf and Ross Drummond's ability to win a PGA tournament. We had no inhibitions. No secrets. He'd even revealed the mysteries of Humming Your Swing and the Do-Instruction. What's more, he liked me well enough to waive his fee for a putting lesson.

Jos pushed me hard and I fell over again. I wasn't enjoying this. 'Come on, my friend. It's only golf,' he said. 'Enjoy yourself, it is a beautiful day in England.'

He was right. June was on its best behaviour, bathing us in a Mediterranean heat. It wasn't really a day for golf but for throwing frisbees and panting in the shade, or eating ice-cream by the seaside. For once the pros could wear their free wrap-around shades and mean it. The sun was a perfect shimmering ball, the azure sky empty but for the feathery wake of a long-gone jet and the manicured landscape shining like a freshly painted door. The Forest of Arden may never have looked finer, except in the days when it was a haunting medieval wilderness and home to vast herds of wild deer. These days it's home to two 18-hole golf courses, a Moat House Hotel and a red-brick conference centre. It is also a near neighbour of the M6 motorway. I hated the place.

The beech and sycamores rustled in the draught of passing juggernauts as I cracked. 'To be perfectly honest, Jos, I can't feel the balance. All I can feel is you pushing me around.'

'Ah, Self One. We must quieten that motherfucker.'

It wasn't just Self One. Every bone in my body was nervous and with good reason. The European Tour Caddies' Association Annual Golf Championship (qualifying round) was due to start in an hour and, inexplicably, my golf swing resembled a caveman killing his lunch.

I say inexplicably because on the very first day I pulled on a caddy's bib I was convinced that I was about to become a better golfer. How this would happen, I confess, was hazier. In my dreamier moments I imagined that Ross would burn off a little excess talent every time he smashed a driver up the fairway – and I would be there, not two club lengths away, breathing in the vapour. By the same quirk of nature that allows an octopus to grow a new leg, he would replenish his skills in time to clip his second shot to within a yard of the flag and I would fill both lungs to the brim. And on we would go.

It was a daft idea, of course, as if milking cows on Paul McCartney's farm for six months would leave me equipped to write 'Eleanor Rigby', and it lasted only for a few weeks. The truth is, being a caddy destroys your golf swing. There is nothing mysterious about this: it is just that caddies aren't allowed to hit a ball within the precincts of a European Tour event. If you're caught you're fined £50. Everyone ignored the rule but however many stolen shots I took on the range or illicit putting competitions I participated in on the practice green my game had slowly crumbled through neglect.

I tried everything to reverse the decline. Videos, magazines, instruction books, even prayer. A few of the pros generously devoted a minute of their time to the cause. Ross, bafflingly, suggested attaching my arms to my body. Philip Walton, the man who won the 1995 Ryder Cup for Europe, said I was dropping my hands at the top of my backswing. Adam Hunter, a devotee of David Leadbetter, insisted I needed a wrinkled left wrist. Paul Lawrie took one look at me hitting balls and advised a holiday, followed by retirement from the game. Jos was my last and best hope but, try as I might, it was hard to see how being pushed around by a ten-franc Belgian philosopher was going to carry me to the caddies' championship.

Who am I kidding? I didn't stand a chance of winning. Some of the caddies were brilliant golfers. A few, like my friend Neil Wallace, had even played pro golf at some stage. (In case you missed it, Neil once came seventh in a South African PGA tour event, five strokes behind Nick Price!) Others had been single-figure handicappers as teenagers but had lost interest. The rest were either too fat to play or fell into the category 'keen but hopeless'.

I placed myself firmly in this last group, though I'd convinced myself that qualifying for the final was not a complete fantasy.

The caddies' championship was held every year at Forest of Arden. The qualifying round was played on the smaller, scruffier course. Martin Rowley had done a grand job scrounging new drivers, golf balls, glossy golf books, computer games and appalling knitwear to give away as prizes. Best of all, he'd got the PGA to agree that the final could be played in front of the paying public over nine holes of the championship course.

The rules, the competition's organizer Grant Berry informed me as he handed over my scorecard, were simple: (1) The best three scores qualified for the final and (2) No fucking cheating.

I was paired with Ritchie Blair, a former assistant golf professional who had taken up caddying to escape the monotony of selling jumpers in the club shop. We skipped off in the direction of the course like two young lovers in search of a haystack. We scarcely noticed the golf balls whizzing over our heads as we crossed the pros' practice ground to get to the first tee.

Ritchie teed off while I had a few practice swings. I felt alive, free, unshackled. Oh, what joy to be playing golf rather than lugging a heavy bag!

My first shot was a high-flying hook that disappeared over the hedgerow way to the left and on to the second fairway of the championship course, out-of-bounds. I couldn't understand how this had happened. My arms had definitely been attached to my body, I was sure I'd felt the balance and that had certainly been the grass I could feel beneath my feet. My second drive followed the same sickening trajectory. The third scuttled across two bone-hard fairways, neither of them the one I was aiming for, and into a cornfield. Ritchie intervened before I had the chance to take another shot.

'We'd better be going.' He grimaced. 'Give yourself an eight, no one will ever know.'

I walked in after six holes, twenty-three over par.

Fortunately, Ross played better than this in the first two rounds of the week's lesser competition, the English Open, though we spent an hour hanging around the course after the second round waiting to see if he made the cut.

This was my first visit to the Sweat-box. This is not, as the name might suggest, a communal sauna but the patch of worn grass in front of the main scoreboard where caddies and players gather every Friday afternoon to watch the hole-by-hole scores of the players still out on the course. It's an ancient tour ritual with strict rules of behaviour. Players act with the utmost dignity and sportsmanship at all times, they never wish ill on their fellow competitors and always accept that if they miss the cut it is entirely the consequence of their own failings on the course. Certainly, they will concede, it would have been nice to play at the weekend and make some money but life is full of little disappointments – there is always next week.

And caddies tell the truth.

So it was that I left Ross quietly calculating his prospects if Player A bogied hole X or Player B birdied four of the last six, and joined a group of caddies gathered round a table groaning with beer glasses. We spent a raucous hour cheering every bogey and abusing any player who threatened our weekend's employment. In the end, someone needed to bogey the last hole for Ross to make the cut. Thankfully, he did.

As the obliging blue (bogey) number went up on the board, my thoughts went out to the unfortunate player who was probably in the car park throwing his clubs in the boot or in the locker room apologizing to his caddy. Another chequeless week, another sorry journey home to his family. Why the fuck do I bother? he might say to himself as the miles scrolled past. Why indeed? It melted my heart to think of him in his penniless plight. On the bright side, though, at least we had made the cut for the third time in four weeks.

Ross finished the tournament in fifty-third place. Believe me, it felt wonderful. The newspapers are forever full of articles bemoaning 'British diseases' like the inefficiency of the railways or sporting mediocrity. Don't believe a word. I once worked for the old British Rail. I slept through a summer of night-shifts, pocketed fares and deliberately got stuck on the Edinburgh express so that I could buy the latest X-Ray Spex single at Bruce's Records. It was the most inefficient and happiest time of my life.

I felt pretty much the same about finishing fifty-third in the English Open. Ross won £2,535. This moved him up to sixty-fourth place in the Order of Merit. He had now made £42,000, enough to make sure he wouldn't be one of the players desperately trying to make a huge cheque in the last few weeks of the season to keep his card. He'd been in that situation a few times in recent years and hadn't enjoyed it. Come to think of it: how could anyone enjoy having to make a cut or hole a couple of six-foot putts to keep their job for another year?

Now that he was safe, a serenity had descended over Ross that nothing could disturb. Missed putts, pulled drives and even the occasional mistake by his caddy just washed over him, leaving behind a wry grin or casual shrug of the shoulders. Off the course, he floated around dispensing bonhomie and generally having a good time. Even his vocabulary had changed. Instead of saying something like, 'Lawrence, I'm not sure if you're doing that right,' he would say, 'Lawrence, you fool, stop that.' He was more decisive and relaxed, a completely different person almost.

Which brings me back to what I was saying before. No doubt fifty-third place in any golf tournament *does* look like the epitome of sporting mediocrity in the Monday-morning results column in the newspaper but from where I was standing it felt like Brigadoon.

It wasn't just me who'd noticed the change in Ross. He could hardly swing a club on the range without other players and caddies passing remarks about how well he was playing or sidling up to ask for an insight into his new-found approach to the game. We even got a good draw in the first two rounds at the Forest of Arden. This is always a sign that the tour hierarchy is taking a player seriously. No more Gianluca Pietrobono! I was beside myself.

Jos was excited too, though for a different reason. The coincidence of his own appearance on the scene and all of this excitement had not escaped him. If the inconvenient fact that the guru-less Drummond had finished fourth at the Oxfordshire disturbed him he didn't show it when we retired to the clubhouse bar after Ross had finished his final round at Forest of Arden.

'I think I have given him the weapons,' he said solemnly. I supped my pint and thought to myself that this is how Oppenheimer must have sounded in the canteen at Los Alamos the night after he invented the bomb.

'Progress has been made. He is a magical guy but I think I can still improve him another forty per cent.'

It is an immutable fact of professional golf that others will claim the credit for a player's performance. It isn't deliberate or malicious, more of a reflex. And it only ever happens when a player does well. I did it myself all the time – I would say 'we came fourth' or 'he missed the cut' – until one afternoon an experienced caddy called Andy Sutton told me to shut up. In the long and glorious history of golf, he said, no caddy had ever won a golf tournament or even finished fifty-third.

Jos was simply under the same misapprehension that I once had been.

We passed another half-hour in the clubhouse until it was time to go. As I got out of my seat to leave Jos grabbed my arm and wagged his finger at me. 'Believe me my friend, he is ready to win. Next week, maybe.'

I would normally have filed this prediction away in the dusty recess of my mind marked 'wonderful news, if only it had been true' but I have to tell you the strangest thing happened the following week. Jos came within a whisper of being right.

*

The Northumberland Challenge at Slaley Hall was far from being the most prestigious event of the season. All the top players were off playing in the US Open. The (relatively) small prize fund, £300,000, gave others an excuse to take the week off. But the tournament did have the imprimatur of the European Tour, a £50,000 first prize and a two-year qualifying exemption. Ross decided it was worth playing. It gave him something to do for the week. If only a South African pro called Retief Goosen hadn't had the same idea he would have won.

Ross started the last day nine shots behind. He played brilliantly, scored a course record of sixty-five and terrified the life out of Goosen. In the end, he finished two shots behind in second place – the closest he had ever come to winning a tournament. Breathtaking! Jos even kissed him.

Still, the real second prize was better than a snog from a Belgian golf guru. Quite a lot better in fact: £33,330.

We spent a drink-fazed night in Drumrossie waiting for the television highlights to be shown on Eurosport. When it was time Ross gleefully grabbed the remote control, switched on and announced in a voice sated with excitement, 'IIIIIIIITTT'S SHOWTIME!'

He spent the next hour chuckling at himself.

'God, look at that, I bend over a lot when I putt.'

Another bottle of wine.

'Good swing that, Ross.'

Down the twelfth hole – 'And here's Scotland's Ross Drummond he's going very well, only four shots behind the leader . . .'

'I knew I needed some birdies but I didn't want to look at the leaderboard.'

'And Drummond has a putt here at the seventeenth to join Goosen in the lead . . .'

'I knew when I missed it that my chance was gone.'

More beer.

The last thing I remember before slipping off to sleep was slurring, 'You're a fairy tale, Ross, do you know that?'

Next morning I wobbled downstairs to find him sitting at the breakfast table. He was wearing a short-sleeved pink T-shirt, black jeans and an ancient pair of black and white gym-shoes. He looked ten years younger than when we had sat at the same table before the season started.

I flicked through a handful of Scottish newspapers lying on the table. The Northumberland Challenge had been assigned to a tiny corner of these rags to make way for less important stuff like devolution and the traffic chaos in Auchterarder when the lights failed. There were a couple of five-paragraph stories underneath daft headlines, 'Drum Beats Record' or 'Drummond Record – Mind Over Matter'. Reading them, it occurred to me that any man who had gone from being the 151st best golfer in Europe to the thirty-second best in the space of a month was worth more than five paragraphs.

Eventually, after breakfast and four Alka-Seltzer, I persuaded Ross to sit down and talk for a while about how he'd managed to turn round not just his season but his career.

Happy?

'Elated.'

Did you think you were going to win your first ever European Tour event?

'Not before I went out on the last day. My target was to finish in the top five. I knew I was playing well against the course but I didn't know how the others were doing. I didn't want to look at the leaderboard. Faldo or Montgomerie would probably be shocked if their name wasn't up there – it's different for me, it could have frightened the life out of me, so I didn't look.

'It was close in the end. If it had gone to a play-off I was definitely favourite.'

Why were you frightened?

'I've been playing in a state of fear for a long time: scared

166

that when I got in a good position I'd blow it, scared that the ball wouldn't go where I wanted it to go. You start thinking, What if I hook it or hit it out of bounds, instead of the good shots you're going to play. It's not just me, you know, it happens to everyone.'

So what changed?

'I spent a lot of time looking at my life and my career. I knew I had to change my attitude. A lot of the guys I started out with had slipped away I was starting to think I was going the same way. It wasn't looking good in Italy, was it? I was spending more than I was making. I was dragging myself down, thinking all sorts of daft things: (a) I was going to lose my card, (b) go broke, (c) maybe have to sell the house and, (d) find another job.'

So how does it feel to have £75,654 in the bank?

'Comfortable. I'm not going to rush out and buy a big car or anything. It's just good not to have to worry about money. I can just get on with playing golf.'

How did you manage to change your attitude?

'Lots of ways. Claire helped a lot, encouraging me. Anthony Robbins helped too.'

Not him again, the guy that looks like Herman Munster on Prozac?

'Yes. I ploughed my way through his book. It was hard work but I got a lot out of it. But then I bought the tape at the Oxfordshire – I went out to the car and played it straight away. That did it for me.'

A £2.99 tape?

'I'm not saying I went into the car as mild-mannered Ross Drummond and came out like a tiger, I'm just saying that it helped me understand a lot of things.'

Like what?

'He talks about making true commitments. You might want to change something in your life but you put off making decisions to change because you know it will cause you a lot of pain. He says you've got to think of the good things that'll happen if you do change. That's what I've done.'

Did Jos help?

'Yes. But I wouldn't say he was responsible for what has happened. I did well at the Oxfordshire before I worked with him. But he helped me focus on what I was doing and not get ahead of myself. He helped me with my putting too.'

What about your new super caddy? Has he been responsible for any of this?

'Throughout my career I've never been too dependent on a caddy. You've got to be comfortable with the person you're with, be able to talk to him . . .'

Just answer the question.

'OK. There has been a long list of things that have helped me this year and a new caddy isn't at the top of it.'

15. Wobbly

This might come as a shock – it did to me – but I was beginning to gain a tiny bit of respect as a caddy. The seen-it-all-done-it-all caddies had stopped looking at me as if I was something suspicious they'd found in the catering van's burgers (like real meat, perhaps). Some of them nodded in my direction as they walked past on the range. A few even spoke to me. Magical things like that happen when your man starts making decent prize money.

What if Ross actually made a fortune? I wondered. Perhaps I would be able to join the caddying élite – the premier league – where first-names are bandied around like, well, like normal human beings. And that's not all. I'd start staying in single rooms at the Holiday Inn. Reporters would talk to me. I'd fly everywhere, I'd get myself sponsorships, hat, clothes, car, watch. Who's knows? I might, like Philip Morbey, buy myself a three-bedroomed house in Yorkshire and call it Augusta.

Morbey – 'Wobbly' – was Ian Woosnam's caddy, one of the seen-it-all-done-it-all brigade but different: open-faced, kind, friendlier than a month-old puppy. It felt like I knew him even before we met. Like the rest of the nation, I saw him on television with his heavy-rock perm, lifting Ian Woosnam off the ground when he holed his putt to win the Masters.

(Which reminds me: what were Ian Woosnam's first words

after he won the 1991 Masters? 'Put me down, Wobbly, you daft bugger.')

I discovered Wobbly lived in a house called Augusta when I detoured off the A1 into the village of Riccall on my way north to Carnoustie for the Scottish Open. I wanted to see how the other half – the premier league caddies – lived.

As you might expect, they live very well indeed. Augusta was tucked away in a cosy horseshoe of new houses just off the main street, a sanctuary for aspirational couples looking for something rustic but also close to the motorway. It was mid-afternoon when I pulled up outside. Most people were at work. Every driveway had a second car, a battered Fiesta or a Nissan Micra, except Wobbly's. His brand new metallic blue Jeep sat outside his house, shouting at passers-by that someone special lived here. He greeted me at the door like an old friend.

Augusta had that barely-lived-in feel, like a show home, for the not unreasonable reason that he had barely lived in the place since he had bought it. Caddying had opened up the world to Wobbly. It had taken him to places that when he was a boy he hadn't even known existed. Best of all, if it hadn't have been for caddying he would never have gone to Atlanta, Georgia, and would never have met his fiancée Christine. I was smitten. Once I'd got over the excitement of even breathing the same air as someone so gorgeous, I sat down with Wobbly and he told me his life story. Christine went off to make some tea.

My efforts at a serious anthropological study of caddies had long been abandoned. No one would tell me anything. It wasn't that they didn't like me, I was repeatedly assured, it was the taxman – who might read anything I wrote – to whom they had an aversion. To be honest, I was glad. After the first flush of excitement I couldn't summon the energy needed to run around being nosy or think deeply about such matters. What I did instead was hang around the locker rooms and caddyshacks long enough, with a half-cocked ear, to form a few vague ideas about what everyone was doing there in the first place. It was hardly Desmond Morris but, for what it's worth, this is what I concluded.

There were three types of caddy:

1. Caddies who were 'not doing this for the rest of my life, no way!'. This group was on its way to somewhere else, either the other side of the world or another job or back home in a couple of weeks once they'd scrambled together enough money to doss around for a while. It included those who didn't really enjoy the caddying but thought they might benefit from the experience, people like John McLaren, a budding golfer who thought caddying on the tour for a year might make him a better player when he turned pro. He was wrong. 'All I've learned is how to be a complete and utter wanker if I really wanted to be one. My player is a good guy but the vast majority of the others are total tossers, wankers or prima donnas,' was his verdict after one spectacularly trying day on the links.

2. Caddies who were 'escaping'. This was the most populous group. Martin Rowley was a member, so was Andy Prodger. Both were escaping the drudgery of their previous jobs. A few years ago it would also have included a fair number of caddies escaping the drudgery of a pregnant girlfriend or a police interview about a break-in at an off-licence. This element had largely drifted off the tour in recent years, which might explain the huge increases in single mothers and domestic burglary in Britain during the summer months.

The toe-rags had been replaced by a huge cross-section of respectable citizenry. I met the lot: Oxbridge graduates, computer experts, civil engineers, mobile-phone salesmen, failed bookies, Australian coal miners, strike-breaking miners, cabbies, failed pro golfers, failed amateur golfers, chefs and insurance salesmen.

3. Caddies who had started off as kids, caddying at the nearest posh golf course to their home for pocket money, discovered

they liked it and then graduated to the tour. I thought of them as 'career caddies'.

Myles Byrne fell into this category. He started caddying at a golf course near Dublin 'in the days when the Irish punt was the size of the *Daily Mirror*'. His brother was a caddy too, and he had followed him on to the tour when he was twenty. Myles could do the *Daily Telegraph* crossword in the time it took the rest of us to tie our shoelaces. He was the cleverest caddy on tour but when anyone suggested that caddying was a waste of a brain the size of Einstein's he would smile wisely and say he planned to sort his life out next year. Maybe. And maybe he will be the Taoiseach next year but I doubt it. He loved caddying too much: the travel, the camaraderie, the quick cash, damp nights in leaky tents, the hangovers, the missed cuts, the lack of money, lack of financial security. Seldom has there been a man so wedded to caddying.

Wobbly was a career caddy. He left school with three O levels, got a job in a supermarket, left that, went on the road, aged seventeen, and had been out ever since. He loved caddying just as much as Myles but at least he had an excuse: £500 a week and $7\frac{1}{2}$ per cent of whatever prize money Ian Woosnam staggered home with in his suitcase every Sunday night.

Not wishing to pry, I asked exactly how much that came to.

'Oh, about sixty, maybe seventy thou' this year,' he said airily. 'With sponsorships.'

'Sponsorships?'

'Ten grand for a wearing a hat, a few quid for wearing clothes.'

This news inspired two emotions as I sat there slurping my tea: envy, foremost, and then puzzlement. I could understand if, say, Hititman golf clubs wanted to pay Ross Drummond ten thousand pounds for wearing a hat. People might see him on television playing brilliantly and think, It's his Hititman clubs, I must buy some myself. But why would they pay his caddy to wear a hat? No one who saw me zigzagging down the fairway in my Hititman hat was going to be inspired to buy a new set of golf clubs, were they? All modesty aside, they'd be mad if they did.

And while I'm in London cabby-mode ... Rumours were floating round the caddyshack that Coca-Cola wanted to sponsor all of the caddies to wear hats. Again, why? Would you, on sight of a caddy wearing a red Coca-Cola hat at a jaunty angle, say to yourself, 'God, I could do with a refreshing Coke'? Of course not. It's not as if caddies even drink the rotten bloody stuff: they drink pints of lager.

Wobbly could see I was taken aback. Seventy thousand was more than most golfers earn in a season, after all.

'I work hard for it, though,' he said, defensively. 'I've contributed to Woosie's success. It's not as though I just walk around the golf course with him. I'm part of the team.'

I had to explain that my temporary thoughtfulness was not a sign of disapproval, more unadulterated jealousy. I asked how I could get a job like his.

There appeared to be two methods. The easy one: turn up in the car park one day and bump into a caddy-less player who happens to be a world-beater and he gives you the job. And then there was the way life actually was: I would have to hang around for years, earn a decent reputation as a caddy and hope for a lucky break – the way Wobbly had done. It took six years working a passage through a veritable *Who's That?* of world golf before he landed Woosnam's bag.

He started working for his local pro, then a Brazilian who broke his finger, then a couple of other guys who didn't do much. The first tournament he won was something called the Car Care Plan International. That took four years.

He was on Ian Baker-Finch's bag when he led the 1984 Open at St Andrews going into the last round. That didn't last. Next stop, Howard Clark – 'I told him his ball was stuck up a tree and he called me Walter Mitty. I thought, Fuck it, I don't need this.' Woosie's best friend, D. J. Russell, gave him a job for a while until, finally, the man himself asked him if he wanted the bag. It was August 1987.

Woosie won three tournaments in their first three months together. He hasn't stopped since. Twenty-odd victories, five Ryder Cups, the World Cup, the US Masters, ranked number one in the world and the first two tournaments of the 1996 season (before I'd even carried a bag in anger). Woosnam had done it all and Wobbly had been there to see it happen and get a lift home in the private jet afterwards if he wanted one. Nine years, not one week apart and only one row: 1993, Lancôme Trophy, two-iron into the bunker on the ninth.

'We didn't speak for four holes. I said sorry for saying it wouldn't reach and he said sorry for losing his rag. See, we've got a different relationship to most of the other players and caddies. We're like friends, really. Just as long as I don't forget he's the boss.'

I asked him what his favourite moment was.

'Gotta be the Masters, ain't it? I had a few tears afterwards and he says to me, 'What's wrong with you, then?' It was his first Major and mine too. Brilliant, especially because we were head-to-head with Tom Watson and all the Yanks wanted him to win . . .' Before I knew it, we were back at Augusta on a hot April Sunday, 1991, replaying every shot.

'He had a six-foot putt on the last to win and he asked me what I thought the line was. I remember the year Sandy Lyle won it he was looking for the line on his winning putt and his caddy said, 'Don't fucking ask me.' I said it were inside the right lip, so did he. As soon as he hit it I knew, I just knew.'

It was time to head north. I'd been there all afternoon and my retina had worn out from ogling his fiancée, my belly was bursting with tea and the story of his success had turned my heart into a huge lump of green cheese. I'd learned what it took to become a premier league caddy – hard work, dedication, enthusiasm, luck – and more than enough to know that I didn't have it.

'I'll see you next week,' I said, walking down the path to the car.

Of course, I never did meet up with Wobbly at Carnoustie. Woosnam won the tournament. He led from the first round and played late every day, so late in fact that I saw him arriving at the clubhouse around lunch-time on Saturday as we were finishing our last round.

The town of Carnoustie happens to have one of the finest golf courses in the world. It also happens to be one of the ugliest places in the world. Imagine, if you will, the Chrysler Building in downtown Halifax. It is supposed to be a holiday resort but I defy anyone to have a good time in Carnoustie. There is no night-life, no shops and an army firing range next door to the beach. One day every year the sun comes out and the wind lies down for a rest. That particular Saturday was not the day.

It was blowing a gale as we played the second last hole. Ross was seventeen over par and almost comatose with exhaustion. It would have been remiss of me to let him wallow in his misery so I slapped on my most sympathetic expression, made a host of disparaging remarks about Carnoustie and asked if he'd ever played in so much wind before.

'Yes. But I've never been so pissed off in my life,' he replied, morbidly. We played the rest of the round in silence. He bogied the last hole for an eighty-one, his worst score of the season. This wouldn't have bothered me normally – we'd have a few days off, rest up and be ready for the next week's tournament – but in eighteen hours we were due to tee off at Southport and Ainsdale in the first round of the Open Championship qualifying. I could've been wrong but I suspected suicidal was not the best frame of mind in which to tackle the world's greatest golf tournament.

*

I drove south overnight. I snatched some sleep at a motorway service station just over the border and ate what was advertised as a full English breakfast, though it looked and tasted like leftovers from an organ-donor clinic. I bought a Sunday paper, turned to the sports pages and the headline 'Sad Ross Fears Being Drummed Out' immediately caught my eye. I read it in the hope that it was a story about Ross Perot.

Sadly, it wasn't. It began 'Ross Drummond will today try to pick up the pieces of a nightmare week . . .' and went on in similar vein, furnished with suitably disheartening quotes. I read to the end, suitably disheartened. I kept heading south but, to be honest, I didn't expect him to turn up.

When I finally pulled into Southport and Ainsdale's tree-shaded car park he wasn't there. It was still only six a.m., mind. Even so, it was light and people were mingling around: officious-looking men in dark suits, a couple of greenkeepers and a few caddies and players. One of the Argentinian caddies was slouched on the wall outside the clubhouse. He was staring into the distance with the kind of expression most people reserve for funerals.

I cajoled him into a conversation. It turned out that his player had only needed to par the last hole at Carnoustie to qualify automatically for the Open but had shanked his second shot. He ran up a double bogey. Worse still, he choked in the play-off for the Open spot. The two of them had driven down to Southport overnight for an eight a.m. tee-time for the qualifier.

'A nine-iron and he shanked it.' He shook his head in disbelief. 'What a useless – how do you say it? – useless cunt.'

The guilty man was ten yards away, practising his putting and whistling with studied gaiety – a sure sign of despair, I thought. He saw me and said hello.

I nodded. 'Bad luck yesterday.'

'Not to worry.' He smiled.

'Stupid bastard,' the caddy said, under his breath. His English had come on a bundle since we'd travelled together in the Belgrano.

I left him practising his swear words and went exploring.

The Open was due to start in four days' time, just across the Ribble estuary at Royal Lytham and St Annes. Southport and Ainsdale was one of four clubs chosen to stage the final qualifying rounds for the main event and it was bristling with the kind of pompous self-importance that gets golf clubs a bad name.

Not that it had ever had a bad name, at least not until now. In fact, it was an historic club, having staged the 1933 Ryder Cup match between Great Britain and the United States. The historic bit is that Great Britain actually won.

The course itself nestled on a narrow strip of land between the Southport–Liverpool railway line and the main road south. It would have been a fair test in the days of feathery balls and niblicks but, by modern standards, it was short. A couple of holes were too 'funky' (tour-speak for a hole more suited to a seaside crazy-golf course) and the fairways had been burned pale gold by the sun.

It was shaping up to be a beautiful day. I wandered across to the practice area, had a browse in the pro shop and bought a yardage book. It was still only seven thirty. We weren't due off for another two hours. I thought I'd go to the clubhouse, have a nice cup of tea and a sandwich and snuggle into one of the heavy armchairs I could see through the window facing out on to the course.

I pushed open the front door and from nowhere a man appeared. He stepped in front of me. He was wearing a black uniform heavily braided in gold, an admiral's cap and white gloves. 'Can't go in there, sir,' he said, apologetically.

Calmly, I asked why not.

'You're a caddy, aren't you?'

'And?'

'No caddies in the clubhouse, sir.'

'Says who?' I asked, with just a hint of menace in my voice.

'Him in there.' He pointed to an office inside the door where I could see a man with a well-scrubbed, middle-aged face sitting behind a desk. He was wearing a crisply pressed pink shirt and a striped tie.

Him In There was an ex-Army officer who ran the golf club. I bustled into his office. The air was thick with efficiency, pomposity and aftershave. I hated him before he even opened his mouth and then he did and I hated him even more. 'Yes, young man. Can I help you?'

'Why can't caddies go into the clubhouse? Are we sub-human by any chance?'

'Well, we caught a few in there yesterday wearing jeans and training shoes.'

'Well, fuck me, that is serious,' I said. 'Mind you, I would have thought it was better to wear something over their socks and filthy Y-fronts. I might be wrong, though. What do you think?'

The Army must train its officers to remain calm when confronted with anything: from maniacal squaddies to maniacal caddies. This would explain why my little tantrum did little to disturb his infuriating air of superiority. He stood up and placed a fatherly hand on my shoulder. 'Tell me what it is you want, young man. How can I help you?'

'All I want is a cup of tea.'

'Why didn't you say so in the first place? The restaurant doesn't open for another hour. Now, if you'll excuse me, I have work to do.'

Ross sauntered up the path from the car park around seven forty-five.

'I didn't think you were going to turn up,' I said.

From the disgusted look on his face I knew straight away that this was just about the worst thing I could have said. Even I knew it was bad form to upset your player before he went out to play.

'Well, after yesterday, you know. And then I saw the paper this morning and –'

'That was yesterday, Lawrence,' he scolded. 'This is the Open – the tournament that got me interested in golf in the first place. I'm not going to withdraw from the Open Championship, am I? Now, where's the range?'

Meekly, I pointed in the direction of the field at the other side of the clubhouse which had been designated as the practice area.

'Good,' he said. 'Let's go – you can shag my balls.'

Fantastic! I had been looking forward to shagging his balls for months (I've been looking forward to using that line for months as well) although I must hastily add that this enthusiasm was entirely bound up with my desire to try my hand at another of caddying's ancient arts.

To shag a player's balls is to stand at the opposite end of the range and collect the balls as he hits them towards you. The practice disappeared from big-time professional golf with the introduction of range balls and little caged tractors trailing a bastardized ploughing machine that magically gathered up the balls. This device made a caddy's life so much easier, which is presumably why the military chaps running the Open qualifying tournament didn't have one to hand.

Not that I minded. I had a wonderful time standing at one end of a field watching shoals of golf balls falling out of the sky towards my head. If nothing else, it gave me a taste of what it must have been like during the Blitz. And I got a chance to make new friends. Tim Culshaw was a building estimator who had taken time off work to caddy for an American pro called Peter Teravainen. If anything, he was even more excited than me at the prospect of being skulled by a speeding golf ball.

'He's promised me I can work for him if he qualifies for the

Open proper. That would be a dream come true,' he said. 'Of course, the real dream is to play in the Open but I'm never going to do that with a nine-handicap.'

I wished that every pro golfer I'd ever heard moaning about a courtesy car being two minutes late or the coffee in the players' lounge being too strong had been standing there beside me. They would have seen the wistful look on Tim's face as he said this. It would have reminded them of just how lucky they are.

I'd have liked to say now that Teravainen qualified for the Open proper, Tim caddied for him, he played with Jack Nicklaus in the first two rounds, Greg Norman in the third and beat Faldo head-to-head on the last day to win the tournament. But, of course, he missed qualifying by three shots and Tim was back estimating buildings, whatever that is, on Tuesday morning.

A small crowd congregated when we stepped on to the first tee. By the time we reached the second green it was reduced to two wheezing pensioners. We were drawn with Duncan Muscroft, a young Yorkshire pro who played on the satellite tour, and Murray White, a former schoolboy prodigy now living out middle age at a driving range in Watford. It has to be said that it was not the glamour tie of the round, at least not when we started.

Ross holed a thirty-foot putt for par on the first hole, birdied the second, third, fourth, ninth, fifteenth, sixteenth, eighteenth and, just to be different, eagled the seventh. He finished with a sixty-three – eighteen shots better than the previous day, only one shot off the course record and three clear of the rest of the field. When he holed his putt at the last I burst out laughing. It struck me that this was what life on tour was meant to be like.

My only regret was that no one would ever be able to say they saw Ross Drummond shoot sixty-three at Southport and Ainsdale except our two loyal pensioners who had shuffled along behind us all the way, despite the heat and the dust. So Geoffrey

Gibbs, retired postmaster of Liverpool, and his best pal John Healey, well done, and did we all have a good time or what!

When we finished, Ross slipped into the scorer's tent. I wandered off to the scoreboard where I stayed for the rest of the afternoon, nudging people in the ribs and saying, 'Look at that, Drummond, sixty-three.' They, in turn, would nudge their friend and point out this startling piece of information. By six p.m., I estimate that everyone in Greater Merseyside must have known.

The following day not all of them made it in time to see Ross tee off. I counted forty-seven spectators, most of them club members who had come along to see what this freak was doing to their course. He only had to stand up to make sure of qualifying for the Open proper but he still played well and shot sixty-eight. In truth, it would have been a boring day if the head of Murray White's driver hadn't flown off on the third tee and nearly brained a spectator. Then there was my little contretemps with Duncan Muscroft, whom I had the audacity to praise for his putting half-way through the round.

Five holes later he sauntered over to me with a murderous look on his face.

'You know when you said I was a great putter?' he said.

I nodded.

'Well, I haven't holed anything since. Put this in your notebook – you're a useless bastard.'

Sadly, Duncan shot 149 over the two rounds and failed to qualify. Nor did he win eight European Tour events during the remainder of the season, or the US PGA Championship, the Volvo Masters or the Sun City Million Dollar Challenge – all of which was obviously my fault for saying he was a good putter. Either that or he's a useless bastard.

Murray was still talking to me when he walked off the last green. He'd shot five over par and broken his favourite driver. To his credit, he was still smiling. He had only made the Open proper once, in 1975, when he made eight birdies, had sixteen shanks (possibly an all-time record) and almost finished stone-cold last at twenty-five over par. At least he wouldn't have to go through all that agony again, much as he would have liked to.

'I suppose it's back to the driving range for me,' he said, throwing his tatty leather bag over his shoulder.

We said goodbye and I watched him walk waveringly down the hill, past the clubhouse and the knot of players and caddies getting ready by the starter's hut to play off for the last few Open spots. He stopped for a few seconds to watch, shook his head and kept walking towards the car park. It was a perfect study in misery and when it was over I got down on my knees and praised the Lord: I was going to the Open.

16. The Van

The Open. Me. Caddying . . .
The words had a dreamlike quality. I drove to Royal Lytham and St Annes almost paralysed with excitement.

After years of painful failure, I'd come to accept that I wasn't any good at sports that required more physical co-ordination than it took to walk. That left darts, and I didn't have the eyesight or alcohol capacity for that.

The fact was that the 1996 Open Championship was to be *the* defining sporting moment of my life, the only chance I'd ever get to participate in an event alongside the very best in the world. I parked my car on Lytham's main street, sat back in my seat to contemplate this terrifying fact, and decided that if I didn't have a sedative within the next five minutes I was going to have a heart attack.

I dived into the nearest pub, a barn-like place alive with the high-frequency chatter of teenagers on a two-drink journey to oblivion. I was contemplating joining them when through the crowd I saw two familiar faces. Colin Byrne and Lorne Duncan, two of the best caddies on tour, were deep in conversation. I shouted over. 'Lads. LADS!'

Colin looked up, saw me and grinned. 'Lawrence. You made it,' he shouted back. Word that Ross had won the Open qualifying at Southport had obviously made the thirty-mile journey to Lytham quicker than I had.

'You made it, you made the Open, you caddying legend, you.'

I bought a drink and pushed my way through to them. Duncan shook my hand. 'Well,' he said in his slow Canadian drawl, 'You're a real caddy now.' It was, without qualification, the proudest moment of my life.

Two hours later I stumbled on to the street, still almost paralysed, though alcohol had kindly volunteered to take over from excitement in the arduous task of numbing my senses. Thankfully, I had a place to stay – an achievement almost as great as making the Open itself. I'd rung around earlier and found the only bed-and-breakfast in Lytham that had a vacancy for the night. When I got there I found out why.

'Forty pounds for this?' I slurred, as the landlady pushed open the door to my room. I say room, it was a glorified broom cupboard with an ironing board for a bed.

'Take it or leave it,' she said, with all the hospitality of a prison guard at Strangeways. It was Open week and the wretched woman knew she could charge anything she liked.

'I'll take it,' I conceded, but somehow a little bit of the Open Championship magic died for me with those three words.

When I got to the golf course the next morning another big chunk of Open Championship magic died. Believe it or not, the caddyshack at the world's greatest golf tournament was a 1975 fish-and-chip van, minus its deep-fat fryer but with added essence of rancid grease and painted-out windows. There were three moulded plastic chairs inside, which someone clearly believed would be enough for all 150 caddies. (If we stuck rigidly to a twenty-four-hour rota everyone would be able to have a twenty-five-minute sit-down every day.) Call me an old fusspot, but I thought this was an insult.

No one else was surprised. Utter disdain for caddies was

apparently a speciality of the Royal and Ancient, the self-appointed group of retired air commodores, amateur golfers and plain old amateurs who organized the Open Championship.

Someone told me a story that caddies were not allowed into the clubhouse at the Open until 1965 when the great American golfer Tony Lema insisted that 'my caddy goes where I go' and pushed his way past the R & A goon who was guarding the door like it was his daughter's virginity. At the time Lema's efforts were seen as the caddies' equivalent of Martin Luther King's civil-rights crusade. Tragically, Lema died in an air crash not long afterwards. Less tragically, but a whole lot more predictably, the treatment of caddies at the following year's Open was as bad as ever.

It has improved in the thirty years since, but not much.

The stench of revolution – and old chips – was in the air as a stream of caddies had a look inside the van and turned away in horror, as if they'd caught their grandparents having sex inside. By mid-morning there was talk of a caddies' strike. This was highly unlikely, but good fun while it lasted. Only the most cold-hearted and humourless person in the world would've been unable to raise a smile at the prospect of a millionaire like Nick Faldo wandering along the fairways carrying his own bag. (Someone like Nick Faldo, in fact.)

The fish-and-chip van was eventually towed away. We were upgraded to an airless portable cabin the size of a table-tennis table. This was far from perfect but at least when I stuck my head out of the door I could see that the rest of the world was having a good time.

I thought I might as well go and join them.

Ross was waiting for me outside the clubhouse. He had decided not to play a practice round until the next day but said he would hit a few balls on the range after he'd registered for the tournament. He sauntered off towards the R & A office, leaving me to soak up the atmosphere.

I can't remember ever being so overawed. Only badge-holders – players, press, caddies and the players' families and friends – were allowed access to the area behind the clubhouse. I stood there for a while and breathed the same air as some superstars: Greg Norman, Fred Couples, Nick Price, Corey Pavin, Tiger Woods, Gary Player, Tom Lehman, Phil Mickelson, John Daly . . .

Jack Nicklaus was the one who finally made me squeal like a Take That fan, though in my defence I should say that he did this by stepping on my foot as he headed in the direction of the range.

'Sorry.' His voice was so familiar, as high-pitched and charmless as a squeaky door hinge.

'It's no problem.'

'Are you sure?'

'Sure, Jack.'

To think, in forty years' time I would be able to tell my grandchildren that I took part in an Open Championship with the great Jack Nicklaus. Of course, I'd have to come clean when the little smart alecs asked me if I'd actually 'played' with the great Jack Nicklaus but the truth was still something to cherish.

When Jack and I had finished our conversation – as I now like to style our little exchange – I spent some time watching the long, excited stream of spectators flooding through the public entrance. How many of them would have loved to have been in my shoes, standing there on this beautiful July morning with their foot throbbing after that clumsy oaf Jack Nicklaus had stood on it? Probably every one of them.

There were some caddies who wouldn't have minded my job either.

I could see Kevin Woodward leaning on the crash barrier by the players' entrance. His man hadn't made it through the qualifying round and he was desperately checking with every player, every journalist, every man in overalls delivering beer to the clubhouse that they didn't need a caddy for the week. I felt guilty depriving such an experienced caddy of a spot in the Open.

Martin Rowley hadn't made it either. Now that *did* make me feel like an impostor. I was about to caddy in the Open and the chairman of the caddies' association had his face pressed up against the mesh fence keeping the public out of the clubhouse.

'Not to worry. Nigel Mansell wants me to work for him,' he told me, nonchalantly.

I knew this already. The talk in the caddyshack was of nothing else. The former world motor-racing champion had announced that he intended to become a full-time professional golfer. This was a bit like me announcing I intended to become a full-time accordionist with the New York Philharmonic on the basis that I could play the theme from *The Godfather* on the squeeze box. To be fair, Mansell was a decent enough Sunday-morning golfer. However, he appeared to think that all that was needed to become a pro was to hire a full-time caddy.

Rowley was good but he wasn't Jesus Christ. I told him he should take the job, if only for the laughs.

'The only problem is he wants a Rolls-Royce caddy for Mini-Metro prices,' he said. 'You haven't heard of any jobs on the go here, have you?'

I shook my head. There had been a rumour that a club pro from Yorkshire made it through the qualifying rounds with his four-months pregnant wife carrying his bag and that the R & A said she wouldn't be allowed to caddy in the Open proper because she was pregnant. This sounded sufficiently sexist to be true. Remarkably, it wasn't, which was a nice end to a nice story, although it didn't help Rowley much.

Ross came back from the registration office. We headed towards the practice range. This was about three hundred yards east of the clubhouse, near the tented village, and to get there we had to walk along a roped-off pathway through the crowds.

As we left the clubhouse I could hear the instruction echoing down the line, 'Player coming, player coming,' and the rope was raised to waist height. This was a signal for hordes of school kids to dash forward with autograph books. A couple craned their necks to see the name on the bag I was carrying. Ross signed their books with a huge grin on his face. Thirty years ago he would have been there with them, scrambling for players' signatures. I kept walking towards the range, quietly proud, stunned by the vast sea of humanity before me. It was Tuesday, still two days before tee-off time. Does nobody work in Lancashire in July?

The practice range had a bigger grandstand than most I'd seen all season and there was still a queue for seats. Those waiting didn't mind. They seemed to be having great fun pointing out the superstars, golfers and caddies, and trying to guess who the others were, such as Ross and I.

The range was busier than the Tokyo underground at rush hour. I picked my way through the psychologists, managers, assistant managers, accountants, physiotherapists, sunglasses salesmen, swing doctors, mind doctors, putting doctors, doctor doctors, alcohol counsellors, stress therapists, wives, mistresses, offspring and caddies. Eventually, I found a place for the bag next to an English pro, Jim Payne, and his caddy, Barry 'The Judge' Courts.

It was a perfect spot. The range was as wide as an eight-lane motorway and we were right on the median line, close enough to watch open-mouthed as John Daly hit drives into the perimeter fence 300 yards off – to think we were competing against that! – but far enough away to retain a little self-respect if by chance he caught you staring.

Beyond the perimeter fence, to the left, the wind snapped at the marquees in the tented village and the flags of the world. The golf course was already lined with thousands of day-trippers dressed in summer whites and lemons, each kicking up dust as they shuffled along beside their favourite four-ball. The haze tickled the throat and, beneath a big blue sky and boiling sun, whispered of excitements yet to come. But standing there I could feel something more, a sense of time and place that seeped through the senses but was impossible to define.

Frustrated, I went to get some balls for Ross. When I came back the Judge nodded and said, 'You made it. Well done.'

'Well done yourself,' I said, delighted.

The Judge was a Londoner, an ex-bookie who'd been on tour for years, someone whom every caddy on tour looked up to and respected. If he was talking to me then I was definitely moving up in the world.

'This is it, ain't it?' he said.

'What is?'

'This tournament. The dog's bollocks, the best fuckin' tournament in the world. It's got the lot, tradition, class, fuckin' everything.'

That's what it was. *That was it!*

I moved out of Lytham. I spent the night in a ten-pounds-a-night bed-and-breakfast five miles along the coast in Blackpool which, if nothing else, is something Nick Faldo or Greg Norman will never be able to say. I had a solitary meal in an Indian restaurant just round the corner and went for a walk along the sea-front. There was a story in the evening paper that for the first time in twenty years the sea off Blackpool had been declared fit for people to swim in. I watched the waves chase gently up the beach, thinking this was terrific news for the town's tourist industry but it must have scared the hell out of the 100 million people who'd visited since 1976.

I walked back to my bed-and-breakfast. The streets were alive with the sights and sounds of raucous holiday-makers, some drunk and the rest completely smashed, but in truth felt lonelier than at any time all season. The Open experience dwarfed anything I'd experienced as a caddy but it lacked the camaraderie of the other tournaments, where it was impossible to walk into a bar or a restaurant and not meet players and caddies. This was too big and impersonal. I dashed home to bed, eager for the morning to come.

And, eventually, it did.

We played a practice round with Steve Bottomley and Billy McColl, an old friend of Ross's who had once played on the tour but now worked at a golf club in Essex. In their own way, both embodied the romance of the Open.

McColl had scraped through a regional qualifying round at Romford, then the final qualifying. He was a decent player, long off the tee, but was there just for the thrill of playing one more time with the big boys. If his luck was in, he might make it to the weekend. If he didn't, then at least he'd had an interesting week off work.

Bottomley, a journeyman tour pro, had greater ambitions. He had come third in the Open at St Andrews the year before. This, without being unkind (oh, all right, just a little bit unkind), was a shock. Even now, twelve months later, people would point him out to me and say, 'That's Steve Bottomley. He almost won the Open, you know!' then shake their heads in disbelief. Previously, his main claim to fame was that he had a sixty-four-year-old caddy who was a member of the Magic Circle – a welcome streak of eccentricity as far as I was concerned, but among the aficionados of the caddyshack it had hardly marked him out as a potential Open champion. Ask yourself, they would say: Would the young Faldo have employed Tommy Cooper as his caddy?

My own ambitions for the week didn't even extend to Ross coming as close to winning as Bottomley had.

There comes a time in every partnership, for better or worse, when we all have to face facts. That time came to me as I stood at the clubhouse gawping at the stars. I didn't tell Ross this (though maybe, just maybe, he knew already) but he wasn't going to win the Open. A top-thirty finish would have been fine but I was prepared to settle for making the cut. Failing that, I would have been happy if he shot 78–74 and played with a couple of big names in the first two rounds. My expectations were quite low. And I still ended up disappointed.

The draw for the Open, like hill walking or the sexual allure that Barbra Streisand holds for gentlemen of a certain age, is a total mystery to sane and rational people. The day before the first round a sheet of paper is pinned to the noticeboard informing everybody when they are teeing off and with whom. It is said to be a great democratic free-for-all in which a road sweeper can be drawn to play with a duke (so to speak) but, of course, it's not. The draw committee takes into account many factors – 'good stories' for the press, crowd control, etc. – when compiling the list. This year, however, its sole consideration appeared to have been to make sure it completely pissed me off.

In my innocence I thought that after winning one of the qualifying competitions Ross might get a good draw. How foolish. We were drawn with Stephen Field and Michael Welsh.

Don't get me wrong, both were fine golfers. Field, especially, was a credit to the sport. Over the months I'd become quite friendly with him. He was a fine chap with a wonderful young family, courteous, quiet and hard-working. I was pretty sure he was nice to his folks and would never kick the family dog. But, God, I was disappointed. I'm sure I wasn't what either of them had hoped for either. Colin Byrne consoled me on the practice putting green. 'It could have been worse – you might have been paired with Irvine Welsh and Gracie Fields.'

He couldn't have been more wrong.

This ill-mannered whingeing brought its just reward, of course.

Field played well for one round and narrowly missed the cut.

Welsh made it to the weekend, when he played with Greg Norman in the third round and Ben Crenshaw on the last day. Both scored better than Ross. In fact, over two rounds only four players scored worse than Ross.

We strode up the final fairway late on Friday afternoon bloodied, unbowed and in fifth last place.

I didn't mind, really, though being first would have been better. And coming last in the Open had an historic ring to it, but I didn't really have the courage to ask Ross if he would mind dropping a few more shots on the final hole. Besides, he'd been managing to drop shots without any encouragement from me for the previous thirty-five holes.

I should take that last remark back. Supposing I live to be a hundred years old, I will never be able to understand how any human being was able to break seventy round Royal Lytham and St Annes that week. To think there were even complaints that the course wasn't difficult enough. Professional golfers may not be the most rounded people in the world, or the most intelligent or well-read or politically aware or sensitive or polite, but, boy, can they play golf.

Twenty-four people broke seventy in the first round. Incredible!

And for a short while – two holes, since you ask – it looked as though Ross would be joining them. He birdied the first hole and was one under playing the third, only to push his drive towards the railway, which ran the right-hand length of the fairway. The ball bounced back off a tree into the rough. He managed eleven yards with the next shot, got trapped in the face of a bunker with the one after that and eventually took seven.

After sixteen holes he was six over par.

'Well, I'm struggling to make the cut now. I suppose I could go home for the weekend, put my feet up, relax and watch it on the telly,' he said, as we walked down the next fairway.

'Come on, Ross, there's plenty of holes to go – we could still make it.'

Any prospect of a miraculous recovery disappeared when I suggested a three-iron for the second shot. As we stood and watched his ball sail comfortably over the flag into the television gantry beyond the green the thought crossed my mind that no matter how badly he could play I could always caddy worse.

'Maybe you're right,' I said, once he'd holed out for a bogey. 'Maybe you're right after all.'

The second round was simply a chance to enjoy the special atmosphere of the Open Championship. I once read a magazine article by the American writer John Updike arguing that golf was a sport of the blue-collar masses. At the time I thought this was dafter than anything Jeffrey Archer had ever dreamed up but that afternoon it struck me that Updike might have been right after all.

When we teed off, it was as if the population of Blackpool beach had been decanted on to the Royal Lytham links. It could have been that they hadn't read the news about the newly revealed absence of turds on the beach but I suspect they wanted to be at the Open. Everywhere you looked there were people. The grandstands were packed and the greens surrounded by ten-deep galleries. Young, old, male and female. The knotted handkerchiefs outnumbered the shooting sticks. And there was noise everywhere, ooohs and aahs and distant cheers, as well as the constant buzz from the vast tented bars. A lone voice by the sixth green screeched as we walked off after a birdie. 'COME ON, ROSS! YOU CAN DO IT.'

Ross blushed. 'Did they call me Russ? I got a fan letter this morning addressed to Russ Drummond.'

Fan letters? He had come a long way since the start of the season.

We reached the eighteenth hole just after seven, as the evening sun was at its richest and the shadow of the grandstands was starting to creep across the final green. He hit a great drive. As we walked towards his ball I could hear television sets in the hospitality tents way to the right, '. . . others to miss the cut include Ian Woosnam, USPGA champion Steve Elkington, Scotland's Ross Drummond . . .'

The grandstands were almost deserted by now. 'Let me hit the last shot. Go on, let me, no one will notice,' I said.

He smiled. 'They'll disqualify me. Let me concentrate. To the pin one three one, a smooth nine-iron, I think.'

He hit it perfectly, right on the line of the clubhouse chimney. I lost sight of the ball as it rose above the redbrick of the clubhouse. I caught sight of it again as it thumped on to the green, ten feet from the flag. A bare-chested man in a white sun-hat sitting seven rows back in the right-hand grandstand started the clapping. Everyone who was left joined it. I tipped my hat to them all as we walked the 131 yards to the final green of our Open Championship. Why the hell not? I thought. I'd never get another chance.

17. Roasting

The word in the locker room was that the Austrian Open had all the glamour of a shell-suit. A couple of weeks before the tournament I asked one player if he was 'teeing it up in the Austrian' and he laughed. 'No, are you?' It was that bad. In fact, the tour was so desperate to make up the field that my old friend Gianluca Pietrobono got a game.

Austria's problem, apart from an unforgivable fondness for Kurt Waldheim, was that its national Open was staged in the same week as the USPGA championship. Even if it hadn't been, none of the top players would have played. The prize fund was a measly £250,000, the golf course nothing more than a buttercup-speckled meadow, and the journey from Vienna airport, as I discovered, gruesome. We were caged in the back of an overcrowded minibus for two hours as it bounced and wove its way to the course at speeds that would have melted rock. This was more than enough for some people to become reacquainted with their evening meal and for me to appreciate fully why Seve and Co. gave the whole thing a miss every year.

Even the not-so-famous were reluctant to pitch up. Ross had warned me months in advance that he was taking the week off. This had supposedly given me plenty of time to find someone else to caddy for and as I risked my life on an Austrian country lane I began to wonder why I had neglected to do so.

It's an odd feeling splashing out £400 you can't afford to fly to somewhere in the middle of the night to look for work, especially when you've no idea how you might do this, no goodwill or professional reputation to help you out, no idea where you are going and nowhere to sleep when you get there. You should try it sometime if you ever want to feel like an irresponsible, spendthrift dickhead.

Actually, I hadn't been entirely irresponsible. I did have a player lined up, an American called Jason Widener whom I had first met in a Spanish hotel months before. I didn't think he was a golfer at first, he looked so bookish. I say this because he was wearing a pair of John Lennon specs, had close-cropped fair hair and was reading a book. What's more, it was a book not written by John Grisham.

If I can generalize for a moment here. Every professional golfer on the planet reads John Grisham books or listens to Phil Collins in his spare time, when they are not watching Eurosport in their hotel room or searching the streets for the local branch of Pizza Hut, that is. They really should get out more, artistically speaking. Not that I ever suggested to anyone they should pack their suitcases with the collected works of Balzac but I would occasionally say to a friendly pro that we were in a particularly interesting part of the planet, with a large selection of historical attractions that might be worth a quick visit.

'We're not here as fucking tourists, Lawrence,' would come the reply. 'We're golfers.'

Widener was a bit different. He read William Faulkner and books on Zen, and listened to R E M on his portable compact-disc player. The other pros muttered suspiciously that he may have visited an art gallery once but nothing was ever proved so they let him play most weeks.

The two of us shared a taxi to the golf course with a curly-haired caddy who had a Gloucestershire accent and claimed to be Fred West's cousin. It was just a guess but I thought it would be a good idea to ignore him and talk to Widener. I was right. He was intelligent and charming, as well as being a superb golfer. He was once the junior champion in North America, better than his contemporary Phil Mickelson at the same age.

Somewhere along the way, Mickelson became one of the best golfers in the world and won millions of dollars on the US Tour and Widener drifted over to Europe. He wanted to play golf but also to broaden his mind, visit art galleries and cathedrals, meet new people, see interesting new places. I thought this was an admirable outlook on life – in fact, I fully intend to broaden my own mind one day – but the locker-room sages saw the danger signals.

As usual they were right. Widener missed the first six cuts of the season. One week he finished sixty-fourth but then went back to missing cuts again. Most Friday nights I would find him in the clubhouse. I would ask if he'd made the weekend, he would squeeze his lips together until they formed a perfect inverse smile and softly shake his head.

At the start of the year, his miserable expression would be followed by a detailed explanation: 'If I'd just holed this putt or that putt.' After a few weeks he switched to 'God knows what went wrong' until, finally, desperation set in.

'Lawrence, I need you on my bag,' he said, after missing another cut at the English Open.

I remember that we'd had this conversation at the English Open because that was the week he'd taken delivery of a new bag from a golf-club company and the wrong spelling of his name had been stitched into the black leather, WIDNER instead of WIDENER. I ask you. It might only have been a tiny little E to Mr X back at headquarters but when you're walking around a golf course with a misspelt name on your bag it must be impossible to feel good about yourself.

How could I refuse a man with the wrong name embroidered on his golf bag? After a couple of near misses and much re-examination of schedules, it turned out that the Austrian Open would be the only chance I'd have to work for him. 'That's great news,' he said, when I called him two weeks before the tournament. And then he phoned back five minutes later. 'I'm sorry, Lawrence, I'm going back to the States to reassess my life.'

I never saw or heard of Jason Widener again. It was as if aliens had arrived, rounded up everyone who couldn't break eighty on the European tour and taken them off to a distant planet for observation. I'm sure he'll resurface one day, hopefully playing as well as Phil Mickelson. If you come across him tell him Lawrence wishes him all the best, that I hope he's got rid of that destructive push off the tee and that his mom has restitched the name on his golf bag. Tell him that I wouldn't have been that bad a caddy, honestly.

With Widener gone my best chance of finding a player was at the airport. I turned up early at Heathrow and scanned the travel agent's list in search of someone I knew, someone who was a decent player but not successful enough to stay at home for the Austrian Open. Sure enough, my eyes fell on Craig Cassells's name.

I found him in the departure lounge reading the *Daily Star*. 'Sorry, mate, I've just got myself a caddy for the week about twenty minutes ago,' he said. He didn't look that sorry. 'Why don't you get yourself up to the car park tomorrow and get roasted for a while?'

Roast (vb): to wait in a golf-club car park all day with a desperate look on your face and sit like a pig on a spit, roasting in the sun. If you really need a job, roasting is the pits – specially if you're in a shitty place like this.

Cassells let me sleep on his floor for the night. The following morning I was standing in the car park at Golf Club Waldviertel by nine. A few caddies were already in place when I got there:

Kevin Woodward, his friend Howard Rosser, who'd driven overnight from Gothenburg, and a South African caddy called Justin, who helpfully provided me with the definition of roasting above.

I thought he was a bit harsh about Waldviertel. It was a beautiful setting for a golf tournament, nestling restfully on the gentlest of rolling landscapes near the border with the Czech Republic. The course was cut through a vast conifer forest. As you would expect for Austria, the sky was a creamy blue, the air as fresh as a mountain stream and the locals healthy-looking and wholesome. It was easy to imagine the von Trapp family skipping over the hills and dales from Vienna in time to perform a concert for everyone on Sunday afternoon. Mind you, if they had shown up they would have been out of luck because the Beatles were on.

I thought it was a bit odd that the world's most popular beat combo should choose a golf tournament at Waldviertel for their reunion concert. Still, when the great day came they were brilliant, especially 'I Vunt To Old Yur Hant' and 'She Lufs You Ya Ya Ya'. But why the black nylon wigs and childish German accents, guys? Grow old gracefully is what I always say.

Another thing I always say is never take a job with someone whose name would leave you wide open to ridicule in the bar at the caddies' hotel that night. This ruled out some of the more exotic-sounding characters on the entry sheet pinned up outside the PGA office: Uli Weinhandel, Romain Victor, Freddy Regard, Max Balti, Fabrice Honnoart de Mai, Frédéric Grosset-Grange.

Also out were the British players, most of whom had their regular caddy or had fixed up someone in advance, and anyone who could not afford to pay a caddy. This accounted for just about everybody else.

We sat outside the clubhouse for most of the morning, sunbathing but with an eye open for a caddy-less player. Kevin read his golf rule book and shouted out questions every once in a while: 'What's the decision if a little furry rabbit comes along and snuggles around the ball? Do you play it as it lies?' This would result in a loud, ill-informed discussion until a player was spotted and everybody would become transfixed, as if Lady Godiva had appeared on a Perspex horse.

After lunch things became really desperate. Gianluca Pietrobono walked past pulling his bag on a trolley and I was tempted. Only tempted, mind. Occasionally, someone would say they were off to the toilet but the rest of us knew that he was sneaking off to get a job. The rivalry was unspoken but intense. I didn't know it at the time but a great deal of animal cunning, shiftiness, evasion and deception was required to get off the spit. No doubt this was why everyone else found a job and I was on my own by late afternoon.

I sat on the steps staring wistfully at the activity on the practice range. My thoughts turned to the millions of unemployed back home. Like me, they would have been feeling worthless and dispossessed. Unlike me, however, the lucky bastards weren't facing the prospect of a slow week in Waldviertel with nothing better to do than watch golf. Just as I was about to give up salvation arrived. What's more he had a lightweight golf bag.

I knew Thomas Gögele vaguely. He'd given me a lift once to a golf course from an airport. He was a bit like Jason Widener, young, earnest and reserved. He didn't make too many cuts either. I knew he liked Albert Camus because he asked me when I was in his car if I'd ever read *Der Mythos von Sisyphus*. I hadn't, but was taken aback by the question which was quite a change from 'What do you think, a six- or a seven-iron?'

Thomas spoke perfect English with a thick Gothic accent. 'Lore-ance, what can I do for you?' he said, when I stopped him on his way to the range.

I cast an approving eye over the blue and white nylon golf bag he had on his shoulder. 'Thomas, old chum, are you looking for a caddy?'

'I don't know. How much do you cost?' he said.

'Cheap.'

He could smell the desperation. 'How cheap?'

'Very, very cheap,' I said.

'OK, then, it's a deal. Let me go and get my proper golf bag.'

18. John Daly's $100,000

There was no stopping Thomas Gögele. If it wasn't *Der Mythos von Sisyphus*, it was Konrad Adenauer's influence on the post-war European settlement or the idiocy of the German Social Democrat Party's opposition to labour market liberalization. And did you know that all Austrians have a secret desire to be German? That's why they dress so badly.

No two ways about it, Thomas was a glorious freak, a social-science buff who read German broadsheets from the front page in. You'd go a long way in professional golf to find another one of those and when he dies he should be stuffed and placed in the foyer of the Natural History Museum.

The affairs of state, any state, were not a hot topic in the locker rooms of Europe. Every once in a while a player would have a bloodthirsty rant about the return of the death penalty or whinge about paying too much tax, which might provoke a response from someone within earshot who had nothing better to do, usually a caddy. A long argument would ensue which can briefly be summarized:

Caddy: 'But if rich sportsmen don't contribute to a redistributive tax system how else can we finance a decent health service or help pensioners fend off starvation?'

Player: 'Shut up, you bloody communist.'

I exaggerate only mildly, the caddy might not have said

redistributive. Thomas Gögele would have, though. I never asked but I suspect he would have given all of his money away to starving pensioners if asked, not that it would have put fillet steak on too many tables. He was always scraping along at the bottom of the Order of Merit. 'The only thing I am worried about, Lore-ance, is not becoming as good a player as I can,' he said, when I asked how he survived on a diet of missed cuts and dreams.

He explained that he didn't play golf for money but for the simple, unblemished love of the game. Honestly, if he hadn't been so tall and strapping I would have laughed in his face. A lot of the world's top pros say this kind of thing when what they actually mean is, 'I play to win Major championships and not for the money. Anyway, I've already got £10 million in the bank.' Most players can't afford to be so pure of motive, not even Thomas Gögele. Let's be frank, *especially* not Thomas Gögele.

'Be serious, Thomas, everyone plays for the money,' I mocked.

'As long as I have enough to survive.' He *was* being serious. 'Ever since I was twelve years old all I have wanted to be is something really special at golf. It would be the greatest thing in the world to look in the mirror and see an Open Champion.'

Call me an old sentimentalist, but I thought this was just about the most touching expression of hope and youthful ambition I'd heard all year. Even now, in the depths of winter, it tingles my toes and gives me something to cling to whenever I'm tempted to believe the world of sport is a cold-hearted, cynical place run by rapacious businessmen for the benefit of greedy superstars. On the other hand, if I ever need confirmation that it *is* such a place I think of the day John Daly tried to assassinate me.

This may sound like a bold accusation to make against the world's most famous golfer but consider the evidence. I was standing in the trees at Hilversum Golf Club when his ball whistled past my head and clattered into a beech, kicked sideways off a pine tree, bounced twice and rolled to a stop next to my foot. It was stamped with what looked like a red rat insignia and, this made me really suspicious, the word KILL in shaky black ink. Then I remembered that he does this to remind himself to smash the ball out of sight.

The woman standing next to me shook her head in disgust and said it was his sixty-eighth shot of the day. She was disgusted because we were only on the fourteenth hole.

In the distance I could see Daly walking towards me, a hunched, sloppy figure moulded by room-service hamburgers and too much television. His shock of gold hair, shorn at the sides and left to grow at the back, was straight out of an Arkansas trailer park. He looked so depressed when he finally got to his ball that I didn't have the heart to accuse him of attempted murder.

'Sorr-ee,' he said, lifelessly. I watched him chip out sideways. He flicked the next shot casually on to the green and finished off with a few putts, one of which actually fell into the cup. We all traipsed after him for the next four holes, a long, unhappy stream of Dutch golf fans and me, and we gave him a great big ironic cheer when he holed out on the last for an eighty-nine.

I don't want to boast but I once scored less than eighty-nine for a round of golf. (22 August 1992, an eighty-five at Highgate Golf Club, London. The scorecard is framed and hangs on my bathroom wall.) Who knows? With a tail wind and some helpful bounces I might have scored eighty-five at Hilversum Golf Club. What was certain, though, was that no one would have paid me $100,000 appearance money so that the locals could come to watch me make a clown of myself as I went about it.

It was perfectly possible that the most famous golfer in the world had been trying his heart out but couldn't stop himself scoring eighty-nine. His two playing partners said as much afterwards. But when I tried to ask the man himself, as he strode purposefully towards the car park, his bodyguard threw me out of the way. I never got the chance to ask him if he was embarrassed about receiving $100,000 for finishing thirty-three shots behind the tournament leader. A big crowd had gathered in the car park to watch him climb into the back of his bright blue saloon car and disappear in a cloud of dust. When the excitement was over I fell into conversation with a jolly Dutchman who happened to be standing next to me. It turned out he was the local property developer who had paid Daly his $100,000 appearance fee. I thought it was very odd that he was still smiling.

'Well, do you think you got your money's worth today?' I asked, preparing to sympathize.

'Wonderful!' he boomed.

'What are you talking about? He was twenty-two over par.'

'So what?' He gestured towards the huddle of photographers and journalists. 'Look at all the attention.'

I checked when I got home and the British newspapers had all carried long stories about Daly's infamous eighty-nine. He was right: Hilversum was on the map. So why did I want to throw up all over his beautifully tailored blue suit? I'll tell you why. I'd been speaking to my friend Chris Hall the night before in the clubhouse bar overlooking the green where Daly had holed out for his eighty-nine.

I liked Chris a lot. He was a first-year tour pro, with a penchant for eastern philosophy (his current swing thought was 'one shot, one kill') and the kind of brutal honesty that made others blush. A club professional from Nottingham, he had decided he wanted to play against the best players in Europe, went to the qualifying school and won his card. He couldn't afford to play on the tour but came up with the ingenious idea of selling shares in himself. Instead of owning the hind leg of a racehorse, people had the chance to own a golfer's buttock. He raised £25,000.

Chris had started the season poorly, then managed a couple of top-twenty finishes and had fallen away again. The Dutch

Open was one of the few tournaments he had left to win the
£20,000 needed to keep his card. 'I was chatting to my wife on
the phone last night and she could tell I was down,' he told me,
miserably. 'She called me back an hour later to tell me not to
worry and she's right. What's the worst that could happen? I
could lose my card. Big deal.'

Standing in the car park after Daly had gone, I pictured the
pained look on Chris's face when we'd talked. The truth was,
losing his card would be a very big deal – all that wasted effort
and unfulfilled ambition, all those shareholders wishing they'd
bought a horse instead. How much easier life would be if a
Dutch property developer came along and handed over $100,000
every once in a while. Of course, only superstars like John Daly
are on the receiving end of such munificence. It's a free world,
people can give their money to whomever they like for whatever
reason they like. But sometimes you just can't help thinking it's
a crazy, fucked-up world too.

Maybe I was being harsh. I was starting to think as much by
the time Ross arrived for his second round. There was no space
at the golf course and the practice range was at a horse-trotting
stadium on the other side of town. We caught the bus. It was
only three miles away but the journey seemed to take for ever,
along densely wooded cart-tracks until, finally, we bounced
gratefully out on to the sunny main street. And then slowed
down even more.

Hilversum was clearly wealthy. Its people looked well fed, its
sex shop was stacked to the roof with interesting, expensive
implements and its homes, all individually designed, were set in
spacious, leafy gardens. It was a pretty place, spoiled only by
long lines of top-of-the-range BMWs crawling along at 5 m.p.h.
To pass the journey, I started to tell Ross about Daly's round.
I was working myself up nicely into a lather of indignation when
one of the other passengers, an English player called Mark Roe,
interrupted.

'That's nothing, I shot ninety-three at a tournament last year,' he said, nonchalantly. 'Out in fifty-three, back in forty. All I wanted to do was the exact opposite of what the game is all about. I wanted to score as many as possible. I had a six-inch putt for six at one hole and I hit it forty yards off the green. I took eleven. My only regret was that there wasn't a camera around to film it all. I got fined anyway, so it would have been nice to capture it on celluloid.'

I knew then I'd been right about the world first time round.

Jos was on the range when we got there, pushing someone else around for a change. He was still adamant that Ross was going to win a tournament but I wasn't so sure any more.

He was the same player, yes, but I sensed that I was becoming a different caddy. The scuffling round for a place to stay, the early-morning starts, the endless hanging around, the faint curl of the lip when the clubhouse steward realized you were a caddy. Gradually, it was all becoming a chore rather than an adventure. A couple of days at home had reminded me that life wasn't all about choosing the right club for a 142-yard shot to the green or lining up putts. It was only a game. I'd almost forgotten that over the last seven months. Oasis had split up, got back together again, split up, back together again, the Government was in trouble, Celtic had a fantastic new team and my six-month-old nephew Conor was growing up. Where had I been when all this had happened? Standing outside golf clubhouses being sneered at by doormen with superiority complexes.

Mind you, none of this would have mattered if Ross had been leading the Dutch Open after one round but he wasn't. He was 146th and hitting the ball everywhere. Well, when I say everywhere, I mean everywhere but where it was meant to go. Not even God was going to cure that in thirty minutes, though Jos tried his best. 'Just go out and have fun,' he implored, as grey banks of rain started to sweep towards us. Somehow Jos seemed a strangely inadequate guru at that moment.

Then Ross hinted he might withdraw with a sore back. Terrific, I thought. There could have been a more tedious way of spending the afternoon than caddying in the rain but I couldn't think of one. Besides, there was an educational biology film on the hotel's adult channel that I was quite keen to see. To get in the mood, I caressed him gently, teasingly, towards my preferred option. 'Go on, throw a bad back, Ross – everybody else does it. Go on, please, please, yes, oh, God yes, yes . . .'

And then he smiled. He was only joking, Mr Goody-Bloody-Two-Shoes. 'No, I couldn't do that. It would be a lie. All I need is sixty-three to make the cut.'

Of course, there was never a chance of scoring sixty-three. I knew it and so did Ross, so much so that he even let me pick the club he used on every single shot – he *never* did that.

I chose so many wrong clubs it became embarrassing and I gave up voluntarily. My heart wasn't in it. By the tenth hole there was nothing left to play for except the bicycle on offer for a hole-in-one at the par-three. I'm sorry to go on about this but doesn't it make you feel pessimistic about the future of mankind when John Daly takes nine at one hole and gets $100,000, and someone else makes a hole-in-one and gets a bicycle?

Ross didn't even come close to the bike, thank goodness. The only remaining excitement was to watch as one of his playing partners, Mark Litton, endured the cruellest torture devised since the first Stalinist jailer attached the first electrode to the first shaved Trotskyite testicle: trying to make the cut at a golf tournament when you really, really, really needed to.

Missing cuts at the start of the year was one thing but, come the autumn, it starts to feel like you're losing your first-born, especially if you haven't made enough money to keep your card for next year. Or, at least, it looks as though it feels that way. I was in the happy position of not knowing for sure. Ross was comfortably in the top sixty of the Order of Merit and we were able to miss this particular cut with the *joie de vivre* of two flappers giggling over spilled champagne. Mark Litton wasn't so lucky. Stranded way down in the Order of Merit, he desperately needed to make money at Hilversum.

As it happened he had a very good chance but with five holes to play he double-bogied, then duffed a chip a couple of holes later. He came to the last needing a birdie. It was early evening by then and the course was empty and silent except for a black wedge of starlings flying north to Amsterdam. Somehow, the world's comprehensive apathy towards this little personal drama added to the agony. He looked – there's no nice way to put this – shit. Grey and angst-ridden. His swing looked scarcely better and knocked his drive to the left rough, squarely behind a silver birch. When I eventually forced myself to look again he had a ten-yard putt for a birdie, which missed the hole by four inches.

Back in the locker room, he asked me for a pen to write a cheque for his caddy. 'This is red ink. Do banks accept red ink?' he said, and then answered himself, 'Who fucking cares?' He gave his locker door a loud metallic kick.

I felt sorry for Litton. He wasn't a great player, he said as much himself, but he was a decent man, placid and polite, and patently in love with golf. He had to be. Why else would he put himself through this agony? It wasn't as if he was making any money beyond what was needed to feed his family and keep him on tour. There has to be a system of rewarding the best players, that's why we call them champions and give them huge bundles of money, but I couldn't help thinking that life would have been more humane if just a little something was shared out to the Mark Littons of the game. John Daly's $100,000 seemed like a good place to start.

Ross took a courtesy car back to his hotel. I had a beer, then set off towards the town centre on foot. It was dark and the clubhouse glowed warmly in the inky light. I could hear the voices shouting at a television set showing English horse-racing.

There was a circle of tents by the exit. I saw one of the caddies I knew. He was filling a bag with rubbish, getting ready to leave.

'Missed the cut?' I asked, needlessly. He had. 'Are you out next week?'

He shrugged. 'Don't know. I'm thinking of jacking it. Fed up living in this.' He nodded at his tent, an ancient army surplus in camouflage green. I opened the flap. There was just enough room inside for a sleeping bag, a hold-all, one carton of apple juice, a packet of sour cream and onion Pringles and Monday's *Daily Telegraph*.

'Can't say I blame you.'

'It's not just that.' He started rolling up the sleeping bag. 'You can only take so much. I like this guy I'm with but he's never going to win anything, is he? And, anyway, I've been with him all year – there's nothing I can do to help him any more.'

I held open the nylon bag while he stuffed the sleeping bag inside. 'I'll tell you what,' I said. 'I know exactly what you mean.'

19. The Death of Don Quixote

Our coach pulled into the centre of Mariánské Lázne as early evening reached its peak of excitement. The main street was deserted but for a handful of elderly couples out for a stroll. Under-employed waitresses enjoyed the last rays of daylight outside their empty cafés and a stray Alsatian pissed on the lamp-post opposite the Excelsior Hotel. A solitary newspaper-sized poster glued to the bus-shelter window advertised the imminence of the 1996 Czech Open. We'd arrived at the very edge of Planet Golf.

The noise of thirty caddies unloading luggage sent everyone scurrying for cover. I grabbed my hold-all and set off in search of somewhere to stay. I was unnecessarily worried: empty hotel rooms were a local speciality.

Mariánské Lázne was once the most fashionable spa in Europe and it was easy to see why. It sat in the base of a valley, surrounded on all sides by rolling hills covered in spruce forest. It felt intimate, snuggled down in a rich green blanket. The air was clean and crisp, like freshly washed laundry. According to my guide book, Chopin visited the town in 1832. He was followed, down the decades, by a host of world-famous artists and writers, Freud, Kafka, Twain, Kipling among others. All came to take the naturally carbonated waters, said to be especially effective for urinary problems. It must have been a wonderful, glamorous place back then, with a spa house on every corner and an incontinent genius on every toilet.

The glory years, alas, were long gone, although the main thoroughfare, Hlavni Trida, still boasted what must have been the greatest concentration of grand hotels outside Park Lane – vast *art nouveau* palaces, each decorated as intricately as a wedding cake. The façades had recently been repainted in jolly lemons and creams but inside they were dark and dog-eared. Most retained the original lifts, light fittings and female receptionists.

Golf was another legacy of that more gracious age. Somewhere high in the hills above the town, King Edward VII had hit the first ever tee shot at the local golf club in 1905 and had given birth to a tiny but surprisingly hardy strain of sporting endeavour called Czech golf. Somehow it survived Nazi occupation, Soviet suspicion of a 'capitalist' game and the supreme indifference of 99.9 per cent of the population to bring us all to this unlikely corner of Bohemia for a tournament ninety-one years later.

Of course, the money helped too. Chemapol, a huge Czech industrial conglomerate and makers of the IRA's favourite explosive, Semtex, had put up a £750,000 prize fund. This was either a staggeringly generous gesture or insanity disguised as sports sponsorship. There were less than two thousand registered golfers in the Czech Republic and the nearest city, Prague, was a three-hour train journey away. Minuscule crowds were guaranteed.

Why had Chemapol spent so much money? 'Golf philosophy – elegance, fair play and professionalism is the driving force of our company and that is why we are here today,' the chairman of the board said, by way of explanation in the tournament programme. So he obviously didn't know either. The next morning, the consensus on the minibus as it wound its way up the valley towards the golf course was that it was insanity, though no one was in favour of handing back the money.

Ivan Lendl was on the putting green when we got to the course. Yes, *that* Ivan Lendl. There was a little gathering of caddies under the clubhouse awning, giggling and making rude remarks about his putting stroke. The Czech-born tennis champion had been invited to play by the organizers in a desperate effort to drum up some interest. His photograph had been used on all the publicity material. This made undeniable economic sense but was grossly insulting to all the proper pros who'd practised hard over the years and contributed much to the growth in European golf, only to find they had been brushed aside for a champion tennis player (a five-handicap golfer on a good day). Didn't these people understand? Winning eight tennis Majors was one thing, breaking eighty was another. As if any true golf aficionado would be taken in by such a cheap publicity stunt.

'Excuse me, Mr Lendl, are you looking for a caddy?' I asked, blushing.

'I'm sorry?'

The voice was so familiar, deep, with a hint of Eastern European menace. I started burbling like a schoolgirl ushered into the presence of her favourite pop star. 'I'm such a big fan. To be perfectly honest I always preferred you to McEnroe. Because it's you, I'll caddy for nothing.'

I've never been in the habit of volunteering to work for nothing but for Lendl I would have made an exception. It would have been worth it to have been the centre of attention just once before the season ended. Ross had been up on the leaderboard a couple of times but even when he'd got there the crowds didn't exactly flock round or expend much in the way of adulation. Lendl was guaranteed a large and fawning gallery, whether he scored sixty-five or eighty-five, practised hard or not at all.

'No, thank you, the sponsor has got me a caddy. Now if you'll excuse me I have to practise my putting.'

I was crushed. 'You certainly do,' I said, walking back towards the clubhouse and the jeers of the other caddies who'd been watching this little cameo in sycophancy unfold.

It was just as well, really. Ross was due at the course in a couple of hours. God only knows what he would have said if he'd seen me swanning off down the fairway with a tennis legend when I should have been on the range fetching golf balls and the occasional cup of milky tea for him. My guess is that it wouldn't have been 'Can you get me his autograph?'

He arrived around lunch-time. The range was a soggy mess and we went out for a practice round. It immediately started to rain and a thin but clingy mist rolled in, blurring the course and any enthusiasm I had for the task at hand.

Somewhere around the seventh hole it dawned on me that I would rather be anywhere else in the world right then, facing anything but the prospect of caddying at Mariánské Lázne Golf Club.

It was supposed to be the best golf course in Eastern Europe but this was like saying the Thames was the cleanest river in London. It felt permanently damp, like taking a Turkish bath with your clothes on. And there were a couple of heart-breaking hills. Not short, calf-stretching bursts but long, aching climbs where your feet slipped and the bag felt half full of water. On a purely technical note, the fairways didn't drain and the greens were about as smooth as a Crimplene suit. Less technically, though more interestingly, there was a brothel by the fifth hole called Club Fantazie.

Being blessed with the kind of good looks and charm that have women whimpering with sexual desire, I've never had cause to visit a brothel in my life and didn't know what one looked like. Never in my wildest fantasies did I imagine any of them would look like John Boy Walton's marital home. Club Fantazie nestled shyly in a forest clearing. The only giveaway was a tiny fluorescent red heart above the front door, which winked invitingly at anyone who happened to snap hook a drive into the trees on the fifth fairway.

The tournament programme was packed with long-winded messages from the sponsor but was curiously silent about this – and I use the phrase carefully – landmark of world golf. Why? It was like airbrushing the lighthouse from Turnberry. How many golf clubs could boast a fully equipped, open-all-day shagging shop within sand wedge distance? What a coup! As far as I could see Club Fantazie was the golf club's unique, indeed only, selling point and its existence should have been emblazoned across the publicity material: *Come to the Czech Open, see Europe's top golfers and, as soon as you can decently leave, get across the road and have your putter straightened.* That would have filled the galleries.

Of course, hardly anyone turned up. Even Ivan Lendl could only attract a couple of hundred people, curious to see him zigzag his way round in eighty-five shots. And when they weren't doing that they were sheltering in the clubhouse from the constant rain or scribbling down directions for Club Fantazie.

What they weren't doing was paying any attention to anything Ross and I were doing. It was unreasonable to expect a thick circle of people round every green but one spectator would have been appreciated, just to make it feel as though what we were doing wasn't entirely pointless. We followed the same depressing routine every day: arrive at the course, visit the range, hit a few putts, step on the first tee and disappear off into an unpopulated drizzle for five hours.

To my shame, I even began to dream that Ross would miss the cut and we could get off home for the weekend. Of course, he just scraped in. This made me feel even more disconsolate.

'What's wrong with you?' he said, when I turned up late for the third round.

What could I say? The forecast for the weekend was more showers, no spectators and fifty-sixth place again. I'd hardly been able to drag myself out of bed. My bones ached, my shoes smelt like a bucket of soiled nappies and I'd run out of clean underpants. I'd looked in the mirror and seen a caddy. Not a modern, clean, professional caddy but an exhausted, sleeping-in-a-hedgerow caddy with a moody hairdo and a personality to match. He was unrecognizable as the person who'd been unable to sleep for excitement before his first tournament in South Africa. That was twenty tournaments and 30,000 miles ago. A lifetime.

Everyone told me that tour 'marriages' hit rough spots. Well, Ross and I had reached ours. What had gone wrong? Petty, irrational things. Marriage things. The way he made me walk all the way back to the tee with the bag, lost his temper when he hit a bad shot and was irrationally happy when he hit a good one, zipped up the bag when it rained, didn't trust me to work out the yardage or guess the direction of the wind or choose a club, hogged the umbrella, the way we'd run out of things to say to each other about two months ago . . .

'Aren't flies stupid?'

'I guess so, Lawrence.'

. . . the way he was never ever going to win a bloody tournament anyway.

Ross was a great golfer but so was every player on tour, otherwise they would have been at home, selling sweaters in the local pro shop or giving lessons at driving ranges to unsaveable hackers. It took something more than talent to win – inspiration, luck. It needed a little iron in the soul, just enough to endure the pain it took to win and fight the voice that said coming fifty-sixth didn't matter, that making the cut was a good week, a nice cheque. *I want to win.* It was easy to say the words, but was he really serious? And if he was really serious what was he doing with a caddy like me on the bag?

These thoughts had been running through my head over the previous two days. I'd hardly said a word in forty-eight hours.

What could I say now – I don't think you've got enough iron in your soul, Ross? We didn't say things like that to each other. Players and caddies don't. They say things like 'Strong five-iron or smooth six?' and 'Aren't flies stupid?'

'No, I'm fine, Ross. Honestly.'

He shook his head. 'Well, you look like you want to slit your wrists.'

I was glad to get to Northamptonshire. That's how much I hated Mariánské Lázně and the Czech Open. Give me the British Masters any day, one of the tour's oldest, most prestigious events. It was odd, then, that the PGA chose to stage it in the middle of a Barratt housing estate, on a golf course where the greens were so bad they had had to be painted.

Here's a golf tip. If you ever fancy seeing someone in authority make a fool of himself buy a tournament programme and read it from cover to cover. These brochures are printed months in advance and always contain little seeds of corporate bullshit waiting to sprout into sunflowers of embarrassment. Here's what a Mr Kenneth D. Schofield, who gloried in the title of executive director, PGA European Tour, had to say about Collingtree Park golf course: 'It has been prepared and presented to the highest possible standard to reflect the importance of the event and the skills of our members.'

Did he really think his members were a bunch of thirty-six handicappers about to compete in the Crazy Golf Open?

That was just one of the questions flying around the locker room when I arrived. There were others, like 'What are we doing here?', 'Why did they waste a perfectly good potato field by building a golf course?', 'Do you think they'll have any paint left when they've finished on the greens? My bedroom could do with freshening up' and 'Aren't the PGA a bunch of fuckwits?'

It felt good to be back among the caddies. I'd ducked out of the German Open in Stuttgart after the Czech Republic and gone home for a rest. There was plenty of news to catch up on. Woosnam, and Wobbly, had won another tournament. Thomas Gögele had finished joint second in Stuttgart and won £42,000. He'd taken the week off to celebrate. I could picture him sitting in a darkened bedroom reading Bertolt Brecht plays and smiling contentedly.

And there were rumours that Bernhard Langer and Pete Coleman were splitting up after fifteen years. It would have been deeply sad if such a long and successful partnership had indeed broken up, although some of the caddies had suspended their grief long enough to club together to buy a German dictionary. They were busily learning how to say, 'Can I have the bag, Bernhard?' and other handy phrases in case the rumours proved true.

Ross had big news too. 'I've finished with Jos,' he told me as we walked out on our practice round. 'I told him last week. Our deal was only for two months anyway. He said that he'd always be there for me.'

'I'll always be there for you too,' I said, jokingly, in a half-hearted attempt at reconciliation after Mariánské Lázne.

It couldn't have been much fun for him having a manic depressive on the bag but I told him I'd had a make-over since then. New shoes, pressed trousers and combed hair. Out with monosyllabic grunts and silence, in with considered advice and animated chatter about the rakish pranks we'd all got up to in the caddies' hotel the night before. I was determined to rediscover the old enthusiasms.

This lasted half an hour, until it dawned on me that it was impossible for any human being to be happy in Collingtree Park. There must be a demand for golf courses built on wasteland in the noisy draught of the M1 motorway, otherwise people wouldn't build them, but for the life of me I will never be able to comprehend it. I'd always thought golf was supposed to be a relaxing stroll in the countryside not a coughing, spluttering walk through a cloud of carbon monoxide. The British Masters was the second tournament we'd played on a motorway links. Forest of Arden was the other. That was just as awful but at least we had been there in the height of summer. It was September now. Autumn had taken the week off and let Cousin Winter romp around for a while in Northamptonshire.

Ross and I had been on the range only for a couple of minutes when it started to rain. A few seconds later it was as if someone had thrown a thick grey veil over the landscape. We dashed for shelter. The rain was followed by hail. In two minutes, we were staring at a Christmas card. Then the sun came out, then it rained again.

Eventually, an icy blue sky appeared from nowhere. It seemed such a waste to go back outside now that we'd thawed out but Ross insisted on playing a practice round – he mentioned something about preparing properly for the tournament, swot! – and we trudged off towards the first tee. After one hole I knew my heart wasn't in it. My legs and lungs were pretty pissed off too, and before long my brain was on the verge of mutiny.

Ross was trying hard to concentrate on his golf but couldn't help but notice something was up. 'You haven't even looked at your yardage book or taken any notes,' he said, as we were walking down the eighth hole.

'What's the point in taking notes? It's cold, it's too windy and the rain's washed the paint off the greens,' I said.

Most players would have taken the chance to inform me that the point was they were paying me hard cash to carry their clubs, perhaps throw in the occasional piece of advice and/or diverting, witty chit-chat and to keep my personal angst to myself. Ross just looked at me like a weary father confronted by his teenage brat. I don't think he had the energy to get annoyed. It had been a long season, he wasn't playing well and his first tournament victory seemed further away than ever. An existential caddy was the last thing he needed at this stage.

*

I spent that night in Towcester with Gary Currie, Paul Lawrie's caddy, in a filthy, musty, overpriced twin room above a pub in the town centre. By remarkable coincidence, we had an overpriced meal in the bar downstairs, served by a musty-smelling waiter. Not that any of this made life any more unbearable since my misery was already complete by then.

Currie, on the other hand, was insufferably cheerful. He was planning to go to Australia for the winter when the season was over, spend time on the beach and caddy in a couple of local tournaments. I said I'd rather drink lukewarm vomit every day for a year than fly all the way to Australia to caddy. He called me a 'one-season wonder'.

'Every year guys like you come out on tour and they think it's all going to be a big adventure. Then they discover it's getting out of bed early in the morning, travelling in the Belgrano, pissing rain all the time, soaking wet, hanging about on the range, missing the cut, no money, crap hotels, and they fuck off back home, never to be to seen again. You know your problem?' He pointed a forkful of lasagne at me. '*No staying power.*'

I was flabbergasted. I'd only met him a few months before and already he knew me better than my own mother.

The first two rounds of the 1996 British Masters will go down in golfing history, if only because of the record number of players who withdrew after one day because of tendinitis. This, according to the medical dictionary I have in front of me, is an inflammation of the fibre by which a muscle is attached to the bone and not, as some newspapers wickedly suggested at the time, an imaginary medical condition dreamed up for the purpose of avoiding the mandatory £500 fine for pulling out of a tournament without good reason.

There was also an inordinate number of 'back injuries', one headache victim (poor lamb), one hip-injury sufferer, two sore shoulders and one 'phoned up for his tee-time at 8 a.m. and was told it was 7.38 a.m., disqualified'.

Acres of newspaper space were devoted to the withdrawals and the terrible condition of the course. Players were queuing up at the press tent to complain.

Ross didn't come down with tendinitis. In fact he played thirty-five injury-free holes over two days in commendably good spirits, only to take four putts for a triple-bogey eight at the thirty-sixth. This changed him in an instant from Cheerful Charlie to Desperate Dan. More prosaically, he went from three over par and a handy thirtieth place to six over and looking like he might miss the cut.

I offered a few sympathetic words but he was inconsolable. While he went off to the scorer's tent to sign his card and make arrangements to have my tongue cut out, I dashed down to the main scoreboard to see if we'd made the last two rounds. We had, just.

Chris Hall was just leaving when I got there. Nothing had gone right for him since we had spoken in Holland. He had missed every single cut since then. He finished the day twelve over par and had just missed another. We went for a coffee.

'There are three important things in my life, Lawrence,' he said, with worrying finality when we sat down. 'Seeing my kids, making sure I have a reasonable amount of money and enjoying my golf. None of them are happening right now.'

'Why not?'

'As Zen said, I am bracing myself for failure instead of focusing on what I have to do. Well, bollocks to that. I've had enough of the tour, I'm going home for good.'

Looking back, I wish we had missed the cut too. That way we would never have played the forty-seventh hole of the 1996 British Masters. Ross would never have hit his drive or taken off his rather smart green sweatshirt and asked me to put it in the bag . . .

And if he hadn't done that, I wouldn't have lied and said, 'You can't put it in there. There's no room in the bag.'

... friend Sancho, pardon me that I have brought upon thee, as well as myself, the scandal of madness, by drawing thee into my own errors ...

Why did I say this? Well, the bag was so heavy it felt like there shouldn't be any room in it. I looked afterwards and found four bananas, two bottles of mineral water, two sets of waterproofs, 122 golf balls, one umbrella, fourteen clubs, one baseball cap and one Richard Ford novel. I'll spare you the details of golf-bag design but, believe me, they are huge. There was still enough room for a Chesterfield settee.

... and persuading thee that there have been and still are knights-errant in the world ...

Who knows? Perhaps the real reason was that this was the moment when a deep, dark voice in my soul screamed, 'Enough!' It was just that this came out as a white lie about the golf bag being full.

Of course, Ross looked in the bag and discovered there was plenty of room. He stuffed the green sweatshirt inside. 'What's wrong with your attitude? It's terrible,' he said, walking after his ball. 'Terrible.'

... for shame, sir. Don't give way to sluggishness but get out of your doleful dumps and rise ...

If he hadn't said this, perhaps my eyes would not have started to water. I might even have stopped fibbing. 'I thought there was no room in the bag. Honest.'

'Your heart's not in this any more, is it? Is it?' he said.

'My heart? My attitude? I'm not the one who's nine over par,' I replied.

... ten to one but behind some bush, or under some hedge we may find the Lady Madam Dulcinea ...

And if none of that had been said, we might not have walked up the fairway in single file, me sniffling, Ross five yards in front, shaking his head, muttering incredulously, 'Now you don't want me to put my sweater in the bag because you can't be bothered carrying it. I just don't believe this.'

As I was saying, I wished we'd missed the cut at the British Masters. If we had I would never have chosen that moment to say, 'Right, Ross, this has got to fucking stop.'

Gentlemen. I was mad but now I am in my senses. I was once Don Quixote de la Mancha but am now the plain Alonso Quixano.

20. Home

. . . friend Sancho I was agreeably disappointed with news of thy wise behaviour . . .

Ross found a new caddy, a Scot called Jimmy Hillhouse. I knew him quite well. We'd shared a hotel room at the Dutch Open. He wore a lot of aftershave and a chunky gold ring on the forefinger of his right hand, which spelled out the initials J. H.

I was thinking about them as I drove through the outskirts of Derby. They would be on a golf course in Paris at the Lancôme Trophy, enjoying the first flush of excitement and goodwill that comes with every new 'marriage'. Jimmy was conscientious, experienced and always smartly turned out. He'd caddied at Turnberry for five years, so he knew what he was talking about on a golf course. After me all of this must have come as a terrible shock to Ross.

I didn't envy them. You will read a library of travel books before you come across this line again but I was glad to be in Derby and not Paris. The Lancôme is the most glamorous week of the year, more of a fashion show than a golf tournament, but not even the prospect of galleries full of finely boned Parisian ladies in Chanel suits would have anaesthetized the pain of having to caddy.

There was a story in the most recent *Golf Weekly* magazine

about an Australian player called Mike Clayton, who'd just given up the tour because he was so fed up: 'There comes a time when you get sick of lying on your back and getting prostituted,' he explained. 'It's time to be home and get on with the back nine.'

I loved the last part of that quote, the huge relief it conveyed, the bitterness, the regret and, if you looked really hard for it, the affection – all encapsulated in a daft, clichéd golfing pun. It summed up my own feelings to a tee.

My own back nine consisted of going back to work at the *Guardian*, where the news editor let me loose on his pages again. This was very kind of him but possibly a bit reckless, considering how out of touch I was. On tour it was scarily easy to become isolated from the real world. I had been in Dubai two days before I knew about the Dunblane massacre and that was only because I overheard someone talking about it on the practice putting green. My horror at the event was tinged with shock at my ignorance of it having happened. I tried my best after that to keep up with current affairs but it was difficult on a diet of three-day-old copies of the *Sun*. How do eight million loyal readers manage it?

Thankfully, colleagues were very patient with me and happily broke off from their own work to confirm that, yes, Bill Clinton was still President, the Spice Girls were indeed a pop group and, of course, Parliament had an 'i' in the middle, just like it used to. It must have come as a great relief when I announced I was taking the day off to go to Derby and visit the world's most laconic golf pro.

When David 'DJ' Russell announced half-way through the season that he was giving up playing full-time on the tour to become the professional at Kedleston Park Golf Club, near Derby, he instantly became the butt of a thousand crap jokes from other players about the price of golf balls.

The list of tour pros' pet hates would fill two sides of A4 paper but club professionals might be at the top, just in front of European cities without a branch of Pizza Hut. It would take Sigmund Freud to get to the bottom of this dislike but my own guess is tour pros just couldn't believe anyone who could play to a high standard would prefer selling golf balls to chasing big prize money.

DJ fended off the jokes with the dry wit for which he had become famed after twenty-two years on tour. 'Piss off,' he would tell his tormentors, before insisting that Kedleston Park was one of the most beautiful parts of the country. Now that I was no longer on tour I thought I'd go and take a look for myself. Besides, there was one final question on my mind about professional golf that DJ was uniquely well placed to answer.

He hadn't lied about Kedleston Park. It was a magnificent sight in the sunshine, an open, rolling landscape on the scale of a First World War battlefield. Its centrepiece was Kedleston Hall, a superb neo-classical mansion based on revolutionary architectural concepts laid down by the sixteen-century Italian Andrea Palladio. The clubhouse at the golf course was an altogether more modest affair, based on the cardboard box, but pleasant enough in a suburban fashion. Jeans were not allowed inside so I was ushered through to a store room at the back of the pro shop while DJ nipped through to the kitchen for two plates of fish and chips. Over lunch, he explained that he'd decided to stop touring full-time because he wanted security. 'For the first time in my life I know for sure there's a few quid coming into the house every week instead of waiting until Sunday night to see how much prize money I've won.'

DJ's best friend for the last twenty years has been Ian Woosnam. They both started on the tour in the late 1970s, travelling around together in Dormobiles and hire cars. They matched each other stroke for stroke for a few years, until Woosnam won his first tournament in 1982. Forgive me if this reads a little like the plot for a Jeffrey Archer novel, but thereafter the two great friends led hugely different lives. DJ hadn't exactly suffered in penury but he didn't own a private jet. Nor had he won the US Masters and £5 million in prize money.

I couldn't understand this. Woosnam was a magnificent player, but I'd seen DJ play and he was a great player too, perhaps the most natural ball-striker I'd seen all season. If I didn't know them and had seen them practising together I wouldn't have been able to say which of the two was the golfing superstar. That was what I wanted to ask DJ: what was the difference between the good players and the great ones? Why was he sitting in a cramped store room with yellow Post-it notes stuck to the wall reminding him that 'Mrs Maddison wants a slip-over cardigan' while his best friend was flying the world in his private jet?

I could tell by the lugubrious expression that settled on his face that he'd never given this question much thought – only every day of his life. Somehow he managed a laugh. 'I remember once when Woosie was driving back from Calais and he had to sell something from the Dormobile to get money for petrol. Changed days . . . back then he was never the best player but he had it up here.' He tapped his forehead.

'Another time we were having dinner in Zambia and people were asking us what we were going to do with our lives. I said I would be happy to make a few quid. Woosie said he wouldn't be satisfied until he was number one in the world. I was embarrassed for him when he was saying this – remember, this was at a time when we celebrated when we made the cut.

'I always felt I could have done what he's done but good luck to him. He couldn't understand why I was taking this job. His attitude is if you don't want to take on the world what's the point?'

The bank manager arrived to see DJ We said our goodbyes in the car park. Kedleston Hall had been acquired by the National

Trust for the nation and I intended spending the rest of the afternoon investigating whether my money had been well spent. I jumped in the car and switched on the car radio, just in time to catch the last item on the sports news.

'And at the Lancôme Trophy in Paris Scotland's Ross Drummond looks very threatening, one shot behind the leader . . .'

I didn't hear the rest. I thought I was going to throw up. Every failed exam, every spurned advance and dismal job interview, every match I ever watched Celtic lose, every Tory election victory, the Stone Roses' second album. Had any of them made me feel this horrified? I was sure they hadn't.

How could he do this to me? Win, that is. Without me on the bag. Jesus, God, please, no. But it always happened, everybody said so. Someone leaves a bag and the next week the player wins.

I drove straight back to London with the radio switched off. I felt better around Newport Pagnell. And then I felt bad for feeling bad about him winning. It was what he really wanted, after all. How could I deny him his life's ambition? Envy, I suppose. But didn't I deserve to be there to share in a victory? Perhaps it was me that had been holding him back all season. But then he wasn't going to win, was he? Was he?

The next day was a nightmare. Have you ever watched golf on Ceefax? I gave up and sat by my desk, waiting for the radio reports from Paris. Ross was never outside the top five – always 'handily placed', according to the correspondent. In between times I stared at next door's washing flapping around in the wind. It seemed to be laughing at me.

Day Four. A hot line to Paris was the only answer, straight through to the press tent. 'What's the score?'

'Montgomerie's birdied the first five holes. He's leading by four.'

Montgomerie? I hated Montgomerie. '*Yeeeeessss!* Come on, Monty.'

228

Parnevik won by five shots. Montgomerie dropped six shots in the last thirteen holes. I was glad about that. Ross finished third. He won £40,000 – the biggest cheque of his career.

He was now thirty-second in the Order of Merit, with £137,114 and six pence, almost three times what he'd made in the previous year. Best of all – and this gave me goose-bumps – he was sixth in the points table for the Ryder Cup. If it had started the next day, he would have been in the team. Ross Drummond against Freddie Couples. What a thought!

I could celebrate all of this, but it was a victory that I would have found hard to handle. That would have been the final confirmation that he had never needed me all along, that my season on tour had been pointless and that we were never a team, no matter how much I had wanted us to be. It was just him, the professional golfer, and the caddy, A. N. Other – like it had always been.

I sat back in my chair and thought about Paris. He *did* have some iron in his soul. It must have been the happiest day of his life and I was glad he wasn't even happier. Never had I felt like such a shit.

I made the decision to drive five hundred miles to Loch Lomond about ten seconds after switching on the television. The BBC was showing golf, the first round of the Loch Lomond World Invitational. Faldo was leading. Guess who was second?

I could see why Ross had almost won in Paris. He was swinging beautifully. Long and slow. He and Jimmy looked so happy together, laughing as they walked down the fairway. He had a putt to go into the lead but missed it. I was disappointed. Genuinely. I'd convinced myself Paris was an aberration. I wanted him to win now. How could I not, after all we'd been through, in Sun City, Morocco and Cannes? All those missed cuts. If he was going to win, I could be happy for him. If I couldn't caddy for him, then I wanted to be there to see it happen.

*

The car park at Loch Lomond was miles from the action. I caught the spectator bus to the course. When I got there. Ross and Jimmy were standing on the range. I watched them for five minutes. I felt like I was seeing an old girlfriend in the street with her new boyfriend for the first time. Already, they seemed to have fallen into a steady, comfortable rhythm. Ross would hit a shot, turn round with his palm outstretched, into which Jimmy dropped a freshly cleaned ball.

Ross looked cool in black trousers, a dark blue sweater and a black cap. He seemed bigger than the last time I had seen him in the flesh, broader, more athletic. He was much happier than the last time I had seen him, that was for sure.

The prodigal returns. I walked towards him. I was apprehensive. What could I say? 'Remember me? I'm the guy who told you that this had to fuckin' stop.'

'Hey, Lawrence! How are you doing?' He had a huge smile stretched across his face. He stopped hitting balls and we chatted for five minutes, a longer conversation than any we'd had in the last few weeks I'd been caddying for him.

'Hard luck in Paris,' I said. 'I thought you were going to win for a minute.'

'Yeh, thanks. Shame, really, wasn't it?'

Was that a trick question? 'Sure,' I said.

He was in fifth place after one round but on the sports pages Ross Drummond was the top golf story of the day. He'd been hauled into the press tent and, old pro that he was, he'd even given them something to write about on a dull day: 'Anthony Robbins. The Scottish golfer was given the volume Awaken the Giant Within by his wife Claire after seeing Robbins on television. Its rousing message has had a rousing effect on Drummond, who has had his best season ever,' one of the papers said. There was a picture of Ross smiling and holding a book, underneath the headline 'Ross Books Positive Future'.

The publicity had obviously had an effect. A small gallery

was gathered at the first tee, waiting for him to play. That had never happened when I was caddying for him. He drove off and we all walked after him, watching from outside the ropes which ran the length of the fairway. Outside the ropes. It felt like an out-of-body experience.

I don't mean to give the impression that Ross and Jimmy cavorted around the front nine like a pair of spaniel puppies but, bloody hell, they looked happy. Even when he duffed a shot into a bunker at the sixth, Ross put his hands on top of his head and started laughing. Jimmy said something straight away and they were into a cheery conversation almost before the ball rolled to a sorry halt in an impossible lie. I knew for a fact that Ross and I would have remained silent after that horror for at least two holes.

While the other players in the group hit their shots, I ducked inside the ropes for a quick chat with Jimmy. 'How was Paris?' I asked.

'Brilliant.' He grinned. 'I made two thousand, eight hundred and fifty-two quid.'

'And Ross, how are you getting on with him?'

'Good, pretty good.'

'No falling out?'

'Not really. I told him at the fifth yesterday to keep concentrating and he said, 'Jimmy, I am concentrating.' Apart from that, nothing.'

'Sounds vicious.'

It was Ross's turn to play. He hit another bad shot and made bogey. In fact, he started to drop a lot of shots. Gradually, the gallery began to drift away. I slipped away myself after ten holes, satisfied that he wasn't going to win this tournament. I arranged to meet him after the round and wandered off towards the tented village. There were a few friends I wanted to say goodbye to.

The first person I saw was Thomas Gögele standing by the

scoreboard wearing the wistful expression people reserve only for Premier League dreams. It turned out he was in tenth position. 'A sixty-five tomorrow, Lore-ance, and I could win,' he said darkly.

I hadn't seen Thomas since Austria. I congratulated him on finishing second in Germany. I'd looked through the tour statistics: the £42,000 he'd won in that one week was almost as much as he'd made on tour in the previous six years. 'I thought I was going to throw up at the end,' he explained. I'd almost forgotten Thomas's uncanny ability to sound like a Lutheran pastor, even at the height of happiness.

Over his shoulder, I could see Jos Vanstiphout sitting in the beer tent with a half-empty glass of lager. He waved me over. I told Thomas I had to go, I had an urgent appointment with my guru.

I bought two beers and went and sat down beside him. The season had finally caught up with him. He looked more weather-beaten than ever, his face stretched over his cheekbones like fine leather and his eyes, which had once sparkled defiantly in the face of his lifestyle, looked painfully red.

'You look tired,' I said, kindly.

'No, my friend. Today I am just a very disappointed man.'

'What's wrong?'

'I can't say.'

'Come on, you can tell me.'

I half suspected what was coming. The newspaper reports. I read them all, right to the end, just in case I'd got a mention somewhere amid all the praise Ross had heaped on Anthony Robbins. I wasn't mentioned, not that I had expected to be.

Jos pulled hard on his cigarette, then released a hard, fast jet of smoke. 'I was first in the players' lounge and read the papers . . .' My hunch was right.

'I couldn't believe it. The first article was about Ross Drummond and how he had done well and then I see he talks about this psychologist and his bloody book, saying that he made the difference. I was very disappointed, my friend.'

'You said that.'

'Very disappointed. I worked my ass off for that guy. I was his teacher, his father, a brother.' He took another drag from his cigarette.

'And then I read another article. This time there was a picture. He was holding a book, he didn't even mention my name. He'd had this book for ages and nothing happens, then I start working with him and he plays wells. There is no coincidence. I added forty per cent to his game. Bloody book. Who is this Robin guy, anyway?'

'Anthony Robbins.'

'Anthony fuckin' Robbins. Who is he?'

'Actually, he's the world's richest guru. He works with Bill Clinton and Princess Di.'

'See? What does he know about golf? Nothing.'

He drained his beer glass. 'I thought Ross was my friend. I thought we could have a Christmas party together. Maybe he'll have a Christmas party with this other guy.'

And so it went on. Jos and I sat for half an hour discussing this Frankenstein monster he had created, how it had broken its bindings and was now charging around in the world beyond the beer tent, playing good golf and dishing out praise to the undeserving Anthony Robbins. The truth was that Ross had given Jos and me credit when he was talking to the press, but this fact, inexplicably, was not deemed by the world's media to be as newsworthy as the Robbins story.

We wandered out into the daylight. The main scoreboard was showing Drummond at three over par, drifting lazily down the field but still inside the top thirty. 'I can switch these guys off as easily I can switch them on. I could make him miss the cut, you know – just by looking at him,' Jos said.

Voodoo is an ugly word, so I didn't use it. I giggled, which made Jos really angry. The skin drew even tighter across his cheekbones. For the first time, I noticed he had thin lips. 'I mean it. I bloody can do it.'

Ross finished the day four over par. He shot seventy-nine, ten worse than the day before.

The strange thing was that he didn't seem too bothered – I guessed this was down to the numbing of the nerve ends that comes with having £135,000 + in the bank. We sat in the players' lounge for an hour chatting, mostly about Paris. Deep down, he said, he knew he couldn't win the tournament. He'd set his heart on the top five at the start of the last day. Third place was just fine.

I still couldn't bring myself to tell him I'd been sitting at home, willing someone else to win. He probably knew I had, anyway. A friend, a professional footballer, had assured me that he once sat in the stand at a cup final silently willing his own side to lose – just because he'd been dropped from the team. What's the point in your team winning if you're not part of it? All professional sportsmen believed that and understood it when others felt the same, he said.

Distance had performed miracles on our relationship. It was early days yet but we appeared to have metamorphosed into something like friends. We didn't have anything in common beyond golf but I saw little seeds of potential. He was the most left-wing golfer I'd met. He was even contemplating voting Labour at the next election. He liked country music and I could live with that. Best of all, he dragged me out to his car and presented me with a brand new set of golf clubs. A present, he said, for all the good work I had done during the year. What a liar, what a generous liar.

I decided he didn't need to know about Paris. What was a little temporary disloyalty between (potential) friends? Besides, there was one final favour I had to ask him. I wasn't about to

234

blow my chances by confessing I had begged God to let Colin Montgomerie deprive Ross Drummond of the very thing he'd always wanted. Ross knew how much I hated Colin Montgomerie. He would have taken the news very badly.

21. Together Again

Some old friends came to visit as our plane thumped on to the Tarmac at Malaga airport and together they formed a creeping, familiar dread. We're here. Where will I stay? How will I get there? Will it be cheap? Will the bedclothes have been changed in the last six months? Who can I find to split the cost of a room? Where is the golf course? How will I get there? Will Ross be there? How will it be between the two of us? Cool, efficient and professional, or ramshackle and Quixote-esque, like the way it used to be?

. . . look yonder, friend Sancho, there are thirty outrageous giants, whom I intend to encounter . . .

Probably not. He was a different player now, thirty-second best in Europe and – this still gave me goose-bumps – in the Ryder Cup top ten.

. . . for God's sake, Lawrence, quit with all that Sancho stuff. I'm trying to concentrate here . . .

My mind was galloping. I'd forgotten that every week on tour started with an anxiety attack. I hadn't missed that part of the life, not knowing what was going to happen beyond the next half-hour. Still, what was a little uncertainty when I was about to make my comeback as caddy? I was back on tour by limited demand: my own.

I had made Ross promise that no matter what happened months

before between us I could caddy for him at the Volvo Masters. I'd only asked him to cheer him up, as a discreet signal that I still thought he was going to be successful, that he could win a tournament. Those were the heady days when I still thought he could. He had to say yes: to do otherwise would have been an admission that failure, another dreary year, was about to unfold.

I should explain. The Volvo Masters was the last event of the European tour season, a valedictory tournament staged every year at Valderrama, the venue for the Ryder Cup. Only the top sixty players in Europe were invited to play. The prize money was huge but that wasn't the point. To play at Valderrama was to gain entry to Europe's élite. From the first week of the tour I overheard caddies talk about 'making Valderrama'. If your man was good enough to play there then he was worth caddying for, financially and spiritually. It meant he was a proper tour pro, not just a journeyman scraping a living, and by association you were a proper caddy.

That was the favour I wanted to ask Ross at Loch Lomond. Was the deal that we made in Dubai still on? Would he make a *proper* caddy of me?

He took some persuading. This was hardly surprising. Europe's 111th best player was more than happy to have someone regular on the bag, if only for the company. But his ranking was much higher now and he was entitled to believe he should have a better caddy than me. God knows, he could afford it.

'I don't know, everything's going so well with Jimmy.'

'But a deal is a deal, isn't it?' I said, brazenly.

He gave in. 'But remember, this is serious stuff. No messing around.'

And so I found myself standing by the baggage carousel at Malaga airport with fifty other players and caddies thinking how come I was the only person who didn't appear to know where he was going, who he was going with and what he would do when he got there?

My bag was last off the plane. I dashed through the nothing-to-declare-except-my-anxiety exit, fully expecting to discover an empty arrivals hall and, beyond that, a cloud of dust thrown up by a departing bus packed with caddies. It was after ten o'clock at night and my Spanish taxi driver was bound to have his meter on the rip-off setting. I had visions of it whizzing round like the third hand on a stop-watch.

Amazingly, the bus was still outside the terminal, revving little puffs of toxic black smoke into the night air. I could see a line of familiar faces through the steamy windows. They had waited for me. I had never felt more loved. I don't doubt that eight months before someone would have said, 'We're not waiting for him, he's not even a proper caddy,' and wished the driver God speed to wherever they were going. Beaming, I climbed on board.

'Where the fuck have you been?' someone said, in what sounded to me like an affectionate voice.

We didn't go as far as Valderrama but to Puerta Duquesa, a tiny marina resort fifteen minutes along the coast. The journey from the airport took an hour, long enough for all of my problems to be resolved. I could stay in an apartment with four other caddies as long I slept on the couch. Of course, they didn't actually have an apartment yet but there was a bar at the resort where someone might be able to supply keys for an apartment, a cheap apartment. Getting to the golf course would be easy. All I had to do was stand by the motorway exit above the town and someone would pick me up eventually. And Ross? Hadn't I heard? He couldn't get a flight from Scotland until the next day. Not for the first time, it struck me that the route to perpetual peace lay in moving the United Nations from New York to the caddy bus. It was the only place in the world I knew where no crisis was without a solution.

Someone threw a pint of lager over my pepperoni pizza but otherwise my assimilation back into the caddy community went remarkably well. The apartment, magically, materialized. The bed sheets were as white as snow and smelled of rosebuds, the couch was as soft and warm as a mother's belly. Under the circumstances it would have been churlish not to sleep like a baby, so I did.

I woke early, threw some water on my face and dashed out into the morning. I wanted to be at the golf course in good time, just in case Ross made an unexpected appearance. It was still pitch black outside and the lights of the village sparkled across the bay. The tacky tourists bars wouldn't be open for hours and all was quiet but for the sound of water lapping against the harbour walls. Caddying had taken me to some pretty places during the year but this was one of the prettiest. It was one of the tragedies of modern Spain that motorway hell lay just a short walk up the hill, like an ugly knife wound across a child's face. Still, at least it meant I could get to the golf course pronto.

Ross, as predicted by the soothsayers of the caddy bus, didn't appear for another day. I spent that morning sorting out a locker for him, collecting new balls, new golf gloves, cleaning his clubs and walking the golf course – the little things a player expected from a proper caddy. I had never bothered with them. Standing in a queue for golf balls was a chore when you were concentrating hard on inspiring your man to victory. God knows, that had been hard work. If only I had known that Ross would have preferred me to queue for golf balls and walk the golf course, checking the slopes of the greens.

Valderrama was spectacular. I'd never seen a golf course with grass as green, or with such well-sculpted trees or water hazards so blue. The rough was thick and glossy, like a sheepdog's coat. A Bolivian millionaire called Jaime Ortiz-Patino had spent a chunk of the family fortune trying to turn it into the best course in the world. He'd either achieved golfing perfection or proved conclusively that a man can have too much money, depending on whom you asked. Personally, I think when someone spends

£250,000 building a waterfall to make a golf hole more difficult it's time to call a psychiatrist. Then have a revolution.

I spent the afternoon on the practice range, catching up on all the news. The evening I spent getting drunk and forgetting most of it.

I woke up the next morning with a team of workmen building a boat inside my skull. It had been a hell of a night. From the wreckage of what was once my memory I recalled Jos saying that he and Ross were friends again, there had been a misunderstanding – it was all the fault of the newspapers. There were other bits and pieces: Martin Rowley had got a new bag (Nigel Mansell would have to conquer the golf world without his help) but he would still be available for bookings in the winter, Andy Prodger had gone to caddy in Japan, Julian Phillips had been sacked, Spanish Paul was now a *very* important caddy to the tenth best player in Europe, Pete Coleman and Langer hadn't split up, after all. Oh, yes, and Ross was no longer the 438th best golfer in the world. He was 196th.

It would be my dearest wish to follow that uplifting statistic by saying the next four days at Valderrama were a fitting climax to the most successful season of Ross Drummond's career. I could tell you that he won the Volvo Masters but that would make me the biggest liar since Richard Nixon. Besides, the truth is in the record books now. He finished fifty-third.

It was just like old times. Ross hit all the shots and got annoyed if they weren't perfect, I carried the bag and cleaned the clubs. The difference now was that I didn't even pretend to believe he was about to conquer the world. I kind of hoped that he would but didn't much mind if he didn't. I knew now what he had known all along – that he was Quixote, the dreamer, the idealist. How else would he have been able to keep going for nineteen years? How else was he able to drag himself from the depths of despair in Bergamo to this, the Volvo Masters?

As for me? Well, I was just someone who wanted to be a professional sportsman. I knew at the start of the season I didn't have the talent. It was obvious now that I didn't possess the other essential: Brian McClair had it, and my old schoolfriends John Colquhoun and Robert Dawson. I was wrong about Ross, he *definitely* had it – Iron in the Soul.

I was an amateur, crap at golf and past it at football, just like millions of others. So what? It didn't mean I couldn't have a good time making a fool of myself on the links or the five-a-side pitch. What was it A. A. Milne had said about golf? It was the best game in the world to be bad at. Let that be my motto. At least I knew now what it was like to lead a world-class golf tournament and be a part of the Open. I'd appeared on *Grandstand* and spoken to Jack Nicklaus and been to Sun City. Best of all, I was on my way to becoming a *proper* caddy.

Ross was delighted. He loved arriving at the course to discover I'd got him a locker and some new balls, that I'd got a new grip on his driver and had walked the course. Most of all, he loved the fact that I didn't pester him all the time with my ceaseless talk about winning tournaments.

The truth was that he didn't mind finishing in fifty-third place. He didn't *want* to finish fifty-third but there wasn't much he could do, it was just that fifty-two others had played better. He didn't need me to tell him that the next tournament would be along soon and that, not to worry, he was good enough to win it. He knew that already, he'd known it for nineteen years, just as he would know it the following season when someone else would be carrying his bag.

We played the last round while the morning dew was still heavy on the fairways. He was ten over par. Our suitcases were packed before the leaders reached the turn. I was glad about that: it meant we could get away from the golf course before the rush. Surprised to hear that? What did you expect me to say? Damn it, if only he'd taken less shots than the other players he would have won?

Not any more. I decided to leave that kind of wishful thinking to the next ingénue who came along thinking that caddy dreams come true.

Heathrow airport felt like an overcrowded lift, airless and bad-tempered. The forecast was for three-hour snow delays. I was standing in the queue for coffee when I caught sight of a familiar figure in the mêlée by the ticket desk.

Andy Prodger was wearing his caddying gear, black cotton trousers, white trainers and a waterproof jacket. In one hand, he had a small suitcase, in the other a white polythene bag. His hair was matted with sweat and his face a worrying shade of heart-attack red.

'Prodger,' I shouted. He turned round, saw me and smiled. 'I thought you were supposed to be caddying in Japan.'

'I am,' he said, breathlessly. 'I've only flown back for the week off to see the family.'

This didn't sound right. Caddies didn't fly home for the week off, especially from Japan. Only players could afford to do that kind of thing.

'Mr Big Time,' I teased.

'Why not? I won a tournament in my first week out there.'

'You're kidding. How much?'

'Ten per cent of eighteen million Yen.'

'Fantastic. Who were you caddying for?'

'A gentleman by the name of Yoshi Mizumaki.'

'Never heard of him. Is he any good?'

He looked at me as if I was crazy. 'Who cares? He won, didn't he?'